Praise for Pole Dance:

'Avery has electrified the exploration world ... He is shaping up to join the ranks of such British immortals as Sir Ranulph Fiennes and Dame Ellen MacArthur'
Sunday Times

'Told with huge enthusiasm and illustrated by some powerful pictures ... a real-life adventure' *Daily Mail*

'Written in diary form *Pole Dance* is a chronicle of a modern polar expedition. It is a chilling reminder of the power and danger of the natural world' *Brighton Argus*

'This book brings home the real heroism of contemporary expeditions and the amazing accomplishment of Avery's journey' *Winning Breaks*

'Written in the present tense in diary form and virtually unaltered from when he wrote it in Antarctica, the book acts both as a record of Avery's achievement and as a very personal outlet for a young man under extreme pressure ... Avery manages to convey the daily traumas of life on the ice with wit and enthusiasm. An awe-inspiring tale of polar adventure' *Geographical*

Tom Avery was born in 1975 and brought up in Sussex, Brazil and France. After graduating from Bristol University with a B.Sc. in geography and geology, he had a brief career in the City before working for a small Swiss ski business. He has organised and led expeditions to the South American Andes, the French Alps, Tanzania, Morocco and New Zealand, but the highlight of his climbing career to date took place in 2000 when he led a pioneering British expedition to the previously unexplored Eastern Zaalay Mountains of Central Asia. The Commonwealth South Pole Centenary Expedition is the ninth major expedition that he has organised. Tom Avery now spends his time giving motivational talks to businesses, raising funds for The Prince's Trust (for whom he is an ambassador). He has just returned from a pioneering dog sledging expedition in the Arctic which recreated Commander Robert Peary's disputed journey to the North Pole of 1909. He is also an official ambassador for the 2012 London Games, and a Fellow of the Royal Geographic Society. Visit his website at www.tomavery.net.

POLE DANCE

The story of the record-breaking
British expedition to the bottom of the world

TOM AVERY

An Orion paperback

First published in Great Britain in 2004
by Orion
This paperback edition published in 2005
by Orion Books Ltd,
Orion House, 5 Upper St Martin's Lane,
London WC2H 9EA

An Hachette Livre UK company

3 5 7 9 10 8 6 4 2

A CIP catalogue record for this book is
available from the British Library.

ISBN 978-0-7528-6499-0

Typeset by Butler and Tanner Ltd, Frome and London
Printed and bound in Great Britain by
Clays Ltd, St Ives plc

The Orion Publishing Group's policy is to use papers that
are natural, renewable and recyclable products and
made from wood grown in sustainable forests. The logging
and manufacturing processes are expected to conform to
the environmental regulations of the country of origin.

www.orionbooks.co.uk

In memory of Terry Lloyd

CONTENTS

LIST OF ILLUSTRATIONS

ACKNOWLEDGEMENTS

Last summer I flew to Mallorca for a week in the sun. Whilst a large chunk of the book had already been completed, I had yet to find a publisher and did not know where to start looking. As I boarded the flight to Palma, I noticed Peter Stringfellow, the nightclub owner, sitting up in business class. I vaguely recalled that he had brought out an autobiography the previous year, so I began writing him a letter, asking, somewhat hopefully, if he had any contacts in the publishing world with whom he could put me in touch. I suggested *Pole Dance* as a possible title, which would link his line of work to our own exploits in Antarctica. Waiting for the moment when the stewardesses' backs were turned, I slipped through the curtain that divides business class from the rest of the aircraft, and handed him my letter. Never in my wildest dreams did I expect anything to come of my cheeky opportunism, so when Peter Stringfellow's publisher Alan Samson (who had recently moved to Orion Books) called me to arrange a meeting three days after my return from holiday, I was totally blown away. The rest, as they say, is history.

Many people have helped put this book together, to whom I owe so much, no more so than my mother who on numerous occasions stayed up until the early hours proof-reading drafts and putting up with my writer's tantrums. I am immensely fortunate to have such loving and supportive parents who have been a constant source of encouragement from the moment I first ventured to the mountains.

David Yelverton's superb book, *Antarctica Unveiled*, was the first in-depth study into the work of the *Discovery* Expedition, and David provided invaluable assistance with the historical element of the book. Others who I must thank include James Gill for all his hard work as my agent, Lucinda McNeile and Angela McMahon at Orion, Paddy Woodrow, Antonia Loudon, Giles Wingate-Saul, Nick Cox, Roly Denman, and Mary, my long-suffering girlfriend. Thanks also go to Nick Whiting and John Gilkes who helped produce the map, and to Lucy Martin at the Scott Polar Research Institute in Cambridge for helping me make sense of the *Discovery* Expedition's reports and photographs. But I will forever be indebted to Peter for getting the ball rolling, and to Alan for having faith in my modest abilities as a writer.

The expedition received tremendous support from individuals, equipment suppliers and other commercial organisations. In particular I would like to thank Rob Wylie and Anna Wright at Mountain Hardwear, Stewart Morgan at Oakley, Carolyn Dunn at Bridgedale, Julian Bickerton at Expedition Kit, John Bernard at Braemar Mountain Sports, Sami Juula at Suunto, Angela King at Fuji, David Cunnington at Burton McCall, James Thompson at Rab UK, Chris Lines at Berghaus, James Massey at Tag Heuer and John Sunley at the Lord Cornwallis Memorial Foundation. I would like to make a special thank you to David Gundlach at Hastings Direct, without whose incredibly generous financial support I would never have set foot in Antarctica in the first place.

During the two long years of planning the expedition, many polar veterans gave up much of their time to pass on their expert advice to us. In particular I would like to thank our patron Sir Ranulph Fiennes, Geoff Somers, Andrew McLean, Ollie Shepard, Roger Mear, Charles Swithinbank, Alain Hubert, Anne Kershaw and Doug Stoup. We would have been lost without them. Gottleib Braun-Elwert in New Zealand and Andy Parfin at Camber Sands provided much assistance with the training. Many more offered support and encouragement before and during the expedition, but Naomi Edler at The Prince's Trust, Faye Sommerville, Sir Kenneth Branagh, Elizabeth Buchanan, Freddy Markham, David Pearson and Emma Ainslie at Ski Verbier, Brian Cunningham, Shane Winser at the Royal

Acknowledgements

Geographical Society, Amanda Pardoe, Mary Bannister at BBC London, Humfrey Hunter, Patrick Ward, Geraldine McGrory, Jonathan Samuels at Sky News, Ally Spry, Jamie Jarvis and Charles Watson deserve a special mention.

To have had the interest and backing of HRH The Prince of Wales himself was a tremendous honour and a further incentive to reach our goal.

My greatest sense of gratitude, though, goes to Patrick Woodhead, Andrew Gerber and Paul Landry for their companionship, commitment, good humour, kindness, hard work, and for making our Antarctic adventure so much fun.

Finally I would like to pay tribute to the key role that the ITN journalist Terry Lloyd played in the success of the Commonwealth South Pole Centenary Expedition. His promise to report our arrival at the Pole for the *News at Ten* represented our only guaranteed piece of post-expedition news coverage. That pledge was vital in securing our sponsorship. His enthusiasm and unwavering support kept us going when it looked as though the expedition might never happen. Twelve weeks after interviewing me from the South Pole, Terry was reporting from southern Iraq when his jeep was hit by friendly fire. He was killed instantly and his death shocked us deeply. This book is dedicated to his memory.

POLE DANCE

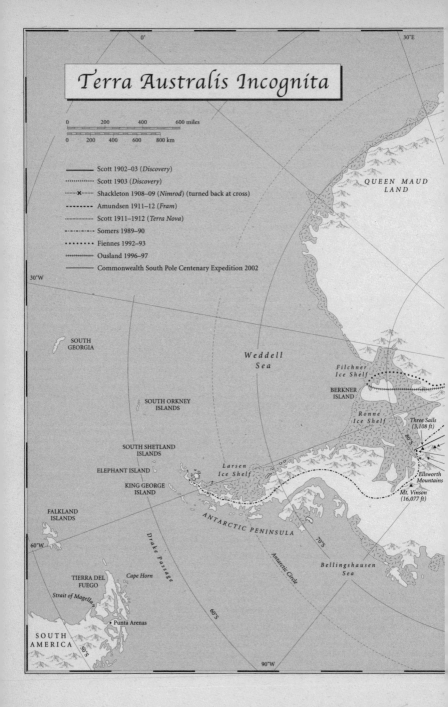

Terra Australis Incognita

0   200   400   600 miles

0   200   400   600   800 km

—————— Scott 1902–03 (*Discovery*)
·············· Scott 1903 (*Discovery*)
········×········ Shackleton 1908–09 (*Nimrod*) (turned back at cross)
– – – – – Amundsen 1911–12 (*Fram*)
—————— Scott 1911–1912 (*Terra Nova*)
–·–·–·– Somers 1989–90
•••••••• Fiennes 1992–93
·············· Ousland 1996–97
—————— Commonwealth South Pole Centenary Expedition 2002

0°

30°E

QUEEN MAUD
LAND

30°W

SOUTH
GEORGIA

*Weddell
Sea*

*Filchner
Ice Shelf*

BERKNER
ISLAND

*Ronne
Ice Shelf*

Three Sails
(3,108 ft)

SOUTH ORKNEY
ISLANDS

SOUTH SHETLAND
ISLANDS

ELEPHANT ISLAND

KING GEORGE
ISLAND

*Larsen
Ice Shelf*

ANTARCTIC PENINSULA

*Ellsworth
Mountains*

Mt. Vinson
(16,077 ft)

80°S

FALKLAND
ISLANDS

60°W

Drake Passage

Cape Horn

Antarctic Circle

70°S

*Bellingshausen
Sea*

TIERRA DEL
FUEGO

Strait of Magellan

60°S

• Punta Arenas

SOUTH
AMERICA

50°S

90°W

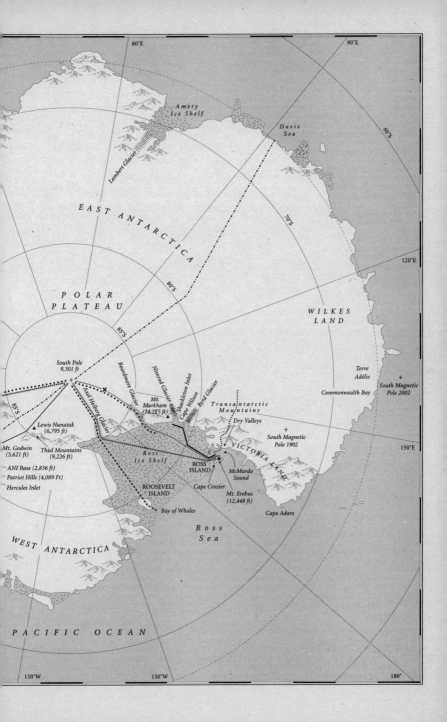

Chapter One

THE LURE OF THE SOUTH

Hope was fading fast. A blizzard had been raging for eight days, imprisoning the three men in their tent. The temperature was in the minus forties and the Antarctic winter was rapidly closing in. Food and fuel had run out days ago and they were starving, desperately weak and frozen to the core. Less than eleven miles to the north lay a depot with enough supplies to restore their strength for the final push but the storm showed no sign of relenting and they were too exhausted to leave their sleeping bags. The end was near. With badly frostbitten fingers, Captain Scott picked up his pencil and scrawled: 'Had we lived, I should have had a tale to tell of the hardihood, endurance, and courage of my companions which would have stirred the heart of every Englishman. These rough notes and our dead bodies must tell the tale.'

I must have been seven years old when my mother gave me the Ladybird storybook about the adventures of Captain Scott. Like most boys of that age, I was far happier kicking a football around than toiling through a boring old book but this one was different from all the others I had been made to read and it gripped me from start to finish. What had compelled these brave men to drag themselves through unimaginable dangers and suffering to reach this barren spot on the Earth's surface? It was a story of extraordinary heroism against a fearsome opponent. I immediately read the book again. A Norwegian called Roald Amundsen might have beaten Scott and his men to the prize of the South Pole, but their glorious failure stirred something deep inside me. Although I didn't really understand why, from that moment onwards I knew that one day I too had to go to the South Pole.

My career as an 'explorer' had not got off to an auspicious start. I was an energetic child and enjoyed climbing things. We were living in a flat in Rio de Janeiro in Brazil when I tried to make an ascent of the north face of my parents' bookcase. On reaching the summit, my weight caused the seven-foot-high structure to tilt outwards from the wall and come crashing to the floor. Mum rushed into the sitting room to find her four-year-old son trapped under the bookcase, crying his eyes out. Luckily I was none the worse for wear, but I vowed to steer clear of items of furniture in the future.

My interest in Scott was rekindled at Harrow School when the polar explorer Robert Swan gave a slide show to the boys about his pioneering expedition to the Antarctic. Along with Roger Mear and Gareth Wood, and without outside support, he had retraced Scott's route from his hut on the Ross Sea to the South Pole, a mammoth journey of nearly nine hundred miles. Captain Scott had also been a childhood hero of Swan's, so I could relate to his passionate obsession. His was a captivating story, brought to life by his enthusiasm and dramatic photographs. But Swan had almost died on the expedition. If this bulldog of a man with shoulders like a rugby prop forward had found things so tough, surely there was little hope for someone like me lasting more than a few hours in Antarctica?

When I was sixteen I joined the 'Marmots', the school mountaineering club. We were immensely fortunate in having an organisation that ran introductory climbing trips to the British mountains. There were many reasons why I decided to give it a go. Although I would eventually grow to six foot two, at that age I was still knee-high to a grasshopper and constantly getting squashed on the rugby field by bruisers twice my size. I desperately wanted to prove something to myself, my parents and my peers and to reach a summit high in the clouds seemed the most eye-catching way of achieving this. Ever since I was a young boy I have loved snow, and mountaineering appeared to be the perfect way of mucking about in the stuff. The rugged hills of Snowdonia, the Lake District and the Scottish Highlands were the perfect playground to get to grips with ropes, crampons and ice axes under the watchful eye of the master-in-charge, Mr Greenstock. Mr Greenstock had over forty years' climbing experience under his belt and his infectious enthusiasm for the mountains rubbed off on all the boys lucky enough to join his well-run trips.

Despite their own scant interest in mountaineering, my parents were always supportive of my ambitions and when I left school they encouraged me to join a trekking expedition to the Indian Himalayas. The four-week trek took us through barren valleys, past ancient monasteries and over high mountain passes, always tantalisingly below the snowline. The one-hundred-mile journey through the Zanskar Range was fascinating, but I found it frustrating not to be up among the glistening white summits.

After saving a bit of money working in the ski and surf department at Harrods, I sought to rectify this by travelling and mountaineering around New Zealand. Despite almost being turned to ash whilst trying to climb the 9,200-foot volcano Mount Ruapehu mid-eruption, my time in this stunning country gave me invaluable experience.

My gap year had fuelled my appetite for the mountains, and shortly after starting at Bristol University I embarked on trying to organise my first proper climbing expedition. Two years later and we had raised enough money through commercial sponsorship and other fundraising events (including a sponsored head shave) to pay for six weeks in the Andes, during which time we climbed a total of six peaks in Ecuador, Bolivia and Peru up to 21,500 feet in altitude.

I was delighted with what our inexperienced team had accomplished. On a personal level, I drew a great sense of fulfilment from having made the expedition happen. There were times when it had looked as though the trip wouldn't even get off the ground, but when we all congregated at Heathrow Airport for the flight to Quito it felt as though we had already achieved something great just to be standing there together. The expedition also taught me a great deal about myself – how strong my body was and how it responded when pushed to the limits, how I coped with the altitude and how I reacted during times of extreme pressure. My climbing skills improved markedly and I forged strong friendships with like-minded people who craved the freedom that the great outdoors provided. The flame of adventure had been kindled within all five of us and we vowed to return to the mountains again.

The long university holidays were filled with smaller-scale climbing trips to the Alps, Morocco, Tanzania and Patagonia which enabled me to build on my experience and extend my mountain skills.

Much of my geography and geology degree course was based on geomorphological processes in the polar regions, focusing primarily on the Antarctic ice cap. I was enthralled with everything I learned, but I never imagined that I would ever get to visit the great white south myself. In my mind, Antarctica was reserved for scientists and a handful of superhuman explorers. This belief was reinforced when I read *Mind Over Matter*, the epic story of Sir Ranulph Fiennes's crossing of the Antarctic continent. For ninety-six days and nights, his body underwent an appalling ordeal, during a journey described as 'Hell on Earth'.

Post-university life as a young twenty-something seemed to be settling into a routine. I became a trainee accountant with Arthur Andersen and moved into a flat in London. Motivating myself for the excitements of accountancy was a hopeless task: my mind would wander when I should have been hard at work. I have always been the inquisitive type but I find there is only so much that I can learn second hand. It is through raw experiences amongst the breathtaking scenery and open skies of the great outdoors that I learn so much about myself and the world I live in. Within weeks of returning from a trip to the wilderness, I find myself planning the next adventure. It is this constant dreaming that gives me my energy, and I dread the day when the ideas start to run out. The daydreaming may have had something to do with my failing a set of key accountancy exams in late 1999, when I decided to leave the City and become a ski guide in the Swiss Alps.

To climb a virgin mountain and tread where no man had been before was one of my lifelong ambitions. At a time when I should have been revising for my financial reporting paper, I found myself trawling through old expedition reports in the libraries of the Royal Geographical Society and the Alpine Club in London. It struck me that there were very few places left in the world where new mountains were still waiting to be explored. Most of the remaining unclimbed summits are located in the remote regions of Antarctica, Greenland, Alaska and the forested mountains of the Congo and Indonesia. The Himalayan kingdoms of Bhutan and Tibet contain some of the highest virgin peaks in the world but because of stringent bureaucracy, mountaineers are dissuaded from visiting them.

I then stumbled across a report by a Russian mountaineer about the new exploration possibilities in the former Soviet republics of Kyrgyzstan and Tajikistan. Due to their location on the sensitive Soviet-Chinese border, barring the odd yak-herder they had been off-limits to all non-military personnel for decades.

Since the break-up of the Soviet Union in the early nineties, the 'Stans' have gradually been opening their doors to mountaineers. A prominent spur of the Himalayas called the Pamirs extends deep into these two small landlocked countries and reaches altitudes of over 24,000 feet. The Pamirs lie alongside the ancient Silk Route trading highway. When Marco Polo visited the region in the thirteenth century he called it 'the roof of the world'. Further investigation revealed a cluster of over forty peaks far higher than anything in the Alps in an area called the Eastern Zaalay range in the southeast corner of Kyrgyzstan. So little was known about the place that only Pik Kurumdy, the highest summit in the range, had been officially named. At 22,000 feet, Kurumdy was one of the highest unclimbed mountains on Earth. I just had to go there.

The British Silk Mountains Expedition of 2000 took the best part of eighteen months to organise. I was amazingly fortunate that several of my Bristol friends shared my passion for adventure. George Wells was one of my closest friends at university, and having proved his worth during our Andean expedition three years earlier he was naturally my first pick when selecting the team for Kyrgyzstan. I also recruited Patrick Woodhead, who had lived with George in the house next door to me. We were joined by one of my Arthur Andersen colleagues (and another Bristol alumnus) Nick Stopford, two experienced Russian climbers called Anatoly Moshnikov and Vladimir Vysochkiy, and our jovial Australian base camp manager, Scott Jamison. Sponsorship was secured only days before departure, courtesy of the internet company NOW.com.

We set off for Kyrgyzstan at the end of June 2000 with the aim of exploring and mapping as much as we could of the Eastern Zaalay Mountains. NOW.com wanted this to be the world's first truly 'live' expedition and sent out a producer and technician to beam back live images and video to the company's website and satellite television stations in Hong Kong and Singapore.

From an idyllic base camp on the banks of a rampant glacial river, which we named the Anduin after the mythical river in *The Lord of the Rings*, we made a total of nine first ascents over a period of six weeks. One of the great treats of the expedition was choosing names for these unnamed rivers and mountains, which might one day appear on a map of this part of the world if the Kyrgyz cartographers get round to it. Mountains were named after my mother Quenelda (following a successful ascent on her birthday), our patron Ranulph Fiennes and even George's lifelong cleaning lady Ethel, who had sadly passed away a few months earlier.

The expedition had been an unqualified success, and we all came home with a real sense of privilege that we had been the first people to visit these secret mountains. The only disappointment was narrowly missing out on climbing Pik Kurumdy, after dangerous snow conditions forced us to retreat less than two thousand feet from the summit. Our time in Kyrgyzstan had been an enormously happy one and fuelled my own desire to organise something on a much grander scale. Having been climbing mountains for the best part of seven years, I wanted to take a break from the mountains and set myself a new challenge altogether. It was then that the South Pole began to fill my daydreams again.

Not long after our return to England, I got talking to Faye Sommerville, an old friend of George's. For the last five years, she had been working for an American organisation called Adventure Network International (ANI), the only private company providing air transport to Antarctica. It caters for climbers, penguin spotters and other 'extreme tourists'. Ever since Robert Swan's 'In the Footsteps of Scott' trip to the South Pole in 1985, ANI has supported every non-governmental expedition to the Antarctic interior. Faye told me that ANI had just begun running commercial trips to the South Pole and that the next one would start in November 2001. For a fee of £30,000, I could join a professionally guided sixty-day journey from a start point at Hercules Inlet on the Antarctic coast to the bottom of the world. With the chores of logistics and team building already organised, all I would have to do to guarantee my place on the 2001 expedition was to raise thirty grand. Faye went on to explain that if the expedition was successful, at twenty-six I would become the youngest Briton to reach the South Pole, and this angle might score points when trying to raise the necessary sponsorship. I knew that if I didn't grasp this opportunity while I had the chance, the South Pole would gnaw away in my mind forever.

After a winter in Switzerland working as a ski guide for the chalet holiday business Ski Verbier, I became part of their London management team. My boss, David Pearson, was aware of my South Pole ambitions and said that provided that my work didn't suffer, I could use the office's facilities to look for financial help to join ANI's commercial expedition. It was an incredibly generous offer, and for the best part of twelve months I made the time, often after work or at weekends, to pester all the companies who had sponsored my previous trips to the mountains as well as hundreds more. Several organisations expressed an interest, but all promises of support vanished after the tragic events of 11 September 2001. I briefly contemplated borrowing the £30,000 before my parents drummed some common sense into me. The expedition went ahead without me. The Canadian polar veteran Paul Landry guided Timo Polari from Finland and Chris Weyers, from Australia, to the South Pole in sixty days.

Seeing my dreams evaporate after so much hard work only made me more determined to have another go the following year, but not on a commercial trip and not with a group of people I had never met before. Without really thinking about what I might be letting myself in for, I made the decision to put my own South Pole expedition together and fill it with fellow adventurers, people I had climbed with in the past.

2002 marked the centenary of Captain Scott's first attempt to reach the South Pole, and I began trying to find a way in which I could incorporate this important anniversary in my own plans. The 1901–4 British National Antarctic Expedition, or the *Discovery* Expedition as it is more commonly known today, was a landmark in the history of Antarctic exploration, but its extraordinary achievements have been completely overshadowed by the tragic events of Scott's fateful return to Antarctica nine years later.

In 1902 Scott and his companions Ernest Shackleton and Edward Wilson were forced to turn back less than five hundred miles from the South Pole. But it was outstanding scientific work that was the expedition's crowning glory, and its findings filled more volumes than the entire Encyclopaedia Britannica. My idea was for our expedition to celebrate the *Discovery* Expedition's achievements by following Scott's route south from McMurdo Sound to the point of his party's 1902 farthest south on the Ross Ice Shelf. From here the plan was to join the *Terra Nova* Expedition's 1911–12 route up the notorious Beardmore Glacier, through the Transantarctic Mountains and on to the Pole. Unlike Scott, who had to retrace his steps all the way back to McMurdo Sound, a ski plane would come to pick us up from the Pole. Only Robert Swan's team had completed this route since Scott's day and we could expect the 820-mile journey to take anything from fifty-five to seventy-five days.

*

Even though the first recorded sighting of the Antarctic mainland took place less than two hundred years ago, man has
speculated about its existence for thousands of years. In about
530 BC the ancient Greek philosopher Pythagoras reasoned that
the Earth must be spherical with a vast southern continent
balancing the landmasses of the north. The name Antarctica,
from the ancient Greek Antarktos, translates as 'opposite
Arktos' – Arktos being the constellation of the Bear that dominates the northern night sky. The Egyptian, Ptolemy, believed
that people of great wealth inhabited what he called Terra
Australis Incognita, the Unknown Southern Land, but that an
impenetrable hot belt of fire and monsters separated the northern and southern hemispheres.

The fearsome Polynesian chief Ui-Te-Rangiora headed south
from Raratonga in his canoe in about AD 650 'until the ocean
was filled with white powder and great white rocks rose high
into the sky.' The notion of a southern continent lost favour in
the Middle Ages, when dissident thinkers risked being burned
at the stake for suggesting that the Earth was anything but flat.
It was not until the momentous journeys of Columbus and
Magellan that Pythagoras's theory was confirmed.

The first known map of Antarctica dates from 1508, when the
Renaissance genius Leonardo da Vinci drew the outline of an
imaginary continent called 'Antarctus' south of Africa. In 1578,
sixty years after Magellan's circumnavigation, Sir Francis Drake
became the first man to sail round Cape Horn. In his boat the
Golden Hind he reached a new 'farthest south' of 57°S. When
the Dutchman Abel Tasman sailed around Australia in 1642–3,
he proved once and for all that if there was a great southern continent it could not be connected to an already known
landmass.

During the early planning stages of our expedition, Pat
Woodhead and I visited the Expedition Advisory Centre at the
Royal Geographical Society in London, where a magnificent
seventeenth-century map of the world adorns an entire wall.
Gazing up at this fabulous work of art, I found it extraordinary

that even though Antarctica had never been sighted at the time the map was drawn, the cartographers of the day had imaginatively pencilled in a vast southern continent, complete with rivers and forests.

It was the Yorkshireman Captain James Cook who threw the concept of a verdant southern paradise out of the window for good. During the second of his long voyages around the world, he became the first man to penetrate the Antarctic Circle, and in 1773 the first to circumnavigate the continent. Cook spent many months searching for land, and after pack ice forced him to retreat to South Georgia Island he wrote: 'The place is doomed by nature never to feel the warmth of the sun's rays, but to lie forever buried by everlasting snow and ice, whose horrible and savage aspect I have not the words to describe.'

Cook had reached 71°10'S, a record that was to stand for half a century. Had it not been for the bad weather, he would surely have sighted land, tantalisingly shrouded in mist less than fifty miles from his ship. Although he never saw it, Cook believed that a southern land must be the source of the icebergs spread over the ocean but that it was unlikely to be habitable. He concluded: 'Should anyone possess the resolution and fortitude ... to push yet further south than I have done ... I make bold to say that the world will derive no benefit from it.'

Explorers were so discouraged that they steered clear of the far southern seas until in 1820 when, as often happens when waiting an eternity for something to arrive, Antarctica was spotted twice in the space of just three days – first by a Russian ship and then by an English vessel. Whether it was Fabian von Bellingshausen or Edward Bransfield who saw it first remains a source of dispute between Russia and Great Britain to this day, but their discoveries opened the way for hundreds of pioneering voyages to the Antarctic. These expeditions were led not by explorers but by ambitious men seeking to make a quick buck from Antarctica's primary resource – seals.

The sealers were roughnecks, lured to the South by the huge bounty that seal pelts could fetch back home. Sealing parties from Britain, France and the United States had slaughtered literally millions of animals for their fur. Having never seen humans before, the seals showed no fear and would inquisitively waddle up to the men, only to be clubbed to death or shot. During one particular voyage in the early 1820s, no fewer than 100,000 skins were taken back to England aboard the *Pegasus*. But by the time the ship had docked in London, the skins had rotted into a stinking mass that had to be shovelled out of the hold and sold on as manure.

By 1822 the seal populations of the Falkland Islands and South Georgia had already been hunted almost to extinction, forcing the sealers to search for new breeding grounds further south. Often the discovery of new lands would be kept secret so the sealing companies could have the seal stock entirely to themselves. The sealers' journeys became ever more daring, and in 1823 the Scot James Weddell sailed south through the sea that now bears his name as far as 74°15'S, over two hundred miles further south than any man had been before.

Within ten years, Antarctica's seal population had been obliterated and the industry collapsed. Amazingly, many seal colonies have since recovered. From a population of around ten animals 180 years ago, the fur seal population of South Georgia has multiplied to over a million, in one of the animal kingdom's great recovery acts.

The departure of the sealers from the south came at a time when scientific interest in the polar regions was on the increase. Following the discovery of the Earth's magnetic field by the Germans in the 1830s, ambitious expeditions were launched to find out more about it. Scientists were only just beginning to realise the importance of the Earth's magnetic field to maritime navigation. Spurred on by the British naval officer James Clark Ross's arrival at the North Magnetic Pole in 1831, several government-funded expeditions headed to Antarctica in the hope of locating the South Magnetic Pole.

The next to cast their eye south were the French, under the command of the wonderfully named Jules-Sébastien-César Dumont d'Urville. Dumont d'Urville had already made a name for himself seventeen years earlier after persuading his government to buy the beautiful statue of the Venus de Milo for the nation, which had recently been unearthed in the Aegean. After penetrating deep into the Weddell Sea and spending a year carrying out anthropological research in the South Pacific, they finally landed in East Antarctica in 1840, hacking off a few pieces of granite from a cliff as proof of their discovery. Dumont d'Urville named the land Terre Adélie after his wife and returned home to great acclaim.

At about the same time Lieutenant Charles Wilkes led an American expedition into the south. His discoveries led him to believe that the lands unfolding before him could be part of a much bigger continent – Terra Australis Incognita. But this could not be proven. Despite charting more than one thousand miles of virgin coastline, Wilkes was court-martialled on his return home for poor surveying techniques and for the rough treatment of his crew.

But neither the French nor the Americans found what they had been searching for. Hoping to reproduce his sensational successes in the north and discover the South Magnetic Pole, the dashing James Clark Ross set sail for Antarctica aboard HMS *Erebus* and HMS *Terror*. In January 1841, he penetrated the pack ice as far south as 78°9'S, becoming the first to see the 200-foot-high gleaming wall of the Ross Ice Shelf. He described this extraordinary ice barrier, which stretched for hundreds of miles in each direction, as 'a mighty and wonderful object far beyond anything we could have thought or conceived'. It prevented Ross from pushing any further south and he concluded: 'We might with equal chance of success try to sail through the white cliffs of Dover.'

Other discoveries during Ross's four-year voyage included new mountain ranges, the 12,000-foot volcano Mount Erebus on Ross Island and the coastline of Victoria Land. Ross was adored by his crew and in 1842 he threw a lavish New Year's Eve party for all on board. After mooring alongside an iceberg, a refreshment bar complete with seating was carved into the ice and the festivities lasted all day.

Around the coast of Victoria Land, Ross's compass started

behaving wildly. His investigations led him to speculate that the South Magnetic Pole was located somewhere on the high plateau of Victoria Land and way out of reach. Ross's legacy was his surveying work of McMurdo Sound off Ross Island and then eastwards along the Ice Barrier, which would one day pave the way for the subsequent British and Norwegian attempts on the South Pole.

Ross was given a hero's welcome on his return to England. On his wedding day later that year, his new father-in-law made him promise to hang up his expedition boots for good. He kept his word and the career of one of Antarctica's great pioneers came to an end. Ross had proved conclusively that there was no hospitable land in Antarctica and it was not visited again for over fifty years.

Interest in the southern continent was rekindled in 1895 when the leading geographers of the day gathered at the Royal Geographical Society in London and passed a resolution stating: 'The exploration of the Antarctic Regions is the greatest piece of geographical exploration still to be undertaken.' Governments were urged to send teams south and a new wave of scientific exploration in the south had begun.

The Belgians were the first to respond, and in early 1898 *Belgica* under the command of Adrien de Gerlache weighed anchor at Punta Arenas in Chile and headed south. A young Norwegian called Roald Amundsen volunteered his services to join the expedition as first mate and without pay. Hoping to discover new lands, *Belgica* headed down the length of the Antarctic Peninsula and into the Bellingshausen Sea, loaded with three years of supplies. With the austral winter fast approaching and a growing danger of the ship becoming frozen in, de Gerlache asked his crew how they would feel about spending the winter stuck in the pack ice. The men went berserk and accused their skipper of plotting their icy imprisonment long before they had set sail from South America.

By early March, the ice had sealed their fate, and more by accident than anything else, *Belgica* became the first ship to overwinter in Antarctica. Penguins were slaughtered to provide fresh meat, enabling the ship's doctor to prove the effectiveness of fresh food at keeping the dangers of scurvy at bay. The ship's physicist ignored the advice, saying that he would rather die than eat penguin meat, which on 5 June was precisely what he did. Narrowly avoiding becoming trapped for a second miserable winter, *Belgica* returned safely to Chile the following March. The expedition provided Amundsen with valuable experience and fuelled his desire to one day claim Antarctica's ultimate prize and be the first man to reach the South Pole.

In 1899 the Norwegian Carsten Borchgrevink overwintered near Cape Adare on Victoria Land with nine colleagues and seventy-five dogs. They took the dogs out on sledging forays, produced excellent maps and carried out research on the Earth's magnetic field in one of the windiest corners of the continent. The expedition showed that in the relative comfort of a wooden hut, men could survive the desperately cold and dark Antarctic winter, opening up numerous possibilities for the exploration of the interior. But the enigma of the great southern landmass still remained unanswered.

Since the International Geographical Conference in 1895, the elderly president of the Royal Geographical Society, Sir Clements Markham, had campaigned tirelessly for a major British expedition to push deep into the heart of Antarctica. He was not alone in his belief that because of the ground-breaking voyages of Cook and Ross, the British had priority in Antarctica. One outspoken campaigner went so far as to say: 'I should not like to see foreign names upon that hemisphere where all civilised points are inhabited by our countrymen and belong to this country.' This was the heyday of the British Empire so it is not surprising to find ripe Victorian arrogance assuming that the polar regions were part of the Empire and the best way of exploring them was the British way. After years of fund-raising and meticulous planning, Markham's dream was finally realised.

At the dawn of the twentieth century, atlases were covered with blanks south of the Antarctic Circle. Despite hundreds of journeys by nineteenth-century pioneers, there had been just a handful of coastal landings and only a tiny fraction of Antarctica's twenty-thousand-mile coastline had been mapped. Were these early discoveries merely islands, or could the dots be joined to reveal Ptolemy's great southern continent?

Following a royal inspection by the new king and expedition patron Edward VII at the Cowes yachting regatta, the SS *Discovery* set sail from the Solent in searing heat on 6 August 1901 on a quest to unravel the mysteries of the far south. The British National Antarctic Expedition was the most ambitious programme of Antarctic exploration ever seen, and one which would ultimately open the route to the South Pole. *Discovery*'s commander was to become the most recognised name in the history of polar exploration. His name was Robert Falcon Scott.

*

ANI's base in Antarctica is located at Patriot Hills near the Ronne Ice Shelf, thousands of miles from Scott's base at McMurdo Sound. Had I found the funds to join Paul Landry's expedition with ANI in 2001, we would have set off from Hercules Inlet, twenty-odd miles from Patriot Hills, on the edge of the Antarctic continent. Following in the footsteps of Captain Scott, as opposed to the standard Hercules Inlet route, would increase our expedition's costs dramatically, as ANI would need to fly halfway round Antarctica just to drop us off at our start point.

Based on a party of four people and a polar guide, ANI quoted me a price of £180,000 to include all logistical support and the placing of two depots at either end of the Beardmore Glacier. Extra equipment and training costs put the budget close to the £200,000 mark. I remained convinced that despite a sevenfold hike in the amount of money to be raised, public interest in Scott's exploits would put us in a strong position to generate significant media coverage and possibly a television documentary. This publicity would all help when it came to looking for sponsorship.

Ranulph Fiennes, who had supported some of my previous trips to the mountains, agreed to be patron of the project, which adopted the grandiose title of the 'Commonwealth South Pole

Centenary Expedition'. Having been working with the Prince's Trust for a number of years, I was keen that the expedition should try to raise a significant sum of money for this worthwhile cause, a task made more achievable after the Prince of Wales gave the trip his backing.

Next came the task of selecting a team. Our expedition to the unclimbed mountains of Central Asia had been as close to the perfect trip as possible – we had achieved far more than we had expected, and despite the day-to-day stresses and hardship, every day was filled with laughter. If we could reproduce the same expedition spirit in Antarctica, then I believed it would give us the very best possible chance of success. George Wells had just started his own property development business in London, and with all the distractions and time away that the expedition would entail, pressing him to join me would be disastrous for his fledgling company. George had been with me on most of my earlier trips and leaving him out of the side this time around was a particularly difficult decision to make.

I hoped that Pat Woodhead and Nick Stopford, the other two Kyrgyzstan veterans, would have fewer work constraints and be able to join the team. We had been through a great deal together and become very close. At the end of 2001, Pat was trying to make it as a freelance television producer, working on documentary subjects as diverse as swimming with great white sharks and the journeys of Alexander the Great. I first met him at the beginning of my second year at Bristol University when I had just moved into a house with five friends. One day the doorbell rang and I opened the door to find a young student, wearing nothing but a towel around his waist and clutching a chicken. He walked straight past me and made a beeline for Amanda and Lucinda, two of the girls I was living with. 'Good afternoon ladies,' he said confidently, with a cheeky twinkle in his eye, 'I've just moved in next door and was wondering if I could borrow your microwave to defrost this.'

Over the course of the next two years I got to know Pat very well, and found out that there was much more to the guy than simply trying to impress members of the opposite sex. Together we competed in the London Marathon, rock-climbed in the nearby Avon Gorge and became good friends. Pat is one of life's great enthusiasts and his limitless energy has seen him work as a rhino tracker in Namibia and run marathons in Arctic Norway. I fired off an email to see how interested he might be in coming to the South Pole. The reply came back within three minutes. 'What makes you think I want to freeze my kahoonas off, eat grim food, burn eight thousand calories a day, never see darkness, have to put up with you as a tent partner, be in danger of falling in crevasses and be savaged by mutated penguins? Yes alright, I'll do it.'

Nick is without doubt the most experienced mountaineer amongst our motley group of adventurers. Even before going to Kyrgyzstan, he had an impressive list of ascents to his name, including Mont Blanc and Mount McKinley, the highest mountain in North America. In 2001 he joined a British expedition to the North East Ridge of Mount Everest, reaching an altitude of over 25,000 feet before bad weather forced the team's retreat from the mountain. Nick's personality fluctuates between that of a serious accountant and that of a giggly teenager. His passion for the outdoors and ability to get on with anybody made him an excellent guy to have on the expedition. The only problem was that he had recently gone to work for Ernst & Young in Geneva. Whilst he was desperate to join the team, it would have been pushing his luck to ask for all that time off before he had settled in to his new job. Nick's girlfriend at the time was living in London, which did at least give him the perfect excuse to fly over for weekends to train and work on the expedition.

My work took me to Verbier for a few days in March 2002, during which time I managed to fit in a day's skiing with some friends who were over on holiday. One of their party was a South African called Andrew Gerber, whom I had never met before. Although you would never have guessed it from his Home Counties accent, he was brought up in Cape Town before moving to England at the age of seventeen. He seemed particularly interested in my South Pole plans and confessed to having wanted to go on a major expedition for years. Later that morning Toby, one of the guys we were skiing with, came up to me and whispered in my ear: 'If you're still looking for teammates, you should seriously consider asking Gerber. He may have never done any of this expedition stuff before, but he is strong, loyal, has plenty of common sense and is a beast on the rowing machine. Trust me, he would be awesome.' By the end of the day I had seen enough of this Andrew Gerber character to ask him to join the team.

It may seem strange to pick someone for such a major venture as an expedition to the South Pole without knowing much about him, but on all my expeditions, I have tried to select people who get along with others and who can stay focused when the chips are down. To me, these character traits are far more important than sheer technical ability. Even though I have been incredibly fortunate never to come to blows with a team member, it is well known that expeditions can be stressful affairs where fellow participants have spectacular fallings out. I wasn't sure exactly what it was, but Andrew had something about him, and I just sensed that he would fit into the team perfectly. With all his sailing, skiing and rowing experience, I was convinced that he wouldn't take long to pick up the technical side of things.

The hardest part of any expedition is finding somebody to pay for you to go. It is usually a two-stage process. First you need to be able to guarantee publicity. Only with the strong prospect of the company's name appearing on television screens or newspaper pages will a marketing director part with any of the precious marketing budget. With Nick in Geneva and Andrew not joining us till the spring, Pat and I set about working on ideas for a television documentary.

Sir Kenneth Branagh had just appeared as Ernest Shackleton in Channel Four's superb two-part television drama about Shackleton's fateful *Endurance* Expedition. Having heard Branagh give a passionate lecture at the Royal Geographical Society about the making of the film and his dream of one day visiting Antarctica, we approached him about the possibility of flying in to join us for the final hundred miles of the expedition.

For two weeks he deliberated before declining because of work commitments. He generously wrote: 'I shall therefore leave it to the real heroes and simply say a huge thank you for the immensely flattering idea that you should even consider me as a team member.' Had he come on board, we felt sure that everything else would have fallen into place.

For months Pat used his contacts in the television industry to set up meetings with documentary makers and production companies. The two of us would then try to sell them the idea of a bunch of young polar novices following Scott's route on the centenary of his first attempt to reach the South Pole. Whilst there was plenty of interest in the idea, the practicalities and costs of filming in Antarctica became the major stumbling blocks every time. We needed to pursue other options.

All the major newspapers and television news channels were approached to explore the chances of our story making the headlines. Every time the answer was the same: 'It sounds an interesting story and there's a chance we might run a report about your story when you reach the Pole, but due to the unpredictable way that news works, it could be that major news breaking on the day would shut your story out. Keep in touch, but for now we can't guarantee anything.'

One of the news outlets I contacted was ITN. I spoke to the journalist Terry Lloyd, who over the years had reported on many of Ranulph Fiennes's polar exploits. After all the setbacks of my other dealings with journalists, his enthusiasm blew me away. 'Tom, I think this is a terrific idea. I would love to report your story for "The News at Ten".

'I'll see what sort of commitment I can drum up from the guys here, but count it as a YES. Now go and get your sponsorship, young man!' Over the course of the next few months, Terry and I spoke regularly on the telephone to set everything in stone. It wasn't the hour-long documentary that we had been hoping for, but it was a start.

The four of us wrote hundreds of sponsorship letters and emails to the marketing departments of every major company with a budget large enough not to take fright at the £200,000 we needed. From telecommunications firms to banks to yoghurt manufacturers, we courted them all and followed every letter with a phone call. Optimistically, we also approached organisations with a polar connection, however tenuous, such as Smirnoff Ice, Guinness Extra Cold and even Fox's Glacier Mints, convinced that we were the answer to all their marketing dreams. Before the person on the other end of the line had a chance to say no, we would offer to come and meet them in person. Mostly we got no further than the switchboard, but on the few occasions when an offer for a meeting was successful, we felt we were far more likely to be taken seriously if we could talk to someone face to face.

Months of schmoozing in office buildings all over the country routinely ended in disappointment. It was a shameless task, and however many meetings I had already had that day I would still try to sound passionate and excited. David at Ski Verbier was wonderfully supportive, and if things in the office weren't too busy he would give me the time off work to meet potential backers. Everyone in the team was doing their bit in our never-ending quest for sponsorship. Occasionally, a company would sound impressed by a presentation and voice an interest in making some form of financial contribution. But when it came to that final commitment, things would always fall through.

One exception was Snickers, with whom Pat and I had several meetings. It was particularly ironic that it should have been Pat who made the initial sponsorship approach. Towards the end of our Kyrgyzstan expedition, food supplies had run out three days before we were due to be picked up from our base camp. Things got so desperate that we resorted to living off wild mushrooms and Strepsil throat lozenges. We had saved one Snickers bar to be split between the team, which we hoped would provide us with enough energy to reach Pik Fiennes, our last summit. Our empty stomachs rumbled from the very first step. I have never been so hungry or felt so weak. For six long hours we staggered up the mountain's snowy flanks, fighting off temptation for as long as possible. A few hundred feet below the summit and we could hold off no longer.

Salivating uncontrollably, we turned to Pat, the custodian of the Snickers bar, and asked him to start chopping it up into equal portions. Looking decidedly sheepish, he bowed his head and confessed: 'Sorry guys, I've already eaten it.' We all have a giggle about it now, but at the time we wanted to throw him off the mountain. By approaching Snickers for a large cheque (and several complimentary boxes of chocolate bars) he was now seeking forgiveness in the most absolute form.

In early July 2002 Anne Kershaw, the president of ANI, was over in London and we arranged to meet her. Anne took over the running of ANI after her husband Giles (the founder of ANI) died in a gyrocopter accident in Antarctica in 1990. This petite, blonde, glamorously dressed and very attractive Scotswoman was nothing like the image of the efficient businesswoman that I had built up in my mind following our correspondence over the past eighteen months. She looked as if she had just left university. For most of our hour-long meeting she was extremely chatty and friendly, almost flirty, as we discussed the logistics of the expedition. Then the conversation turned to money and her steely professionalism kicked in. I tried to find ways of bringing the expedition costs down, but hers is a cut-throat business and she had learned to stand her ground. Before bidding us farewell, she said: 'You've got two months to get the funds together, or I'm afraid the trip is off.'

The route via the treacherous 120-mile-long Beardmore Glacier is the most difficult of all the approaches to the South Pole. Of the eight people who have reached the Pole this way, only Robert Swan's small team returned alive. The glacier is littered with giant crevasses from which Scott had many narrow escapes. Choosing the safest line was of vital importance and I approached Professor Charles Swithinbank at the Scott Polar Research Institute in Cambridge for some much-needed advice. Having spent many years surveying Antarctica from the air, he knew the intricacies of the constantly changing Beardmore Glacier better than any man alive, and he passed on some particularly useful aerial photographs and up-to-date glacier surface information.

I had read much about recent expeditions in Antarctica that used kites to improve travel speeds, and thought it would be worth us trying to do the same. The theory is that when the wind is blowing in the right direction, these mini-parachutes can be raised into the air and used to propel a man on skis, dragging a sled across the snow. As with the new extreme sport of kite surfing, with good handling the kites can help one travel great distances given favourable conditions.

Roger Mear had been part of Robert Swan's three-man In the Footsteps of Scott Expedition to the South Pole in 1985. Roger had used kites in some of his more recent expeditions to great effect, once covering over one hundred miles across Greenland in just six hours. When I asked him if an outfit of polar amateurs such as ours would be able to cope with the technicalities of the new sport of kiting, he could not have been more positive. But Roger also highlighted the importance of training with the kites, stressing in an email to me: 'If you are intending to go to Antarctica this coming season then you have to get going with the kites NOW! It's a big learning curve, even if you are all good downhill skiers.'

I also contacted the Belgian explorer Alain Hubert, who in 1997–8 made the longest unsupported crossing of Antarctica with his partner Dixie Dansercoer. After reaching the Pole from the East Antarctic coast, they descended the Beardmore Glacier before deploying their kites to help them cross the Ross Ice Shelf to McMurdo Sound. He told me that the winds they experienced on the Ross Ice Shelf typically blew from the west. As we would be travelling in the opposite direction to Alain and Dixie, if we were to take kites with us we would be able to use these crosswinds to our advantage. Alain also recommended we use a special type of kite called a NASA-wing that had been developed by NASA as a way of landing spacecraft.

Whilst living in Cape Town, Andrew had spent much of his free time on the beach flying kites very similar to the ones we hoped to use in Antarctica. Pat had also tried them out in the past and the four of us spent several Saturday afternoons on

Clapham Common getting used to the art of flying these king-duvet-sized pieces of paper-thin material. Roger suggested arranging some kite-buggying instruction on the large tidal flats of Camber Sands, not far from my parents' house in East Sussex. Over the course of a hot July weekend, Pat, Nick, Andrew and I slowly got to grips with the kites to power the buggies along the beach. Translating our newfound skills into 'kite-skiing' on snow would be a different task altogether, but our South Coast trials had brought home what might be achieved in Antarctica if the winds blew in our favour.

It was all very well honing our skills in the warmth of the British summer, but we needed to acquire some cold-weather experience before we headed south. Following a search on the internet, I managed to track down a German alpine guide by the name of Gottlieb Braun-Elwert. Gottlieb ran specialist polar training courses in the Southern Alps of New Zealand and had trained a Singaporean team that had successfully reached the South Pole in 1999. I arranged an intensive three-week programme for the four of us at the end of August – the middle of the New Zealand winter. At that time of year Greenland was the only other part of the world where we could have trained for a polar expedition, but the huge costs involved in getting there made this unfeasible.

A fortnight before we were due to leave for New Zealand, Snickers withdrew their support because of 'internal problems'. This hammer blow was particularly heartbreaking as we had received provisional guarantees that they wanted to make a financial commitment of £100,000 to the expedition. The one company who continued to show an interest were the car insurance specialists Hastings Direct, who I had heard were eager to support Sussex-based sporting projects. They had just signed a deal to sponsor the prestigious WTA tennis championships at Eastbourne, and I thought with my own links with the county it was worth approaching them.

Over the course of the summer, I had had several meetings with their colourful American chairman, David Gundlach. Having done a lot of climbing in the Rockies in his younger days, he shared our passion for the great outdoors and said that he would like to become involved in the expedition. David told me that his business commitments made it impossible for him to find the time to climb again but that our expedition was his way of continuing his adventures. He very generously agreed to provide the £8,000 we needed to go to New Zealand 'to keep this terrific enterprise alive.'

Our three-week trip to New Zealand proved to be a great success. After a few days ski mountaineering around the Harris Mountains above the sleepy town of Wanaka, we based ourselves in a small corrugated iron shack called the Centennial Hut, high in the Southern Alps. The only way in was by helicopter. Located amongst large ice fields, with biting winds and regular snowstorms roaring off the rocky peaks above, the place resembled a sort of mini Antarctica and was the perfect place for us to train. We spent a lot of time ski mountaineering, learning to build igloos (a vital skill in case our tents blew away in Antarctica), practising crevasse rescue techniques and building up our fitness levels in temperatures down to −20°C. In the perishing hut every evening, Gottlieb continued the instruction with some invaluable lessons about polar clothing, equipment, nutrition and survival.

Our time on the ice fields also gave us the perfect opportunity to try out the kites on the snow. It was a strange but exhilarating sensation to be pulled across the flat surface by a thin piece of material fluttering thirty yards above our heads. We experimented with the NASA-wings in New Zealand but found they had a narrower wind-range than the more conventional 'wind foil' kites, which allowed us to ski at an angle of ninety degrees to the wind.

It was also clear that if the kites were ever deployed, drama was never going to be far away. Nick and Andrew, both hurtling along in opposite directions at breakneck speed, managed to have a head-on collision, skis and bodies flying through the air in a cloud of powder snow. Thankfully, other than dented pride, neither of them suffered injury and they were soon back on their feet in fits of laughter. Moments later, Pat managed to wrap

£600-worth of kite round the one rocky pinnacle protruding through the ice field. We spent the rest of the afternoon fixing ropes to the rock so that he could abseil down the cliff face and recover the kite.

Although we hadn't been given the chance to travel for days on end across a polar ice cap, we returned to England pleased with everything we had learned and almost ready to take on the harsh Antarctic environment. Our sessions with the kites confirmed their huge potential, and we made the unanimous decision to take them to Antarctica. The training gave Andrew a hands-on introduction to expedition life, and he proved himself to be more than up to the job. Most important of all, everyone got on extremely well in New Zealand and the three weeks had been an invaluable team-building exercise.

With just seven weeks to go before the planned expedition departure date, there was still a huge amount to do. Shortly after we returned home from New Zealand, Geoff Somers agreed to join us as our polar guide and came down to London to meet us. Having somebody in the team with polar experience was going to be vital to the success of the expedition and Geoff was one of the very best in the business. His quiet, unassuming character belies an incredibly tough interior that has seen him achieve far more than any other British polar explorer in recent times. Geoff has not become a household name in this country in the way that other British explorers have, simply because he does not like the attention. After many years working for the British Antarctic Survey, he began leading trips to the Poles. The highlight of his expeditions took place in 1989–90 when, along with five colleagues and several dog teams, he made the longest traverse of Antarctica. In an extraordinary feat of endurance, they finally reached their destination after an unbroken 220-day journey of nearly four thousand miles.

It wasn't just his vast experience that made Geoff my first choice as our expedition guide, it was the fact that four years earlier he had travelled hundreds of miles with kites in Antarctica. We liked Geoff enormously and spent a useful weekend with him talking logistics and flying the kites in Hyde Park. He also suggested a fitness regime to build up our strength and stamina. Geoff's ideas were so unconventional that at first we weren't sure if he was being serious.

Following Geoff's recommendation, Pat managed to track down some old minibus tyres, which we tied together and attached to a waist harness. Geoff told us that dragging them through uneven terrain was the best way of building up the muscles we would be using to pull our sleds in Antarctica. Over the course of the next few weeks, we met up in the evenings for tyre-dragging sessions around the sandy horse rides of Rotten Row in Hyde Park. With a ski pole in each hand, we walked along at a brisk pace, doing hour-long laps of the park. Choking clouds of dust rose from the tyres as they reluctantly slid through the sand. It was mind-numbing, sweaty work, and we must have looked a truly bizarre sight, but we soon learnt to ignore the comments from American tourists and people walking their dogs.

When we met Geoff, one of the first things he told us was: 'You lads need to bulk up a bit. You're way too scrawny for polar travel.' He recommended putting on weight fast, by whatever means possible. For somebody with a sweet tooth like me, I thought all my Christmases had come at once. Rather than pour the usual semi-skimmed milk on my cereal in the mornings, I used double cream, before tucking into a second helping. Throughout the day, I would gorge on cakes, biscuits and jam-filled donuts, go to McDonald's for lunch and eat large steaks and ice cream for dinner. But it wasn't working and my excesses saw me put on only three pounds of weight over a month of feasting. I had read how Ranulph Fiennes had lost nearly four stone during his Antarctic crossing. If the same happened to me, I would surely blow away in the wind.

I cannot begin to imagine how complex it would have been for Scott and Markham to put the *Discovery* Expedition together. To start with, the British National Antarctic Expedition needed to raise the best part of £6,000,000 (in today's money) to get off the ground. After dedicating six years of his life to the job, Markham eventually secured the funds from the government, the Royal Geographical Society and a multitude of businesses and individuals. Scott's officers were largely made up of men who had served under him in the Royal Navy. One notable exception was his young ambitious third lieutenant Ernest Shackleton, who had served in the Merchant Navy since he was sixteen. The scientific staff had an important role to play on the expedition, none more so than the expedition's zoologist and assistant surgeon Edward Wilson. There was little time for any training, although nine months before *Discovery* set sail, Scott and Markham travelled to Oslo for a series of invaluable meetings with the legendary Norwegian explorer Fridtjof Nansen.

Whilst all the preparations for our expedition were coming together, Anne Kershaw was still on my back for the money. Not long after our return from New Zealand, I was asked into the television studios of BBC London to give an interview for the evening news about our recent South Pole training trip. When I was told that the programme was going out live, I went sheet white and shook with fear. Plastered in countless Hastings Direct logos, and with the newsroom filled with tents, kites and skis, I stumbled my way through the interview. The weatherman Peter Cockroft gave a special Antarctic weather forecast and the ordeal of being in front of the cameras turned out to be far less terrifying than I had first feared.

The following day I spoke to David Gundlach, who was tickled pink with the exposure that the interview had given his company but he added that he had yet to make up his mind over sponsoring the expedition itself. He said he was also talking to 'other parties' about possible joint sponsorship deals but would let us know shortly. All our other leads had now dried up – David was our last hope.

With one month to go before departure, I began to write a journal of each day's events and my thoughts at the time. That is where this book goes on from here. Some of the historical, factual and geographical information about Antarctica was written up in my journal, but much of it was incomplete or inaccurate at the time of writing and had to be more thoroughly researched back in England. Otherwise, I have tried to keep the journal as close to its original form as possible. In certain cases, it needed to be adapted to make events more easily understood but I have tried to keep these changes to a minimum. My journal was sometimes written at times of great difficulty and stress, and I believe it reflects these conditions well.

Chapter Two

ICEBOUND

It's D-Day. Yesterday afternoon David Gundlach met with
Lesley McCormack of IMG (the sports marketing specialists)
and Sir Patrick O'Reilly, the Chairman of Heinz, about a co-
sponsorship deal to support our Scott route idea. Heinz was
one of Scott's principal sponsors and we hope that they will be
interested in continuing their association with the South Pole.
We've put all our eggs into one basket and the expedition's
hopes lie with this one phone call.

'So how did the meeting go?' I ask David.

'Look I'm really sorry, Tom. It's just not going to work. Heinz
liked the idea but they aren't prepared to stump up the money.
Between you and me, I think they're missing out on a great
opportunity here. We did think about what sort of a financial
commitment Hastings Direct could make but I'm afraid two
hundred thousand is out of our league now. I'm so sorry.'

I'm devastated. I've wasted another year and again have
nothing to show at the end of it. I call Pat with the bad news.
He says he had been half expecting the sponsorship to fall
through and had already been thinking of alternative plans. He
now hopes to join ANI's guided expedition along the standard
route to the Pole from Hercules Inlet and has some contacts that
seem interested in funding him. The trip will be far less likely
to generate publicity than Scott's route, making it less attractive
for a potential sponsor. Nevertheless, Pat seems quietly optimistic that he will be able to raise the necessary £30,000.

Andrew would very much like to join Pat on the ANI commercial expedition – he has some sponsorship interest in South
Africa and hopes to fly to Cape Town any day now to see

what he can find. Nick says count him out. His employers had provisionally given him three months off to join the expedition, but he can't keep them waiting any longer for the elusive sponsorship to materialise.

Drive to Cornwall for the weekend. So many calls of support from friends during the long journey down. They've all lived this expedition with me over the last few months and their disappointment is obvious.

SUNDAY 6 OCTOBER

Spend highly entertaining weekend in Cornwall for annual Bristol University v. Durham University golf match. Helps take my mind off one of the biggest setbacks of my life. The golf is very competitive, I play pretty well, Bristol reclaims the Challenge Cup and we hardly talk about Antarctica at all.

MONDAY 7 OCTOBER

The weekend has cleared my mind of all the disappointment of not being able to follow in Scott's footsteps, so I'm going to have one last crack at seeing if I can go to the Pole, albeit via a different route.

In to work early. I plan to approach all the companies who have shown an interest in the expedition over the past few months to see if they are able to sponsor, or at least part-sponsor, me to join the ANI trip. I still have that guaranteed interview with Terry Lloyd on the ITN's *News at Ten* and the *Sunday Telegraph* is making positive noises about a possible article – I just hope it's enough publicity to get sponsors onboard.

Feels strange to be doing this alone now. We have become a very close-knit bunch over the past few months, especially since New Zealand, and working together with everyone has been so much fun. Suddenly we are on our own and looking for our own sponsors. Nick has now pulled out altogether and whilst Pat, Andrew and I still speak to one another on the phone most days, it just doesn't feel the same.

Turn on my computer to find an email from Geoff Somers. I had left a message on his answer machine at the weekend saying the trip was off and his words this morning give me great encouragement. The email reads: 'What a bummer. You must be gutted. Do not give up the enterprise. It may not be happening this year but there is always next year or the year after ad fin. Your time has not gone to waste – some company out there does have the funds. Keep going.'

I am still desperate to go to Antarctica but my situation is not good. I've used up every business contact I can think of, I have just £32.74 in the bank account, talk of a second Gulf War and an impending recession is everywhere and I've got less than three weeks to find £30,000.

Nevertheless, I'm in a positive frame of mind. On all my previous expeditions, the funding has miraculously come together in the final few days. If I have learnt anything from this experience, it is to keep on trying until the bitter end. When we went to the Pamirs in 2000, the cheque from NOW.com only cleared the day before we boarded the plane to Kyrgyzstan. But never before have I had to raise a sum this size.

There's also an email from Anne Kershaw. David Gundlach had apparently been in touch over the weekend explaining that he had originally hoped to be involved in the sponsorship of our proposed expedition to follow Scott's route to the Pole, but that idea was now beyond Hastings Direct's financial means. None of this comes as a great surprise to me – David has bent over backwards in his efforts to get the likes of Heinz signed up, but it just wasn't meant to be. The email goes on to say that David was still keen to be involved in South Pole expeditions and would instead be sponsoring someone called Andrew Cooney to join ANI's commercially guided trip.

Andrew Cooney? I'm in complete shock. I first heard about a guy called Andrew Cooney a few weeks ago. He had considered joining a North Pole expedition earlier in the year and was now looking to retrace Scott's route to the South Pole at exactly the same time as us. As only one expedition has attempted to do this in the last 90 years, I thought it would be worth speaking to him to find out more about his plans. It turned out that he was just 23 and was also aiming to become the youngest Brit to walk to the South Pole. He told me he was hoping to join ANI's commercially guided trip to the South Pole from Hercules Inlet. When I pointed out that Scott actually began his South Pole attempts from the other side of the continent at a place called McMurdo Sound, he seemed unconcerned. He told me that his plans were at quite an early stage, he had no sponsorship and would probably have to wait to put off going to Antarctica until next year. When he said this, I relaxed.

For 15 minutes, Andrew Cooney and I shared information about equipment, training regimes and logistics. There is an unwritten rule amongst the expedition fraternity that we are all in this together and that no expedition would ever get off the ground without the useful suggestions and help of fellow adventurers. When I began planning our South Pole adventure, I had no idea where to start. It was the advice and encouragement I received from Antarctic veterans like Ranulph Fiennes, Roger Mear and Geoff Somers that gave our ambitious plans the kick-start they needed. Cooney asked me how our own sponsorship was coming along. Because I had been covered in their logos a few days earlier for the BBC London News interview, I had no hesitation in telling him that Hastings Direct had sponsored our training in New Zealand. It was hardly a big secret.

'And are they sponsoring the expedition itself?' he asked.

'Hopefully. We've been working closely with them for nearly six months now and are just in the process of pulling everything together,' I replied nonchalantly.

He seemed perfectly pleasant and asked me to bear his name in mind if anyone should pull out of our own expedition. I said I would keep him posted and that was that.

Following on from Anne's email, I do some investigating. It turns out that whilst we were still in talks with Hastings Direct, Andrew Cooney contacted their marketing department to ask them to sponsor him to go to the South Pole. He also travelled to Hastings to meet David in person. We will never know what sort of financial commitment Hastings Direct was considering making towards our expedition's £200,000 budget, but the business arguments for sponsoring just one person over us probably made financial sense. Whilst it is unlikely that Cooney would generate anything like the sort of publicity we could have expected for following Scott's route, it would be more cost-effective for David's business to finance one person than four. But it had been me who had approached Hastings Direct in the first place and discussed plans for an expedition months ago.

After rereading Anne's email for a third time, I gather my composure and call David to find out more about his meeting with Andrew Cooney. I tell him: 'I have to say I feel let down by Andrew Cooney. If you are going to be so generous as to fund someone to join ANI's trip to the Pole, I would hope that it would be one of us. Please will you reconsider?'

'Come and see me on Wednesday, Tom. We can talk about it then.'

Never before in all my years of fundraising for expeditions have I come across a situation like this.

Spend the rest of the day cursing myself for being such a naïve idiot.

WEDNESDAY 9 OCTOBER

6.30 pm meeting with David Gundlach in Hastings.

'Tom, I feel bad about what has happened and I would like to sponsor you to go to the South Pole after all,' he says.

I jump up off my chair. 'Thank you, thank you David so much.'

Just as I'm about to give him a big hug, he adds: 'Not so fast. It's on one condition – that you take Andrew Cooney under your wing. I would still like him to go but I want you both going in the same team. He hasn't been on an expedition before and I want you to show him the way it's done. The press would love it.'

What a dilemma. I am ecstatic that I have been offered the chance to fulfil my dream and go to the South Pole, but my teammates won't be the three guys I have been planning the trip with for the last twelve months – I will be doing the expedition with Cooney and a handful of total strangers.

Possibly risking everything, I say: 'I'm afraid that given all that's happened over the past few weeks, I would find it difficult to be part of the same team as Andrew Cooney, let alone take him under my wing.'

He tells me: 'Tom, there's a phrase out west which goes "Bury the hatchet." Get over it.'

I drive back to London, still unclear if I'm going or not. Get flashed by a speed camera on the A3 late at night. Great.

THURSDAY 10 OCTOBER

10 am. Pat calls to say that he has secured his funding to join ANI's South Pole trip. His sister had a contact at the jewellers Omega and they have come on board as his main sponsor. Other bits and pieces of funding have fallen into place too. But he doesn't sound happy. I ask him what the matter is.

'I feel so bad the way things have worked out, Tommy. You put this whole idea together, you got me on board, and now I'm the one going to the South Pole. It's not the same. You know I would much rather be doing it with you than with Cooney and a bunch of random punters.'

Appreciating his honesty, I reply: 'Pat, don't worry about it – better that one of us goes than no one. And besides, Hastings Direct haven't made their final decision yet. It's looking like there may be as many as seven people going to the South Pole this year, and ANI could well lay on an extra trip. I'm still desperate to join you!'

Later. I'm at a friend's engagement party in Picadilly. Everyone here seems so successful – lawyers, fund managers, equity traders. Makes me realise how much growing up I have to do. Here I am trying to go off gallivanting across Antarctica, whilst all of my friends are settling down and getting on with their lives. 'But why the hell do you want to go to Antarctica, Tom? It's so damn cold!' I've lost count of the number of times I am asked that question and have given up trying to answer it properly. Very few people seem to understand. But I know why I want to do this and that's all that matters.

9.30 pm and I'm just leaving the party when the mobile rings. It's Anne Kershaw. 'Sorry Tom, bad news I'm afraid. I've just heard from David Gundlach and it's all off.' There's a long pause before she adds: 'Only kidding! You are going to Antarctica after all.'

'I always knew you were a devious little so-and-so Anne Kershaw, but that was a tad below the belt!' I reply gleefully.

'David has changed his mind and is sponsoring both you and Andrew Cooney. But you'll be pleased to hear that you and Patrick will be travelling in a separate team to him. Thanks to Hastings Direct's generosity, we've decided to run two trips this year.'

I am now VERY excited. Walk all the way back to the flat as opposed to taking the bus – must be good training. I'm on the mobile the whole way, telling friends and family the good news.

Pat is the first one I speak to. 'Pat, I'm coming with you! I've just had the call.'

'This is awesome news! I'm so pleased for you mate,' he replies, sounding even more over the moon than me.

'And Anne has confirmed that we can have our own private trip. Cooney will be in Antarctica after all but he'll be in a team with the rest of the punters. We've got shitloads to do to get ready in the next three and a half weeks – buy all our kit, find a new guide, book flights, get fit and try to persuade Gerber to join us as well. But we can worry about all that in the morning!'

The parents are on holiday in Turkey this week so I leave a message on Dad's mobile. I then speak to Andrew, Nick and George. Then I ring Granny. As soon as she picks up the phone, I can tell something's wrong. She seems distraught. She tells me that Uncle Derek (her 80-year-old brother) died yesterday afternoon at his house in Cheshire in deeply distressing circumstances.

All celebrations are put on hold and I dash round to Granny's flat to see if she's OK. The facts surrounding Derek's death are still unclear and there are a lot of rumours flying around in the local press. He had been suffering from leukaemia for some time and despite having only just given up tennis and skiing, he was finding the increasing number of blood transfusions more than he could cope with. Derek had always been a very impatient man and it looks as if he took matters into his own hands. Apparently he had gone down to his sauna at home with some aluminium phosphide tablets, normally used as rat poison. He locked the sauna door and mixed himself a lethal cocktail. The whole mess is too awful for everyone and has put me in a sombre mood.

FRIDAY 11 OCTOBER

Not really in expedition mode today. Very upsetting to see Derek's bizarre death all over the papers. It turns out the whole A&E department at the Wirral Hospital had to be evacuated by firemen wearing protective clothing because Uncle Derek's body was so toxic. He certainly went out with a bang.

Email from David Gundlach confirming he is sponsoring me to go to the South Pole. He writes: 'I ended up in a bad position with Andrew Cooney. I am going to ask him to apologize to you. He is leaving a week before you. With only a one week head start, you and your team should be at the South Pole about two weeks ahead.'

I tell David Pearson (my boss at Ski Verbier) that I will be going away for three months. It's asking way too much of him to hold my job open whilst I am away and he has said I can stay on until the end of the month whilst he looks for a replacement. Realistically, he knows that my mind is no longer going to be on selling ski holidays and he shows enormous patience by letting me use the office as the unofficial expedition HQ.

After all the ups and downs of the last eighteen months, I hesitate to write the words 'I am going to Antarctica'. But I am, and we're off in just over three weeks' time.

MONDAY 14 OCTOBER

It's time to start ordering all our expedition equipment. Over the last few months I have been drawing up an extensive list of everything we need, complete with everyone's sizes. I have managed to negotiate various discounts with several specialist clothing manufacturers but have been waiting until we got the green light on the sponsorship front before making the orders. After each phone call, I tick each item off an endless shopping list of skis, jackets, woolly hats, socks, thermal underwear, gloves and countless other bits of stash.

Our specialist polar boots have to be ordered from an outdoor clothing company in Norway. Norwegian shoe manufacturers obviously use a completely different sizing system from the rest of Europe as the suppliers have no idea what a UK size 12 or a European 47 is. To get over this problem, Pat and I trace the outline of our feet onto pieces of blank paper and fax them through to Oslo. Just to be on the safe side and to make sure we have a selection of sizes to choose from, I order four pairs for the two of us.

Send an email to Anne saying we would like Paul Landry to be our guide. Having been there last year, he knows the route well, and now that Geoff has said he would not be interested in guiding the Hercules Inlet route, Paul would fit the bill perfectly.

TUESDAY 15 OCTOBER

Dinner with Mum and Dad who have just returned from Turkey. First time I've seen them since the good news. They are thrilled. Like most parents would be, they are understandably anxious about the dangers but are genuinely pleased that I've managed to get this far. 'But one thing that never changes, Tom,' Dad revels in saying, 'is you always leave everything in your life to the last minute!'

WEDNESDAY 16 OCTOBER

Receive call from marketing department at Hastings Direct saying they are not going to sponsor Cooney to go to the South Pole after all. Apparently he has 'let Hastings Direct down on several issues.' I wonder what he could have done?

Speak with Paul Landry for the first time. Seems a really nice bloke. Very professional. When I mention our original idea had been to use kites, he says: 'No way! I'm just getting into kiting myself. There were a few days on our expedition to the South Pole last year when the winds would have been perfect for kiting and it really annoyed me that we hadn't brought any kites with us. I've got a few contacts here in Canada so if you are interested I could try to order some kites for us.'

THURSDAY 17 OCTOBER

Telephone call from Humfrey Hunter, an old Bristol University friend who now works for the *Sunday Telegraph*. He has managed to get the half-page article that he wrote several weeks ago about our expedition published in the main section of the paper this coming Sunday. I'm surprised that they should want to write an article given that we are no longer following Scott's route. Still, this is excellent news.

Andrew still hasn't made up his mind whether to join the expedition or not. I'm desperately keen to keep him involved so go on a tyre drag round Hyde Park with him this evening. Feeling much better doing these now than I did three weeks ago but they still hurt.

FRIDAY 18 OCTOBER

Wake up with sore hips after yesterday's tyre drag.

Call Humfrey just to make sure he knows we are no longer following in Scott's footsteps. He replies: 'I had absolutely no idea! If my editor had known about your change of plans, the article would never have been written! But it's too late to change things now – it will just have to go in as it is.'

A large package of Hastings Direct logos arrives for me to start attaching to my polar clothing. The first of the kit has started arriving at the Ski Verbier office – two pairs of ski poles with alarmingly sharp ends come in this afternoon. The rest of the gear is due to arrive from various parts of the UK next week. My one major concern is our large Meindl polar boots that are on their way over from Norway. I just pray they arrive on time.

SATURDAY 19 OCTOBER

Go on a tyre drag round Hyde Park on my own. First time I've done it during daylight hours and being a sunny autumnal day, the park is packed. The batteries on my minidisk pack up after half an hour, which means I can now hear the questions and abuse that come my way. Being on my own, it's far worse than usual. The majority of those who ask me what I am doing laugh in disbelief when I tell them that I'm training for a South Pole expedition. By the end of today's two-hour stint, I resort to saying that I have just stolen a car and am in the middle of stripping it down. It still prompts exactly the same reaction.

Andrew flies to Cape Town today to see what sort of sponsorship he can drum up at home.

FRIDAY 25 OCTOBER

The doorbell at Ski Verbier has been ringing all week with kit deliveries and the office is now full of large cardboard boxes and bubble wrap. Pat has been round here almost every day to try on the latest piece of clothing. Unfortunately, some of the gear is the wrong size so will have to be repackaged and sent back. David and Emma are being incredibly tolerant and trying to get on with their work – not easy with a polar fashion show going on around them.

Two pairs of boots have arrived from Norway. Neither pair

fits me, but Pat seems quite happy with the size nines. Apparently the other two pairs will be with us any day. They'd better be.

The other excitement is that Anne got remarried on Wednesday – to an American snowboard instructor called Doug Stoup. Anne being Anne, she took the day off yesterday to celebrate and is back in the office today. She rings to say that Andrew Cooney will be joining the other ANI team after all but that his parents are now paying the bill.

Sunday 27 October

Text message from Andrew in South Africa. 'I'm coming. 50% discount from ANI. Please can you order kit Monday morning. Back in UK Tuesday. Bring it on!'

This is such good news. Our original three-man team of Pat, Paul and myself would have worked well, but having a fourth man adds a completely new dimension to the trip. He's done amazingly well to haggle a discount off Anne Kershaw – surely the first in history. This means his expedition costs are down to just £15,000. One or two bits of South African funding have come in and once he's sold his car, he'll be pretty much there. I am so pleased – he will be brilliant, I'm sure of it.

Thursday 31 October

Every piece of equipment and clothing has now arrived – apart from the second box of boots. The other pair of Meindl boots in our first delivery fits Andrew's feet perfectly. I'm getting very worried that the damn things are not going to arrive.

Friday 1 November

Still no boots. Think I'm going to have to fly to Oslo this weekend to see if I can track down another pair from the suppliers. Call up British Airways but all flights are full. Don't know what I'm going to do without boots. Panic setting in.

Big leaving party at the Settle Inn in Battersea. We are incredibly fortunate to have such a tight-knit group of friends and we shall miss them dreadfully. Everyone buys us drinks and by the end of the night Pat, Andrew and I are blind drunk and unable to walk.

Chapter Three

THE LAND THAT TIME FORGOT

There's a hell of a lot to do today. So many things keep crossing and recrossing my mind that I haven't slept properly. I've been up since four trying to finish off my packing. I'm sure I've forgotten something. Our flight takes off at 7 pm and there are still a million things on my checklist, but as usual I've left everything to the last minute.

8 am and it's drizzling. I'm stuck in traffic in South Kensington and running out of time. The minicab in front screeches to a halt. I slam on the brakes, but skid straight into the back of it. Let out some truly filthy expletives. Thank goodness nobody is hurt and the damage doesn't look too bad. Precious minutes are wasted exchanging insurance details and surveying the damage. I'm kicking myself with utter frustration. I could have really done without this. Bits of headlight and bumper lie strewn across the road. Other drivers harangue me by beeping their horns whilst passers-by simply stare at the scene. Nobody seems to realise what's at stake here. There's a real danger that I won't get everything done before that flight. I want a hole in the ground to appear and swallow me up. Dad will be spitting mad when he hears about this, especially as he'll have to deal with the insurance and get the car fixed whilst I'm away. More expletives.

The car is still roadworthy, so, utterly deflated, I head round to the Ski Verbier office in Fulham on the off-chance that the boots have been delivered and to say my goodbyes. No sooner have I arrived than the doorbell rings. I open the door to find a Parcel Force deliveryman, clutching a large box and a clipboard.

'Mr Avery is it? Delivery for you from Norway.'

'I don't bloody believe it!' I exclaim, scarcely believing my luck. I want to hug the man.

Like a child on his birthday, I rip off the packaging to find two pairs of brand-new Meindl boots, one of which is a UK size 12. I try them on and clump about the office. Incredibly they fit, so I won't have to traipse across the Antarctic wearing just my socks after all.

'You are such a jammy git, Avery!' jokes David. 'Now piss off to the South Pole. We've got work to do.'

The rest of the morning is a whirlwind of telephone calls, more packing and last-minute panic buying. My random assortment of purchases includes 120 of my favourite chocolate bars (Double Deckers, Toffee Crisps and Biscuit Boosts to name but some), four books (including Richard Branson's autobiography), a couple of tubes of sunblock, a whole alphabet of vitamins to keep the scurvy at bay and, what every expedition base camp should always have, a large pot of Marmite.

We all pitch up at Andrew's flat off the Gloucester Road at 3 pm. Everyone is jumping around with excitement. We're finally on our way. Any minute now and Mohammed, the man from the local taxi firm, is supposed to be arriving in his minibus to drive us to Heathrow Airport along with our many blue equipment barrels and ski bags. Luckily the airline has given us unlimited excess baggage. Our long passage to Antarctica will take us to Santiago, the Chilean capital, and on to ANI's headquarters in the town of Punta Arenas at the southern tip of South America.

Pat said goodbye to his parents in Suffolk at the weekend, and with Andrew's family all living in Cape Town, the farewell party at Heathrow consists of Mum, Dad, my sister Jessy, brother Leo and Pat's girlfriend Robyn. BBC London have sent a camera crew down to see us off, making the goodbyes not quite as private as we had hoped, with big furry microphones thrust in front of us mid-hug. Saying farewell to the family is a difficult, emotional moment, and after years of going away on expeditions it never gets any easier. Mum always thinks the worst is going to happen and she invariably gets in a state about me not wearing enough clothes when it's cold. The next two and a half months might test her a bit.

There's a payphone at the boarding gate, and just as we're about to board our very smart Lan Chile Boeing 777, I telephone David Gundlach at Hastings Direct to thank him for believing in me and giving me this incredible opportunity to fulfil my childhood dream.

'Hey, it's a pleasure,' he says in that distinct American drawl of his. 'I think it's also going to be a good investment on our part. That's as long as you don't get yourself killed out there!'

TUESDAY 5 NOVEMBER: SANTIAGO TO PUNTA ARENAS

We're less than an hour from Santiago now as our plane cuts through a gash in the Andes mountain chain. I'm really excited to see the 23,000-foot Aconcagua again, a giant door-wedge of a mountain and the highest in South America, looming high to our right. I point out a small col to Pat, no more than a few hundred feet below the summit, that marks the highpoint of my solo attempt to climb the mountain in 1998.

Aconcagua is a technically straightforward mountain that is climbed hundreds of times every year. Even though it was well before the start of the climbing season when the temperatures are far lower, youthful exuberance got the better of me and I thought that I had enough experience to reach the top. I foolishly gave myself just ten days to climb the mountain, allowing very little time to acclimatise to the altitude. Things were going well until I realised that my toes had gone completely numb, the altitude was affecting my vision to the point that I could barely see, my head felt as if it was about to explode and the only other person on the mountain was 6,000 vertical feet below me. I was forced to admit defeat just two hours from the top, but not before I had scared myself silly.

For some reason we're late touching down in Santiago, leaving us barely an hour to collect our luggage, clear customs and check in at the domestic terminal for our onward flight to Punta Arenas. It's an oppressive 33°C outside and we're dripping with sweat as we race across the airport car park, dodging taxis and trying desperately to stop our equipment barrels falling off the trolleys.

Breathless, we arrive at the Lan Chile desk to find that they have just closed the flight. The check-in girl takes one look at all our kit and tells us that unless we are travelling in business class, we won't get on the plane. Pat flutters his eyelashes and cheekily asks if we might be upgraded, which would solve everyone's problems. Much to our amazement she agrees, and we run off to the boarding gate hooting with laughter like excited school children.

It's a four-hour flight to Punta Arenas and we are enjoying a glass of Chilean Merlot in the comfort of our spacious business-class leather seats. Chile has been blessed with bright sunny weather today and we're treated to a breathtaking spectacle of the country's natural wonders. A thin runner bean of a country, Chile is 2,700 miles long and rarely more than 100 miles wide, cut off from the rest of South America by the Andes. The Andes is the longest mountain chain in the world, stretching almost uninterrupted from the Caribbean to Cape Horn. It forms the backbone of the continent. Chile's vast range in latitude and altitude has produced an extraordinary geographical diversity, from salt lakes and deserts in the tropical north to the Alaska-like scenery of the deep south. The landscape below us has already changed from the imposing wall of rocky peaks around Santiago to the eroded snow-capped hills and endless vine-yards we see now. Blessed with a Mediterranean climate and rich alluvial soils, this is the most populated part of Chile and the heart of the country's agriculture and industry.

An hour later and we are amongst steep forested valleys that snake their way to the coast. Symmetrical volcanoes, cloaked in snow from top to bottom, rise up to meet us before plunging away again to verdant farmland and deep blue lakes. On more than one occasion, I have to drag Pat away from his in-flight entertainment system so he doesn't miss out on this geo-graphical extravaganza.

The Andes reassert themselves south of the city of Puerto

Montt with gigantic tongues of ice extending all the way from the Patagonian Ice Cap through a labyrinth of black peaks and fjords to the Pacific Ocean. The pilot tells us that the Torres del Paine are coming into view on our left-hand side and helpfully tilts the plane to give us a better look. We can clearly see the colossal yellow pillars of granite that have made this the most famous national park in South America. The Torres are a 'must see' destination for tourists to this part of the world, and I was lucky enough to spend a few days here trekking amongst the turquoise lakes, spectacular glacier systems and impenetrable forests during my South American visit four years ago. It is a wild, beautiful place alive with giant skunk, llama-like guanaco and puma. This is also the home of the condor, and as we begin our descent into Punta Arenas Airport I scan the skies in the optimistic hope of catching a glimpse of one of these masters of the air.

Two reps from ANI are waiting for us at the airport and drive us to the Hostel El Bosqué that will be our base for the next few days. They are obviously a hardy bunch down here, and we walk into the kitchen to find the landlady, Isabella, chopping up a conger eel for her two-year-old daughter.

'*Quieren congrio?*' she asks, wondering if we would like to join them for dinner. Tempting as it looks, we politely decline.

As Andrew and I stack our kit into the corner of the room, I notice that one of the ski bags is a bit on the thin side.

'Gerbs, you did manage to fit all the skis into the two ski bags didn't you?' I ask.

'We've got three ski bags,' Andrew replies.

'Yeah, funny one. Seriously though, did you manage to get three pairs into each bag?'

'No, I'm being deadly serious.'

'Well, we only took two bags to Heathrow so where the hell is the third one?' I ask, now going weak at the knees.

There's a moment's silence as the realisation starts to sink in that we've left them behind in Andrew's flat in Earl's Court.

'Remember you asked me to buy you a ski bag from Snow & Rock yesterday?' asks Andrew.

'Yes. Isn't it that black bag over there?' I reply, pointing at the brand new Snow & Rock ski bag propped up against the wall. My stomach is starting to turn inside out.

'No, that's mine. I decided to get myself a new one too. I put your skis in their own bag and left them right by my front door. You couldn't have missed them!'

'Well thanks for telling me! You were the last to leave your flat and I asked you to double check that we had everything. I don't believe it.'

Pat steps in before a scrap breaks out. 'Guys, guys, guys, stop this! Please. This isn't achieving anything. We've got a problem, a serious problem. Now is not the time to start pointing the finger. But how the hell are we going to get those skis all the way down here?'

There's nothing we can do tonight. It's 1 am back in London and everyone will be asleep. After all the dramas with the ski boots, it's absolutely devastating that we've shot ourselves in the foot by stupidly managing to leave two pairs of skis at home. What a bunch of piss artists. We're each meant to be taking two sets of skis on the expedition – one for pulling our sleds and another for kiting. If we don't get hold of those skis then we will be forced to ditch our kiting plans before we've even set foot in Antarctica. All that work with the kites over the past six months would have been for nothing.

To avoid further argument, Andrew and I agree to split the blame. Considering our joint cock-up is now seriously jeopardising the success of the expedition, Pat has shown remarkable restraint in all of this and, ever the optimist, he seems hopeful that we will get the skis back before we fly south. I hope to God he's right.

WEDNESDAY 6 NOVEMBER: PUNTA ARENAS

Operation 'Ski Recovery'. Chile is just three hours behind GMT so the alarms have been set for 4.30 am, when we hope our friends in London will be getting ready to go to work. Their help is going to be vital if we're ever to see the skis again. We absolutely have to get the skis to Punta Arenas before we fly to Antarctica and it's making us all feel sick. The main problem is that Andrew's two housemates are out of London this week and whilst Andrew's girlfriend, Rowena, has a spare house key, it's going to be impossible for her to find a courier company during office hours because she is a full-time teacher. Andrew telephones Rowena and gives her specific instructions to collect the skis from his hallway and drop them off at Amanda's house on her way to school. I shared a house with Amanda for two years at university and I know I can rely on her more than most. She works for an estate agency in Belgravia and unless the London housing market has suddenly picked up, she should be able to find the time this morning to contact Federal Express. I just pray her boss will be understanding and take pity on us.

I call up Amanda. 'Mandy, we've got a bit of a problem. In about half an hour's time, Rowena is going to give you a ski bag containing two pairs of skis. Please can you take it in to work and arrange for a courier to get it down to us in Punta Arenas as fast as possible?'

'You absolute muppets!' comes her sympathetic response.

She seems to have got the message though, and a few hours later Amanda calls back to say the skis should be with us on Friday. 'I looked like a right wally carrying your ski bag on the Underground. And I was late to work! You owe me dinner when you get back to London!' What an absolute angel. Let's just hope the skis get here on time.

Punta Arenas feels, and is, a long way from anywhere. Located at the southern tip of the South American mainland, a sharp bend in the Andes mountain chain cuts this once important port off from the rest of Chile. To the east the large island of Tierra del Fuego (Land of Fire) lies across the tempestuous seas and currents of the Straits of Magellan. The only way of getting to Punta Arenas without going the long way round through Argentina is by air or sea. Constantly battered by storms that sweep across the Southern Ocean dropping huge quantities of rain on the mountains behind us, this remote town must be a pretty bleak place to live. The 110,000 inhabitants have done their best to brighten things up though, and every house in this surprisingly vibrant town seems to have been painted in a different colour.

After breakfast we go for a stroll. With a temperature of just 6°C, it's a far cry from the searing heat of Santiago – time to put on the long trousers. Imposing colonial mansions in the centre of town are legacies of the wool boom of the late nineteenth century. The port also profited from the California gold rush, Punta Arenas being the only port for thousands of miles on the long route round from the Atlantic to the Pacific. However, the opening of the Panama Canal in 1914 led to a reduction in shipping traffic and a gradual decline in wealth.

Magellan was the first European to visit the area in 1520 during his voyage around the world and the main square is dominated by an immense bronze statue of the man himself, cape billowing in the wind and gazing purposefully towards Tierra del Fuego across the 20-mile-wide strait that bears his name. Local legend has it that to ensure a safe return from Antarctica, travellers must kiss the big toe of one of the Tehuelche Indians sitting at Magellan's feet. Being superstitious types, we each give the weathered digit a tentative peck. We're going to need all the luck that we can get.

Nothing much has changed in Punta Arenas since I was last here four years ago. The schoolgirls who stroll the streets in large gangs still haven't got used to the sight of fresh-faced westerners in their town and any glance in their direction is met with a seductive grin, followed by fits of giggles. It's good to be back.

We pay a visit to a haberdashery near the main square and are greeted by a beaming munchkin of a lady called Maria. Looking not unlike a Tehuelche Indian herself, Maria gets very excited when I explain to her in my broken Spanish that we are heading off to Antarctica and need her help attaching a couple of sponsor logos to our jackets, that we never got round to doing in England. '*Vamos al Polo Sur*,' I say, pointing out of the window. She's clearly done this before and chirps, '*Si si si, comprendo*,' grabbing Pat's fleece from his hands. One of the few commitments we have to our sponsors is to ensure that they gain maximum exposure in our photographs and video footage. We are all pretty incompetent with a needle and thread, so we're thanking our lucky stars that we've discovered Maria.

Following a hearty chicken burger at the interestingly named 'Lomits Steakhouse', we return to the hostel where Paul Landry is waiting for us. After 18 months of email correspondence and phone calls, I had built up a mental picture of what he might be like. But this is not the man I was expecting. Of moderate height and build and with a striking blond ponytail, Paul looks more like a guitarist from a heavy metal rock band than a polar guide. He is a far cry from my preconceived image of the stereotypical bearded polar explorer. But Paul's weathered looks can only come from having spent a large part of his life outside in the cold. Not only has he completed three successful expeditions to the North Pole and one to the South Pole (meaning he has more poles under his belt than any man in history), but his hometown of Iqaluit in Arctic Canada experiences one of the most hostile climates on Earth. In the depths of winter the sun barely appears above the horizon and the sea is frozen solid for seven months of the year. He lives there with his wife Matty McNair, their two teenage children and a dozen husky dogs, running an outdoor adventure company called Northwinds, which specialises in polar training courses. We are in good hands. Matty is no slouch either, having led the first-ever women's expedition to the North Pole in 1997, and this year will be guiding four clients (including Andrew Cooney) on the official ANI South Pole commercial trip.

Paul talks to us in a very matter-of-fact way about the things we need to do before we fly to Patriot Hills. His gentle manner and warm smile belie a total self-confidence I have never seen from a mountain guide. When Andrew asks him why he's not taking skins for his skis, Paul's reply is simple: 'I'm a very good skier. I don't need them. I don't care how much skiing you guys have already done but you will need yours. And another thing, no matter how fast we travel on the Ice, just remember this – I will always be able to go faster.' This is not arrogance or pretentiousness. It's the air of a very professional man who has total conviction in everything he does. We like him a lot.

Paul has brought down some dog fur from Iqaluit that, when attached to our hoods, should help cut out some of the piercing Antarctic wind. Paul throws a dark strip my way and without expression says: 'He was called Portagee and was one of my favourite dogs. He got run over by a snowmobile in the spring. Look after him.'

I'm quickly realising that Paul's lifestyle is completely alien to our own. There's never going to be a good time for this, so we decide to tell Paul about our little mishap with the skis. With the faintest hint of a grin, he shakes his head in despair. Goodness knows what sort of a first impression we have given him.

Some friends of Andrew and mine are passing through Punta Arenas tonight, en route to the Torres del Paine National Park and we arranged to meet up with them weeks ago. It's great to see Caroline Lawson and her brother Mikey again and we enjoy a boozy dinner together in a dingy seafood restaurant on the outskirts of town. As so many people in their mid-twenties seem to be doing at the moment, they have packed in their jobs in London to travel the world. Mikey tells me he has just put a deposit down for an apartment in Verbier that he is planning to rent for the season. 'Mate, why don't you take the spare bed and spend a few months skiing in Switzerland after your expedition?' With no job to return to, it's a tempting offer.

THURSDAY 7 NOVEMBER: PUNTA ARENAS

The ski situation isn't looking great. According to our friends at the courier company, the errant ski bag has yet to leave the UK. It should be on a plane later today, but with our Antarctic departure date looking like 12 November, fears are growing that those skis are not going to be here in time. For once, luck is on our side, and Paul comes round to the hostel with the amazing news that ANI have unearthed a couple of old pairs of fluorescent yellow Fischer skis that were left behind by a

German expedition a few years ago. Despite the odd bit of rust, they are in pretty good condition and Paul seems to think that if the ski bag doesn't arrive from London on time, we should at least be able to use these.

Paul is clutching a clipboard this morning, which can only mean one thing: it's kit-packing time. Every square inch of the hostel's floor space is soon covered with a plethora of cold-weather gear from thermal underwear to down jackets to ski poles to kites as we lay out all our equipment for Paul to tick off his list. Isabella looks on, very confused. I'm amazed at how little clothing Paul thinks we need to last two months in Antarctica. Mum would hit the roof if she knew I was only taking three pairs of socks to last all that time. It's vital for the sleds to be as light as possible and it comes as a psychological boost when surplus items are discarded. We can worry about the hygiene implications another time. Pat suggests adopting the practice of our patron Ranulph Fiennes, and cut our tooth-brushes in half to save a few precious grams. 'You will probably burn more calories cutting the thing in half than you'd save by carrying a lighter washbag all the way to the Pole,' Paul jokes.

There is still much to be done and we head into town loaded with more work for Maria. Dog fur needs to be attached to hoods, leather nose-protectors stuck to sunglasses, and a layer of windproof material somehow needs to be fixed to our goggles to give further protection to our faces. The western big spenders have arrived in town and she is only too happy to take on the extra business.

Later, we find ourselves in a leather shop. Apparently, there's somebody here who might be able to fasten extra straps and buckles to our kiting harnesses, which are no more than adapted climbing harnesses. This is all Andrew's design and his superb handyman skills come to the fore as he talks the señorita through the necessary adjustments. Meanwhile, Pat seems more interested in buying a gaucho lasso and trying on a pair of studded leather chaps. Looking up at a gun case behind the till, he rather hopefully asks: 'Do you think they will let me have a go with one of those revolvers?'

ANI has hired a hostel in the centre of town for the guides and support staff. Paul takes us to a dark storeroom where we find crates of food piled high to the ceiling. This is where we will be based for the next few days, preparing the provisions for our 60-day expedition. All surplus packaging has to be removed and then food split into individual meals. Daily rations must be weighed individually and accurately and it's a time-consuming, fiddly process. More than once I catch Andrew stealing a piece of flapjack from the tray.

Geoff Somers is in town at the moment and it's great to see him again. He's just returned to ANI's hostel after a ten-mile run, showing no sign of sweat or breathlessness. The good news is that despite the cancellation of our Beardmore Glacier plans, Geoff has managed to find work helping a BBC film crew on a documentary about penguins. This will keep him in Antarctica for two weeks before he returns later in the season to guide an Englishman and an American the final 120 miles to the Pole. He seems genuinely pleased for us that things worked out all right in the end and bears no resentment whatsoever that Paul will now be guiding us instead. 'In Paul Landry,' says Geoff, 'you've got the best polar guide in the world. He's immensely fit and professional so you're in excellent hands.' Coming from a man of Geoff's standing, this is a very strong endorsement indeed.

This evening we join Matty and the five other members of ANI's official expedition to the South Pole. They were due to fly to Patriot Hills on 1 November but the notorious Antarctic winds have made it too dangerous to land a plane and the group has been stranded in Punta Arenas for nearly two weeks now. Before meeting up in South America they were complete strangers, so this delay has at least given them time to get to know each other a little. They finished their final kit and food preparations days ago and are on standby for the first flight of the season. Weather delays seem to be the norm for trips to the great white south and Paul reminds everyone at the table that last year, when he was guiding Chris and Timo, he had to wait here in Punta for four weeks until the wind abated. I hope we don't suffer the same fate.

As well as Paul, Geoff and Matty, there are some very experienced and impressive people with us at the table. Devon McDiarmid is another native of Arctic Canada and has led 'last degree' expeditions to the North and South Poles before. He is working as Matty's assistant guide on the ANI trip. I am sitting next to Graham Stonehouse, a tall and athletic, well-spoken man in his late thirties who resigned from his high-flying London banking job so he could fulfil his lifelong dream and try to ski to the South Pole. He is no stranger to endurance events himself, with a host of multi-day rowing races under his belt as well as having completed the infamous Marathon des Sables earlier this year. This 135-mile run across the Sahara is about as gruelling as it gets, but Graham downplays his achievements in a modest, almost embarrassed, English manner.

At the end of the table are two Basque climbers, Willie Bañales and Angél Navas. Between them they have made five attempts to climb Mount Everest as well as a host of successful ascents of some of the world's highest mountains. They are both immensely strong, and Willie in particular is built like an oak tree. Neither can speak a word of English and their Spanish isn't much better, but we somehow manage to communicate through a combination of smiles and elaborate charades.

The final member of Matty's team is Andrew Cooney, who looks just like a Grand Prix driver. Whereas everyone else at the table is casually dressed, he is wearing a beige poloneck, festooned with a multitude of sponsors' logos, union jacks and large emblems that read 'Andrew Cooney South Pole Expedition'. After a few nervous looks in our direction, he walks round to our side of the table and says: 'I would just like to clear the air over everything that happened with the sponsorship. Basically, it was a complete coincidence that I happened to contact Hastings Direct shortly after I spoke to you on the telephone. They just happened to be the next company on my long list of sponsorship approaches.'

Having suffered his last-minute setback with Hastings Direct, he's done remarkably well to get all these sponsors together.

Pat's keen to find out more and, pointing at his impressive collection of logos, asks: 'So who are Development Consultants International then?'

'They are a major property company in the Midlands and one of my primary sponsors.'

'That sounds great,' replies Pat, 'I haven't heard of them myself. How many properties do they run?'

'Just the one at the moment,' comes the slightly tentative reply.

'Oh right. I presume it's one big development then. How many people work for them?'

'Well, just me actually. It's the company I set up to buy my flat in Nottingham.'

FRIDAY 8 NOVEMBER: PUNTA ARENAS

There's still no sign of our skis. Even though we have found some replacements, I would feel much happier using our brand-new skis than the tired used ones ANI have generously provided us with. I call the couriers to find that at last the ski bag has left the UK and by last night they had made it as far as South America. The bad news is that the delivery plane's propeller developed a problem somewhere over Colombia and the plane has been grounded – in the middle of the jungle. A new propeller has been ordered from Europe and will be delivered in the next few days. Apparently. I'm pulling my hair out.

It's nearly a week since I've done any exercise so I go for a run around town this evening, leaving Pat and Andrew to check their emails in an internet café in town. The run proves to be much more of a workout than I had planned. Punta Arenas has a sizeable stray dog population and large gangs have gathered on the shingle beach. This is clearly their patch and they make it quite obvious that they don't want a jogger gatecrashing their Friday night beach party. For the next ten minutes I am pursued along the waterfront, through dark alleys and disused buildings by a mob of mangy dogs. A giant poodle even joins the chase.

Eventually they get bored and I return to the Hostel El Bosqué a breathless but very relieved man.

The Punta Arenas dogs are probably the southernmost canines in the world, but this has not always been the case. Scott brought 23 dogs to Antarctica during the *Discovery* Expedition and dog teams were instrumental in helping Amundsen become the first man to reach the South Pole. Since Antarctica's 'Heroic Age', dogs were used extensively by the various scientific bases to transport men and equipment across the continent. They often proved more reliable than mechanised transport, particularly in rough terrain, and although a small number of seals had to be killed each year to provide food for the dogs, their environmental impact was considered far less detrimental than that caused by heavy machinery.

Everything changed in 1994 when all twelve governments with scientific operations in Antarctica signed a treaty that banned all non-indigenous animals from setting foot on the continent ever again. The official reasoning was that the debilitating disease canine distemper might spread from dogs to seals. This drastic decision made by bureaucrats thousands of miles away caused uproar amongst the scientific community, as there had not been one recorded incident of canine distemper being transferred to the seal population in a century of close interaction. As well as being more practical than machines, dogs were great for morale in the science bases, particularly during the long dark winters. Many believed that the men in suits had other reasons, more linked to the public perception of the government-run scientific programmes.

Two Americans, Will Cross and Jerry Petersen, arrived at our hostel today and we join them for dinner at the palatial Chinese restaurant that overlooks Punta Arenas from the hill on the east side of town. Will is a remarkable man and aiming to be the first diabetic to ski to the Pole. His only problem is that his diabetes is making it very difficult to find an insurance company to cover him. ANI will not fly them to Patriot Hills without insurance and they are anticipating a long wait in Punta until the situation is resolved.

Will and Jerry's training regime can only be described as unorthodox and for the last four weeks they have stopped exercising completely and concentrated instead on piling on as much weight as possible, to the point that they have developed impressive bellies. Sweet and sour pork, crispy duck and gassy Chilean beer should aid the fattening process further, and as another round of *cervezas* arrives at our table, this is quickly turning into yet another boozy night.

Our table affords a spectacular uninterrupted view down the Strait of Magellan, past rusting tankers and the disused oil refinery by the beach and on to an archipelago of snow-covered islands far away on the southern horizon. The other side of Cape Horn and the treacherous Drake Passage lies the Antarctic mainland less than 800 miles away. There is a real frontier feel to this place and the white continent feels very close. Having said that, at 53° South we are as far away from the South Pole as Macclesfield is from the North Pole.

SATURDAY 9 NOVEMBER: PUNTA ARENAS

For a third successive morning, we wake up with hangovers. The tedious job of packing food at ANI's hostel is made all the more tiresome with a throbbing headache. There's very little in the way of chatter as bags of breakfast cereal are individually measured out in 800-gram rations and evening meals prepared. Matty's team are still twiddling their thumbs waiting for a break in the Antarctic weather and looking increasingly bad-tempered.

Before we left the UK, Mum asked me where I would like to be buried if the worst happened on the expedition. I had told her that I rather liked the spot by a young fir tree in the wood behind the house. I pick up an anxious email from her this morning saying she's in a panic because she can't find the four-foot-high sapling anywhere.

Later. I'm in the middle of chopping up salami when the telephone rings. It's Rachel Shepard, ANI's head of operations in Punta Arenas, and she wants to speak to Matty urgently. A minute later Matty emerges from the office grinning from ear to ear and says to her team who are lying on the lawn under a warm sun: 'Guys, you're never going to believe this but the winds at Patriot Hills have died down and tonight we will at last be flying south. Paul, Rachel also wants to speak to you.'

Moments later and an equally smiley Paul tells us: 'Apparently, there's also room for us on the plane if we want to go too. We're on!'

'But we've still got loads of packing to do,' says Pat, pointing at the mountain of food piled up against the wall.

'We can carry on with that at Patriot Hills. I don't want to be stuck here for another four weeks again. You'll be picked up from your hostel at 7.30 pm. That gives us two hours to get everything ready. Let's go for it!'

I make one last desperate call to the couriers but the plane (minus propeller) is still somewhere in the Colombian jungle. The Fischers will have to do. I call home to tell the family I'm catching the next flight for Antarctica but I get the answer machine.

There's no time to waste. Whilst Paul and the others chuck all the remaining food supplies haphazardly into barrels, I dash off to the supermarket to stock up on loo roll. I'm completely unable to focus on calculating how much toilet paper four men will use in two months. To run out halfway through the expedition would be a disaster, so I load the shopping trolley to the brim and race to the checkout.

Back at the Hostel El Bosqué, Andrew and Pat are sealing the barrels of equipment with gaffer tape and double-checking that we've left nothing behind. Every few minutes someone asks: 'Have we got the skis?' All this commotion has attracted Isabella's attention, and she seems more confused than ever seeing us rushing about the hostel in our thermal tops and heavy-duty polar boots. Because of the strict baggage allowance on the flight to Patriot Hills, jeans, T-shirts and trainers must be left behind. In a mixture of Spanish and gobbledygook, Isabella starts ranting away and it's clear that she thinks we're going off to stay at another hostel. In my pidgin Spanish I ask her if she can look after our surplus luggage for the two months we're in Antarctica. The message still hasn't got through and she shrugs her shoulders, muttering something about the former Chilean dictator General Pinochet that I can't understand. Despite living at the gateway to Antarctica, she seems completely unaware of the frozen continent on her doorstep. We bid Isabella farewell and tell her we will be back sometime next year. She stares back blankly.

En route to the airport in an old farm truck, we ask our Chilean driver what he normally gets up to on a Saturday night. In perfect English, he unashamedly explains: 'Oh I'll probably end up in the red light district. You know, Punta has more brothels per head of population than any other city in the world, except for Amsterdam and Bangkok. There's something here for everyone. You should check the girls out when you get back. I'd love to go to Amsterdam one day.'

The last internal Lan Chile flight left some time ago and the only people left milling around in the half-lit departure hall are on our flight to Patriot Hills. We're a real mixture – climbers, guys hoping to reach the Pole, Russian flight crew and half a dozen ANI staff. Geoff Somers is also here. Sadly, the BBC has had to pull the plug on the wildlife documentary, so he'll be flying back to England tomorrow. The cameramen had been hoping to film emperor penguin chicks, but all these weather delays mean that they will arrive at the rookery just as the last of the grownup chicks is leaving for the ocean. Geoff remains positive and says: 'The very best of British, lads. I'll be thinking of you.'

For a few weeks every year, Anne Kershaw employs one of Pinochet's retired generals to facilitate the customs process and the polite officials wave us through passport control without a fuss. There's an air of childish exuberance as we are ushered across the tarmac. Towering high above us, the Ilyushin jet is very different from the plane I had envisaged would be taking us to Antarctica. 'Kras Air' proudly adorns the side of the aircraft in huge blue lettering, along with some incomprehensible Russian hieroglyphics. Andrew shouts out over the noise of the engines: 'I hope they left the letter H off on purpose.' As we clamber up the narrow metal ladder, I wonder when we'll next be on Chilean soil and if our return will be a jubilant one.

The inside of the plane is no more than a dimly lit shell. Everyone and everything is travelling cargo class tonight. We buckle into one of the 40 or so seats at the front that look as though they were bolted on only this afternoon. Behind us, hundreds of black aviation fuel barrels, ski bags, equipment barrels and food boxes are stacked up and covered in a giant net.

How polar travel has changed over the years. As I fasten my seatbelt, I cast my mind back to *Discovery*'s very different journey to Antarctica. The ship sailed from the Solent in early August 1901, not reaching the site of their base camp at McMurdo Sound until a long five months later. The journey of Scott and his men was far from a comfortable ocean cruise and those men had to battle against storm-force winds and thick pack ice much of the way. Much to the resentment of his team, Scott's leadership was extremely firm, and he insisted on daily deck scrubbing, however cold the temperature. The *Discovery* Expedition came close to an early end when a major leak sprang in the hold as they were rounding Senegal. Thank goodness for Kras Air.

Given that the weather could have left us stranded in Punta Arenas for days, if not weeks, we've been very lucky to get on board.

I just hope we packed enough loo roll.

SUNDAY 10 NOVEMBER: PUNTA ARENAS TO PATRIOT HILLS

Midnight. I'm extremely jittery as we accelerate down the runway with 200 drums of aviation fuel rattling around at the back of the plane. I glance across at Andrew, sitting across the aisle, studiously poring over the Kras Air safety card. It's all in Russian, and with only the one diagram (a moustachioed man putting on an oxygen mask) I would be surprised if he understands much. Wires hang from the ceiling, some of which are wrapped together with gaffer tape, and swing from side to side as we gather speed. It feels as though the engine is under my seat. Everything shakes.

We have been provided with earplugs to dull the sound of the takeoff to just below the eardrum-piercing level. Towards the front of the plane the Russian crew sit pensively on tatty stools, dressed in white shirts and navy moth-chewed jumpers, pressing buttons and looking important. Their headphones would be more at home on the deck of an aircraft carrier than on a tourist flight. Three boiler-suited crew members sit behind me and have been asleep since we boarded. There is Russian writing all over the drab inside of the plane. I have no idea what it means but it could be graffiti written by previous traumatised passengers, warning of the Kras Air experience. Or it could just be the directions to the toilets.

Our Ilyushin jet has been chartered by ANI for the three-month Antarctic summer. Normally based in Siberia, the aircraft and her crew are well versed in landing on icy runways and keeping her fully operational in the cold. ANI's base camp at Patriot Hills is located next to a blue-ice runway, making it one of only a handful of places on the continent where wheeled aircraft can land. Discovered in 1986 next to a small range of 4,000-foot peaks by Giles Kershaw, the two-mile strip of rock-solid turquoise ice has been formed by the notorious winds that have stripped all snow from the surface.

Antarctica experiences the strongest winds on the planet, with intensely cold, dense air rushing off the 10,000-foot-high polar plateau and accelerating down to the coast. These descending katabatic winds can reach speeds of over 200 miles per hour and are at their strongest when forced to veer around an obstacle such as a mountain range. All the electronic equipment at ANI's camp is powered by wind generators, with some help from solar panels, so the blustery conditions do have some benefit. Occasionally there is a lull, and for the first time in twelve days the wind at Patriot Hills has abated enough to give the Ilyushin a brief window in which to fly in, drop us off, and return to Punta Arenas. The plane has a vast fuel capacity and is able to make the 3,900-mile return journey on just the one tank. This means that if the winds pick up during the flight south and the pilot is not confident of making a safe landing, he has enough fuel to circle the runway for up to an hour, turn around, and return to Chile.

We are now airborne and the noise level has dropped enough for us to take our earplugs out. Over the din of the engines, Pat and I just about manage to have a conversation with Rodrigo Jordan, who is leading the Chilean Antarctic ski mountaineering expedition. With looks and an accent not unlike those of Antonio Banderas, he explains with tremendous passion his plan to make the first complete ski traverse of the Ellsworth Mountain Range with his three companions Kiko, Pablo and Ernesto. His team of experienced climbers also plan to make a number of first ascents in the range and will carry 60 days of food, fuel and climbing gear with them for the 240-mile journey. It is without doubt the most ambitious of all the expeditions taking place in Antarctica this summer. Rodrigo's expedition pedigree blows me away. He led the first successful Chilean expedition to climb K2, and in 1992 reached the summit of Mount Everest via its most technical side – the Kangshung Face. Unlike a lot of the climbers I have met in the past, he is extremely modest about his achievements and seems more interested in listening to our plans and talking about Manchester United. It is wonderfully refreshing. They hope to begin their expedition this afternoon, so sadly we won't be able to spend much time with them at Patriot Hills.

It's 2 am and the sun is up. We are given the opportunity to visit the navigation pod – a glass bubble underneath the cockpit with room for the navigator and one other, giving an almost 360-degree view. As I crawl in, I feel like a rear gunner in a Lancaster bomber, half expecting a patrol of Messerschmitt fighters to emerge out of the sun. We are flying down the length of the Antarctic Peninsula that juts out 1,000 miles into the Southern Ocean from the predominantly round continent of Antarctica like the tail of a giant comma. Since World War Two the area has seen an alarming 3°C temperature increase, with the result that many of its ice shelves have started to disintegrate. The view from up here is quite incredible. There are mountains everywhere, interspersed with a white ocean of snow. I've got goose pimples and cannot wait to get down there. I can just make out wind-blown ridges in the snow – sastrugi,[1] which will no doubt be giving us headaches over the coming weeks. Unlike Pat and Andrew, who have long since passed out, I find it impossible to sleep. I think it's the excitement more than the noise.

Three hours after takeoff and we have crossed the Antarctic Circle. We are entering an unknown world. Beyond this invisible line lies a place so remote and inhospitable that most world maps don't even bother including it. This is hardly surprising when one thinks that Antarctica is the coldest, driest, highest, most windswept continent on the planet. Temperatures plummet to the minus eighties, whilst its average precipitation is less than in most deserts. Nobody owns Antarctica, and whilst a handful of scientific research stations have been set up in recent years, it has never had a native human population. With its gigantic ice shelves and icebergs, rugged mountain ranges, wildlife still fearless of humans and vast empty interior, Antarctica is like nowhere else on Earth.

The landing is even more petrifying than takeoff and just as noisy. The Russian crew can hardly speak any English, and after five hours in the air, a giant haystack of a man, kitted out in dungarees, gestures to us to attach our seatbelts. I have no idea how high we are off the ground and am desperate to peek out of the two solitary windows at the front to see where we are. A few hundred feet below us, a member of the Patriot Hills camp staff, and Antarctica's answer to air traffic control, is standing on the edge of the blue-ice runway, guiding us in to land using no more than a small bathroom mirror to reflect the sun into

---

[1] Sastrugi: fluted ridges of concrete-hard snow formed by prevailing wind. Size varies from a few inches to six feet and is dependent on strength and duration of wind as well as local snow conditions.

the pilot's eyes. When the Ilyushin last flew in two weeks ago, a crosswind sent the plane into a slow spin, so I'm more than a little apprehensive as we brace ourselves for touchdown.

We hit the ground with a thud. We're careering down the ice and showing no sign of slowing down. The runway is far from flat and littered with countless shallow depressions in the ice. Touching the brakes on this frozen cobbled street would be asking for trouble, so the pilot can only slow down using the throttle.

There's lots of clapping when we finally come to a halt but we're bemused to see the cabin crew shaking hands and patting each other on the back as if they're surprised we made it in one piece. 'Thank you for flying Kras Air, we hope that you will choose to fly with us again,' says our dungareed friend in a thick Russian accent, grinning from ear to ear. Unfortunately, we have no choice in the matter. If it is still airworthy, the same rust bucket of a plane will take us back to civilisation in two months' time. But for now there are other things on our minds.

It's the best part of 40°C colder here than it was when we took off from Chile and we've changed into our expedition gear for the 20-minute stroll to camp. As the rear of the plane drops down and we take our first tentative strides into the cold, I feel as though we've been transported to another planet. The first thing we are struck by is not the chill, but the light. Coming out of the drab interior of the Ilyushin, we find ourselves having to squint in the bright sun, even though we're wearing sunglasses. There's not a breath of wind and, despite it being −21°C, the apparent temperature feels nothing like as severe. My rubber-soled boots offer next to no grip on the pitted blue-ice runway and my first steps on Antarctica are more of an undignified stumble. I steady myself and take a deep breath. The cold air hits the back of my throat and it feels fantastic. We've arrived.

A convoy of skidoos arrives as we shuffle across to the more secure snowy surface by the runway. We are met by a burly Scotsman called Jamie who introduces himself as the Camp Manager at Patriot Hills. We newcomers cannot contain our joy at having arrived in Antarctica and, despite it being five in the morning, Pat and I run around like mad things and perform a jig for the video camera. Paul seems somewhat subdued, as later this evening he will be saying goodbye to Matty. Not only will they be away from each other for the best part of two months, but they will also have to face the daily worry of wondering how the other one is coping with the Antarctic conditions. It must be very difficult for them.

The Patriot Hills camp itself is about half a mile from the runway and the mountains, where the prevailing winds are not as strong. The Patriots are just foothills to the much more alpine-looking Ellsworth Range, and poking over the top of the rounded hills I can see a series of sharp icy summits peering down at us.

We are the first ANI guests of the season and are welcomed with open arms. A long blue mess tent is the focal point of the camp, with a series of operational tents (communications, medical, vehicle maintenance, toilets, etc.) close by. As we stroll into camp, the multicoloured 'clam tents', which are used to house guests in moderate comfort, are being set up by members of staff. They are comfortable in that they have a solid floor and a mattress, and if you're lucky enough to be less than five foot tall you can stand up in them as well. The 30 or so staff are housed in individual pyramid tents, almost identical to the ones used by Scott 100 years ago. Someone has clearly taken great care over their spacing and they must look like a giant chess set from above. Behind camp, a sea of brilliant white stretches away to a depthless horizon.

Like me, Paul didn't get much rest on the flight and is keen to get a few hours' sleep before we carry on with the food packing from where we left off in Punta Arenas. Rather than stay in the giant clams, we all agree that it would be best to set up our polar tents in order to get into the routine of expedition life.

We will be taking three tents with us for the journey. Paul likes his privacy on a long expedition and he has brought with him his own purpose-built tunnel tent that takes no time at all to pitch. Setting up the two yellow North Face tents is more time-consuming because, unlike Paul's, the flysheet is not already joined to the inner. I hope this doesn't cause problems later in the expedition when the wind will make the process of setting up camp much more of an ordeal. Andrew volunteers to sleep in the single tent for the time being, whilst Pat and I will share the larger tent, which, once we set off, will double up as both the kitchen and dining room at mealtimes. So that we can have some privacy of our own during the expedition, the three of us will rotate beds every six days. Pat christens the single man's tent the 'gunner's tent' and ceremoniously hands Andrew a porn mag that he picked up in Punta Arenas yesterday afternoon. From now on, the tent's occupant becomes the custodian of *Chicas Eroticas del Sol* when he moves in and it is his responsibility to look after it during his residence.

It is a dramatic sight when the Ilyushin takes off. Although its tail is over three storeys high, the plane looks more like a remote-controlled toy against the craggy backdrop of the Patriot Hills. Even from this distance, a deep roar can still be heard as it hurtles down the runway before it climbs confidently into a deep blue sky.

During the Antarctic summer, the Ilyushin will probably make over 20 return flights to Patriot Hills. Around half of these will be to drop off or collect ANI clients. As ANI is the only commercial outfit offering flights to Antarctica, all non-scientific visitors to the continent's interior will fly with them, and use the Patriot Hills camp and ANI's infrastructure. Most of these will be climbers, hoping to scale Mount Vinson, the highest mountain in the Antarctic. As well as the handful of annual South Pole expeditions, a number of people will be flown to the Pole in one of ANI's two De Havilland Twin Otter ski planes, waiting obediently in the snow on the other side of the mess tent. Other visitors will visit the emperor penguin colony at the Dawson-Lambton Glacier on the Weddell Sea coast and some will take in the Antarctic experience by spending a week at Patriot Hills. In addition to these 'tourist flights', the Ilyushin will make a number of separate flights carrying hundreds of barrels of aviation fuel to Antarctica. These will be used to run ANI's flotilla of smaller aircraft, which fly visitors all over the continent.

Before we jump into our sleeping bags for the first time in Antarctica, we say our goodbyes to Rodrigo, Kiko, Pablo and Ernesto before they set off on their great trip. In that brilliant over-the-top South American way, we are given great big bear hugs and wished every success. With his dark skin, thick jet-black hair, killer lamb-chop sideburns and bandanna, Ernesto resembles a youthful Elvis, and when Pat says he looks like The King, the four of them crack up with laughter. Soon after, their Twin Otter ski plane takes off from the snow runway barely 100 yards from our tents and flies away to the start point of their expedition at the northern edge of the Ellsworth Mountains.

The rest of the morning, and a large part of the afternoon, are spent relaxing in the tents and trying to catch up on sleep – it's very important that we're well rested before the start of the expedition. After supper, everyone makes their way out to the snow runway to wave off Matty's team who are making the short flight to their start point at Hercules Inlet this evening. They have taken provisions for just three days, as they plan to return to Patriot Hills for a rest before continuing southwards. I wonder if we will still be here when they return or if our paths will cross en route to the South Pole. After another round of hugs and 'Good Lucks', they are on their way.

Later. I'm now in my tent, writing my diary, tucked up next to Pat. It's past eleven and the sun is still up – something we'll have to get used to on the journey ahead. I still can't quite believe we're here. It's all happened so quickly. I find it hard to think that barely a week ago I was relaxing in front of a roaring fire, reading the Sunday papers at home with Mum and Dad. It was only 24 hours ago that we were still very much in the civilised world and now we are here in the loneliest and most desolate land there is.

Pat and I talk about the fact that there will be another team very close to us on the Ice. I would say that Andrew and myself, and Pat to a lesser extent, are naturally quite competitive. To have another group a few days in front of us will give us a real incentive to make good progress and to slowly reel them in. This is no more than friendly rivalry, although after everything that's happened, it would be just great to reach the Pole before Cooney's team.

MONDAY 11 NOVEMBER: PATRIOT HILLS

This is the land of the midnight sun, where the days merge seamlessly together, and I haven't slept well. Since going to bed last night, the sun has shone continuously with a blinding brilliance I never knew it possessed. Matters have been made worse by the fact that our tent is bright yellow and both Pat and I left our eye patches behind on the flight from London. Snuggling up to a car headlight would have been more conducive to a good night's sleep. It is something we are going to have to become accustomed to on the journey ahead. The Lonely Planet guidebook to Antarctica (yes, this really does exist) has warned us to beware of a condition called 'Big Eye', a period of disorientation and sleeplessness caused by the 24-hour daylight. The idea of stumbling our way through those crevasse fields around Hercules Inlet still bleary-eyed is a bit of a worry. We must try to track down some more eye patches before we get going.

The colourful little tents of camp look so serene against the stark backdrop of the rocky Patriot Hills. It's hard to imagine that from early April the sun will dip below the horizon, plunging this place into the depths of the polar winter for five long, depressing months. Fierce katabatic storms and temperatures as low as −70°C force this small community off the continent. The entire camp is taken down at the end of January and stored in a complex network of tunnels deep within the ice. ANI even keeps a small Cessna ski plane down there. We've been reassuringly told that if it takes us longer than the anticipated 60 days to reach the South Pole and the weather prevents us being flown back to Punta Arenas before the onset of winter, there should be just enough food and fuel underground to last us until next November.

We've got a lot to do today. Skins need to be attached to skis, we need to make final kit checks and alterations, and there's still a lot of food that needs weighing and repackaging. We hold a team meeting in the mess tent to discuss the plan for the first phase of the expedition. Paul has a suggestion: 'OK, the way I see things, we've got two options. Either we can do what Matty's team have done, take three days' provisions to Hercules Inlet and stop off at Patriot Hills on our way south. Or, we can cut out Patriot Hills altogether, load up our sleds with supplies for 30 days and go straight for the Thiel Mountains.'

There are about half a dozen recognised routes to the South Pole and, because of ease of access, the Hercules Inlet version is by far the most popular. Having said that, around half of the 120 or so people who have skied to the South Pole came this way, so it's hardly a well-trodden path. In much the same way as North Pole expeditions are only considered 'to count' if they start from the shores of the Arctic Ocean, there's an unwritten rule amongst the polar fraternity that for a South Pole expedition to be authentic, it has to begin from the edge of the continent. Some would argue that a trip must start on the perimeter of Antarctica itself, where the sea is no longer covered by ice, whilst the purists would say you have to go there and back without being resupplied. Others will ask what's the big deal.

Unlike the strictly controlled world of ocean racing, the rules of polar travel are still very much a grey area, and in recent years have been a source of petty squabbling amongst adventurers vying for records. As Paul illustrates on his map, if one draws a straight line between Hercules Inlet and the South Pole, it passes more or less right through both the Patriot Hills and a cluster of peaks called the Thiel Mountains, conveniently located halfway to the Pole. Most expeditions who follow this route ask ANI to drop a month's worth of provisions by Twin Otter at a predetermined grid position next to the mountains. We shall do the same. This resupply should then last us for the second half of the journey. We decide against stopping off at Patriot Hills on our way south. Of course it would make things easier, because the steep climb from Hercules Inlet onto the continental ice would be done with very light sleds. It would be so tempting to put our feet up at camp and be pampered by the ANI staff before loading up the sleds and heading towards the Thiels.

'For me, once this expedition begins, we're on our way. We're all up to the hard slog at the start and I think we should head straight to Thiels. I think it would be kinda cool,' says Paul.

'I don't want to come back to this place until the expedition is over,' I say, anxiously glancing over my shoulder just in case Jamie might be within earshot. 'What do you guys reckon?'

'Yeah, I'm well up for that,' replies Andrew, showing no hesitation.

Pat also shows his enthusiasm for the plan and it's agreed. Our departure time is set for Wednesday morning, when we shall say goodbye to Patriot Hills for two long months.

After lunch, the four of us go for a short ski around camp. We won't be walking to the Pole, but skiing there. The concept of 'walking on skis' is so impossible for us Brits to get our heads round that in the press polar journeys are typically described as 'treks' or 'walks' to avoid confusion. With their long history of Alpine pursuits, our European cousins are well versed in the practice of ski touring, or ski mountaineering, where one can ski uphill or on the flat. The simple bindings allow the heel of the boot to be lifted without restriction, and we fitted these to the skis earlier this morning, along with the final nylon skins that are screwed to the underside of each ski. This material consists of thousands of tiny synthetic hairs that glide smoothly over the snow when slid forward, but like stroking a cat the wrong way, the skins offer resistance when pulled back. It's possible to climb slopes as steep as 30 degrees thanks to the purchase that the skins provide. However, the terrain that we shall be crossing during our journey south will be predominently flat.

We ski along the groomed piste of the Twin Otter runway next to camp and it feels great to be able to stretch our legs again, although the three of us are all a little unsteady on the very thin skis. Paul has a skiing style all of his own, developed after years living in the Canadian Arctic. Everything about him is so still and economical, with skis never leaving the ground. He later confesses that he was a cross-country skier in his younger days and competed at national level. It shows.

On the other side of the parked Twin Otters lies an old Douglas DC3 aircraft lurching awkwardly on its side. We ski towards it. Closer inspection reveals that both landing gears are completely mangled and one of the wings has been partially covered by snow. The DC3, which has been flying since the 1940s and underwent a major refit during the winter, flew in from Punta Arenas a fortnight ago with a small team of staff whose job it is to begin setting up the camp at Patriot Hills for the new season. Only a handful of tents had been erected on the snow when a terrific storm arrived out of nowhere. A powerful katabatic wind with gusts of over 90 knots (104 mph) ripped through camp, forcing everyone to take cover underground in the ice tunnels. It must have been absolutely terrifying down there, not to mention freezing. Eventually the storm blew itself out, and they emerged to find that all the tents had blown away. The wind had been so strong that it snapped the steel moorings that were supposed to chain the DC3 securely to the snow, before picking it up like a toy plane, carrying it along for about 50 yards and dumping it unceremoniously onto the hard ground. The damage is so severe that she will never take to the skies again.

Next week the engineers arrive to strip this once magnificent aircraft of its reusable parts before it will be left to a slow, natural burial by the Antarctic snows. 'Guys, do you realise,' I point out, prodding a bent propeller with my ski pole, 'had we been following the Beardmore route, as we had initially set out to do, this is the plane that ANI would have used to fly us from here to McMurdo.' Only the DC3 has a range long enough to make the flight from Patriot Hills to the other side of the continent in one go, so had we managed to get the sponsorship together for our initial expedition idea, we would have really struggled to find a plane to get us to the start line.

A keen wind is turning things pretty unpleasant out here so

we head into the warm shelter of the mess tent to continue sorting out the food supplies. Barrel-loads of salami and cheese have to be cut up into edible chunks, nuts and dried fruit divided into equal rations, and we haven't even made a start on the chocolate yet. Talking to Christian, ANI's mountain guide, offers a welcome distraction from the mind-numbing task of counting peanuts into ziploc bags. Christian is a powerfully built guy from the Austrian Tyrol and about to spend the next ten weeks taking people up Mount Vinson, 70 miles to the north of us. He hopes to climb it as many as seven or eight times whilst he's there. 'It's a beautiful mountain, the Vinson,' he explains in a thick Germanic accent. 'But it's also very dangerous. Many avalanches and rockfall. Altitude affects many people on the mountain. I hope to ski off the summit one day.'

At over 16,000 feet, Mount Vinson has become a must-climb peak for the increasing number of 'Seven Summiters' – people aiming to climb the highest peak on each of the seven continents. Ever since the American tycoon Dick Bass first achieved this in 1985, countless climbers have caught the Seven Summit bug and tried to emulate his feat. The result is that a multi-million-dollar industry has sprung up amid the peaks of Everest (Asia), McKinley (North America), Aconcagua (South America), Kilimanjaro (Africa), Elbrus (Europe), Carstensz Pyramid (Australasia) and Vinson (Antarctica), with countless commercial climbing outfits guiding clients to their summits. Many have already completed the full set. Since the mid-eighties, nearly seven hundred mountaineers have climbed Mount Vinson and ANI has built its business around getting people to the top. Christian leans across to Andrew and me and whispers: 'When you guys get back from the South Pole you must climb the mountain with me before you return home.' He must be kidding.

As the 30 or so residents of our strange little community start traipsing in for dinner, it becomes clear what a diverse bunch we are. A handful of leathery Canadian pilots wearing overalls and baseball caps are sitting in the corner, drinking coffee and not saying very much. Then someone bursts in through the front door, wearing a bright red oversized toddler's jumpsuit and several layers of headgear. It's not immediately clear if the occupant is male or female. Eventually, a bearded man emerges from beneath a second balaclava and a scarf, shouting: 'Christian, get your arse over here. It's injection training time.' Like so many of ANI's workforce, Gareth has spent several years working for BAS (the British Antarctic Survey) and is doing the season with ANI because he 'just fancied a bit of a change'. As well as being the camp's doctor, he is also the only dentist, plumber and marriage guidance counsellor for 600 miles.

Pat, Andrew and I sit down at a table of climbers, camp staff and other misfits. Patriot Hills must be the only place on Earth where you would get Chris and Don sitting at the same dinner table. Chris left BAS last year having just done a continuous 18-month stint as the base's chief engineer. 'The worst part was the winter,' he says in a soft West Country accent, picking engine grease from his finger nails. 'I've never smoked so many cigarettes in all my life!' he adds, his face contorting with laughter. Chris is a wizard at fixing everything mechanical from skidoos to aeroplanes to kettles, and without him this little polar village would soon stop functioning.

Don couldn't be more different. He has wanted to visit Antarctica since childhood and has taken two weeks off work to join ANI's 'Antarctic Safari', which involves skidoo trips, walks around the Patriot Hills, igloo-building lessons and a host of other practical polar activities. I don't think I've ever seen a man so excited. 'My wife would hate it because there are no hair salons in this place,' he says, stroking his thick moustache. Being a highflying New York investment banker in his mid-fifties, the timelessness of Antarctica must seem otherworldly, and I have great admiration for him making his dream trip happen.

Everyone here is so friendly, chatty and wonderfully relaxed. If Pat had his way, he would stay up until the small hours talking motorbikes with Chris. I have to remind him that 36 hours from now we're supposed to be starting an expedition to the South Pole and we need our beauty sleep. The wind has picked up noticeably this evening and things have turned positively chilly. Miraculously, I have managed to track down some nasty polyester eye patches for Pat and myself, so no excuses for a bad night's sleep.

We're now tucked up in our sleeping bags and ready for bed, kitted out in fleece hats and our new wasp-like eyewear. It's a good look.

TUESDAY 12 NOVEMBER: PATRIOT HILLS

Some time during the night I wake to hear the most almighty storm pounding our defenceless little home with a vengeance. Pat's already awake and looking genuinely scared. One of Antarctica's infamous katabatic windstorms that we have heard so much about is sweeping off the mountains behind us and right through camp. 'I want my Mummy!' whimpers Pat, trying to lighten the mood. The tent poles are straining to the awesome power of the wind, and any minute now I am fully expecting the tent to be picked up and carried away. Shortly after we went to bed last night, Chris drove round camp in his big orange snowplough, scooping the snow into windbreaks to protect the tents from the impending onslaught. This does at least offer some protection but with the wind making the most appalling whining sound as it whistles over the protective snow wall and round the tent, we can't help but feel very vulnerable. This is a tempest of biblical proportions and is like nothing we have ever experienced in our lives. The bad news is that my stomach has been signalling its displeasure since last night's beef stew and the bathroom facilities are 100 yards away.

After much procrastination I pull on the minimum number of layers of clothing I feel I need to survive the next five minutes and peer outside. Antarctica is very agitated at this early hour with snow blowing about wildly. I zip up my jacket and head out into the maelstrom. More than once, the wind sweeps my feet from under me, sending me spread-eagled on the snow. Luckily nobody's watching. I'm walking downwind, and much to my relief it's not long before I've arrived at my destination.

The place is a work of great craftsmanship, with expertly constructed ice-brick walls, a wooden roof and a canvas door helping to make this sanctuary blissfully peaceful. With pegs to hang my surplus clothing, a wooden loo-seat and a copy of Wednesday's *Times* to enjoy, reaching this ice haven has been well worth the effort. ANI has to minimise its impact on this pristine environment and all human waste is flown back to Chile. As I put the wooden lid back down a few minutes later, I wonder which one of us will be the first to make it back to Punta Arenas.

The return journey to the tent is an expedition in itself and I am forced to lean at 30 degrees into the wind just to stay on my feet. Straight away the cold powder snow stings my bare face and I have to fight to catch my breath. Remembering there has been more than one incident of scientists in Antarctica's research bases becoming lost after a seemingly straightforward foray into a blizzard, I'm quite pleased to make it back to the tent in one piece.

I am reminded of Scott's first steps in Antarctica a century ago. After *Discovery* dropped anchor in McMurdo Sound in February 1902, the crew spent a fortnight erecting three wooden huts and several dog kennels on a rocky bank just 200 yards from the ship. With all 48 men spending the winter in the cramped confines of the ship, the hut was primarily used for scientific work. The men were wary of the impending winter weather and the hut was stacked with provisions, just in case something were to happen to the ship during a storm. A length of rope covered the short distance between the hut and the ship so that the men could carry out their scientific work during the winter darkness.

On 23 April 1902 the sun slipped below the horizon, where it would remain for four, dark, depressing months. No man had spent a winter this far south before and the men of the *Discovery* were to face constant batterings from hurricane-force gales and temperatures in the minus fifties. Returning to the ship from a visit to the meteorology hut in a particularly nasty midwinter blizzard, the ship's chief engineer Reginald Skelton and the physicist Louis Bernacchi accidentally dropped the safety rope. Unable to find it again, they quickly became disorientated. They yelled at the top of their voices for help, but though the ship was just a few yards away they couldn't see it and nobody onboard could hear their cries for help. Over an hour later another group happened to be on their way back from the huts and stumbled across both men kneeling in the snow, alive but terribly frostbitten. During one particular storm in July, the wind never once dropped below 75 knots (85 mph) over a twelve-hour period.

After breakfast, we are introduced to our sleds, which have spent the winter months in the depths of the ice cave. They seem sturdy enough, but at 35 pounds each they aren't half heavy. By midday, we have finished work on the supplies and can start loading them onto the sleds. Everything from evening meals to powdered milk to loo roll to teabags has now been stripped of all its packaging, carefully divided into rations of equal weight and repacked into lighter and more practical ziploc bags. These will be stored in large stuffsacks at the bottom of the sleds. These bags have been carefully labelled in thick marker pen to make sure we don't start breaking into the wrong week's rations. Group equipment, food and fuel make up the majority of the total load, leaving little room for personal gear. As well as all the food, the kitchen box, 24 litres of white spirit cooking fuel and the stoves themselves, the tents, shovels, solar panels, satellite phone, the Argos (a sort of back-up radio), medical kit and rope still need to be divided equally amongst us.

We will all be carrying exactly the same weight – mainly so we all travel at the same pace but also so there's no bickering about who's got the heaviest sled, something polar travellers are renowned for taking extremely seriously. Everything is weighed to the nearest gram and Paul, ever the meticulous planner, ticks everything off on his clipboard as it is loaded into the sleds. There are separate barrels and crates for provisions that will be taken to our resupply depot at the Thiel Mountains sometime next month. Individual clothing, sleeping bags and our kiting equipment will somehow be squeezed into the sleds in the morning, by which time they will weigh the best part of 175 pounds – exactly the same load as that pulled by Scott, Shackleton and Wilson during the return march to *Discovery* on their Southern Journey of 1902–3.

Later. Pat, Andrew and I are enjoying a brew in the mess tent and excitedly discussing what we might be up to this time tomorrow when a yeti pulls up a chair and asks if we would mind if he joined us. Pat pours him a cup of tea and tentatively slides the plate of custard creams across the table. The giant bundle of hair pulls back his hood and introduces himself as Doug. He is dressed from head to toe in caribou fur and we request an explanation. With great excitement he enlightens us on his life in the far north of Canada, where he traps and shoots Arctic foxes, wolverines and caribou for their fur. An opportunity arose to work in Antarctica, and with his skills in igloo building and polar survival Doug had the perfect credentials to work as a field guide for ANI. His only request was that he could bring his furs.

Doug takes everything immensely seriously. By holding our attention with a hypnotic wide-eyed stare, it feels as if these are the most important words we have heard. His greatest talent is diverting the subject of any conversation towards caribou hunting. It's a truly fascinating subject nevertheless, and he describes it so passionately and in such spectacular detail that we could listen to him for hours. Caribou is Doug's life. It's what he wears, it's what he eats, it's what he sleeps in, it's his main source of income, it's pretty much all he can talk about, and looking at him now, you wouldn't be surprised if he got down on all fours, walked out the door and started grazing the plains outside. Doug is a quite unique character and in Andrew's words, 'The guy is an absolute legend.'

Jason is a young South African radio operator cum meteorologist and arrives from the communications tent with the news that he believes the worst of the winds are over. He tells us that at the storm's peak early this morning, a gust of 91 knots (105 mph) was recorded next to the runway. Paul is naturally concerned for the welfare of Matty and her group and is visibly relieved to hear from Jason that they camped after travelling for four hours this morning, just six miles from Patriot Hills. Having just spoken to his wife on the radio, he says that they are tired but doing fine, and hope to be back here sometime tomorrow.

The winds have also got us talking about the great Australian explorer Douglas Mawson's *Aurora* Expedition of 1911–14, which established a base at Commonwealth Bay in East Antarctica, unaware that this spot was one of the windiest on the planet. The katabatics roared off the ice cap day after day, sometimes touching 175 knots (200 mph). He was later to give the place the memorable name, 'The home of the blizzard'.

By early evening, the winds have abated enough for us to practise flying the kites for the first time. The kites that Paul has brought along from Canada for us are quite different from the ones we have used for our training. They are standard 'foil' kites in the shape of a squashed letter 'D' that inflate on contact with a breeze, much like a paraglider. The four lines that run from each corner of the kite mean that we can control both the speed of the kite through the air and its direction by subtle movements of the handles. A short length of rope connects the two handles. To take some of the weight from our arms, this rope is then hooked round a specially-designed bar on our waist harness, similar to the one used by windsurfers. This half-hour exercise is a very useful revision of our kite set-up and flying skills, but the wind is still too strong to try skiing with the kites as well. We head off to supper feeling as ready as we're ever going to be and hopeful that the conditions tomorrow morning are calm enough for the Twin Otter to take off.

It's bedtime and I lie awake with a million thoughts rushing around my head. Like the night before a big exam, I am beginning to feel very uneasy with the knowledge that the time for preparation is over. Only the test itself lies ahead. My main cause for concern is probably my own physical condition. I would like to think I am reasonably fit, and it normally doesn't take much in the way of physical training for me to get into

TOP LEFT: Making the first ascent of Pik Quenelda in Kyrgyzstan
TOP RIGHT: A young boy having fun in the mountains
ABOVE: On the summit of Pik Fiennes. From left to right: Vladimir Vysochkiy, Anatoly Moshnikov, George Wells, Pat Woodhead, me, Scott Jamison, Nick Stopford

TOP: Tyre-dragging with Pat in Hyde Park
ABOVE: Kite-buggy training at Camber Sands, East Sussex

TOP: Ski mountaineering under clear skies on the Franz Josef Glacier, New Zealand…
ABOVE LEFT: …until things turn nasty
ABOVE RIGHT: The *Discovery* Expedition's Southern Journey gets under way – man's first concerted effort to reach the South Pole

CLOCKWISE FROM TOP LEFT: Me, Paul Landry, Andrew Gerber, Pat Woodhead

TOP: ANI's camp at Patriot Hills, Antarctica. The blue-ice runway can be seen glistening at the foot of the mountains
ABOVE: First footsteps in Antarctica

TOP: Pat struggling up one of the blue-ice steps above Hercules Inlet
ABOVE LEFT: Crevasses: best avoided
ABOVE RIGHT: Checking the strength of a snow-bridged crevasse

TOP: Sledging past the Ellsworth Mountains

LEFT: Typical pit-stop. Much food eaten, few words spoken

BELOW: Tents and sleds half-buried after our first polar storm

TOP: Weaving our way through a field of sastrugi – the bane of our lives
ABOVE LEFT: Having a bath Antarctica-style
ABOVE RIGHT: Paul helping Andrew with yet another broken ski binding

shape before a big trip. But this is the South Pole, the ultimate test of physical endurance, and if I'm being brutally honest with myself I know I could, and should, have trained harder. Barely a month before the scheduled start of the expedition and still with no sign of a sponsor, the incentive to keep training was fading and I had almost resigned myself to spending the English winter behind my desk at Ski Verbier. I really had to psych myself up to continue training. When we finally got the green light, I managed to refocus, and, avoiding the temptation of heading to the pub with my mates, returned to Hyde Park to drag my tyres through the sand with renewed energy and purpose. I just hope I did enough.

The others appear to be in excellent shape. Even before we started training, Andrew's idea of a good time was to go on a strenuous run before work every morning, whilst Pat has been lifting heavy objects in a gym (ideally with lots of mirrors) since he was in his teens. As for Paul, well by all reports he's a machine. There's an old explorer's adage that says that the fitness required to succeed on a polar expedition is 30 per cent physical and 70 per cent mental. The psychological side doesn't worry me so much. If I can just survive the first three days and stick with the group pace, I know that barring injury or illness, my physical fitness shouldn't be a problem. The two things I can be absolutely sure of are that the next two months are going to be very cold and they are going to hurt. But I am in wonderful company and I know that we will all do our very best to enjoy this unique experience.

After years of daydreaming and planning, I can scarcely believe that at last I'm about to embark on a journey to the Pole, the South Pole, the last place on Earth. Just think of it. The greatest challenge of our lives is about to get underway. I wonder if we will do it?

Chapter Four

IN THE FOOTSTEPS OF HEROES

The alarm goes off at 6.30 am but I'm already awake. Pat is still out for the count, with a slightly scary grin on his face. The tent is cold and a thick layer of frost coats every surface. Despite the recent gales, the sun has shone relentlessly day and night since we arrived in Antarctica, warming the tents like a greenhouse. But today is a different story altogether and a blanket of high cloud absorbs what little warmth the sun has to offer. The wind is still blowing but it's nothing compared to the gales of the last 24 hours. Before I have the chance to wake Pat, Boris (a portly Chilean guy working as a field guide for ANI this season) lets out a yelp and starts shaking the tent vigorously. 'Wake up Ingleses. You got a plane to catch.'

I want to make the most of our last decent meal for a while and am the first into the mess tent. No sooner have I sat down at the breakfast table than Boris thrusts a plate under my nose, piled high with the best fry-up in the land – fried eggs, bacon, thick Patagonian sausages and homemade bread. I'm already on my second helping and Andrew is wolfing down a bowl of steaming porridge when Jamie bustles into the kitchen tent to tell us that the wind has abated enough for the plane to fly. However, there is going to be a delay of about an hour; it was −22°C last night and the plane's engines need to be defrosted. A thousand butterflies suddenly take off inside my stomach. Whilst part of me is desperate to get the expedition under way, there is another part that wouldn't mind delaying our impending two months of suffering and could do with another day sitting out the weather in the luxury of the mess tent. Andrew and I peer out of one of the tent windows to see three engineers removing the black covers from the Twin Otter's engines and filling her up with aviation fuel. There is no turning back now. He puts an arm round me and exclaims: 'Bring it on!'

The tension continues to build. We have a terrific send-off from the Patriot Hills staff who have looked after us so well during our three days here. Despite the early hour, they are all there to see us off. Lana and Mairi, the chefs who have ensured we will begin the expedition on full bellies, are the last to say goodbye. I doubt that we will see a member of the opposite sex again this year.

The sleds have already been loaded onto the Twin Otter by the time we clamber on board. Despite countless checks and double checks, I am convinced I've left something important behind, like my sleeping bag or kite. But it's too late now. As we taxi down the snowy runway, I glance back at the others. Everyone is sitting in complete silence, deep in thought. I'm not the only one who's nervous.

Twin Otters are the workhorses of the polar regions. These twin propeller ski planes are extremely tough and, because they are capable of landing on both snow and ice, they are used by all the scientific bases in Antarctica. ANI has chartered this particular aircraft from a Canadian operation called Unaalik Air, and it took our pilots Russ and Amy nine days to fly her south from the wilds of the Canadian tundra half way round the world to Patriot Hills. Amy is a remarkable girl – she's been flying for 15 years in some of the harshest environments on earth, spending nine months of the year on the wing. She has such an enviable lifestyle, which involves delivering provisions in her Twin Otter to remote communities in the Canadian Arctic and flying tourists around Antarctica. During the summer Amy lives alone with her dog in a little log cabin on the shores of the Great Slave Lake, where she sails her wooden sailing boat and fishes for salmon. It sounds such a tranquil way of life, and that is reflected in her laidback manner and outlook. She's also very attractive, although her padded Unaalik Air boiler suit is not the most flattering (these are obviously standard issue for flight crews in the cold). What makes her even more extraordinary is that she is just 28.

The plane will be based on the Ice for the next three months, during which time Amy will cover tens of thousands of miles flying climbers to Mount Vinson's base camp and tourists to see the penguins on the Weddell Sea. Some will fly with her all the way to the South Pole itself. The Twin Otter has a relatively short range though, and it wouldn't be able to reach the Pole in a single flight. It therefore has to refuel halfway there at the Thiel Mountains, a sort of polar petrol station, where ANI keeps a cache of aviation fuel barrels.

The 22-mile flight to Hercules Inlet takes less than 15 minutes. Peering through the frosted-up window we can just make out Matty's team, strung out like ants across the snow below us. Paul tries to identify which particular termite is Matty, but we are too high to distinguish who's who. 'She'll probably be the one at the front,' says Paul. 'My wife has to be in control of everything!' It looks as though they will arrive at Patriot Hills this evening, where they will have a day's rest before loading up their sledges again for the onward journey. Following our decision to avoid Patriot Hills altogether and head straight for our resupply at the Thiel Mountains, 310 nautical miles to the south, this will be the last time we see our base camp until the end of the expedition.

It's a bumpy landing and everyone leaps out of the plane as soon as we grind to a halt. Russell and Amy are in no mood to hang around, and after helping us unload the sleds, they are quick to bid us farewell. The Twin Otter pulls away into the sky and soon disappears behind one of the imposing snow ridges that guard our route to the south.

Suddenly we are completely alone. Everything is eerily quiet. Never before have I felt so far from civilisation and the real world. Except this for me has become the real world, and standing on the soft snow of Hercules Inlet, with nothing except dazzling whiteness in every direction, feels incredibly invigorating. Bizarrely, it doesn't feel very much like an inlet here. We are on the very edge of the Ronne Ice Shelf, formed as the

Antarctic ice cap flows off the continent and onto the sea. Thanks to this giant blanket of ice, which floats on the surface of the Weddell Sea, the ocean is barely half a mile below our feet, whilst the actual Antarctic coast lies over 250 miles further north. A few hundred yards from us, the gradient increases dramatically and we know it will be a tough start to the expedition. But all nerves have faded away, and from the animated looks on the guys' faces, it's clear everyone is eager for our great adventure to begin.

So without further delay we clip into our chest harnesses and set off in single file with Paul leading the way. The GPS[1] tells us our starting latitude is precisely 80°01'.655 South, which as the crow flies, equates to a mind-boggling 598½ nautical miles (about 700 statute miles) to the South Pole. Because our route won't be following a perfectly straight line, our actual journey will be marginally further. And like all polar expeditions, we shall measure our progress in nautical miles. Andrew and I share our mild irritation at not having begun our march a tad further north at about 79°59'.900. The extra mile and a bit would have added less than an hour to our overall journey time but it would be far more satisfying if our start point was in the 'seventies' and not the 'eighties'. At school, it was a source of frustration that for quite some time, the highest mountain I had climbed was the 999-metre Glyder Fawr in Snowdonia (more a hill than a mountain), and mathematical imperfections on expeditions have wound me up ever since.

The initial pace is good and I am relieved at how much easier it feels to pull our sleds across the snow than it had been to drag those minibus tyres back in October through the sand in Hyde Park. How Ranulph Fiennes and Mike Stroud ever got their monstrous 485-pound sleds moving during their crossing of the Antarctic continent is beyond me.

20 minutes later the climb begins, marking the beginning of the continent proper. I remember Dr Bamber, my glaciology

---

[1] A Global Positioning System (or GPS) is a mobile phone-sized device that uses satellites to pinpoint our exact position on the Earth's surface.

lecturer at Bristol University, describing the Antarctic Ice Cap as being flat. Even though the Pole itself is the best part of 10,000 feet above sea level, any change in gradient is supposedly very subtle. Not here. The continent rises from the coast in a series of steps, before flattening out in the centre, but because we are surrounded by an infinite expanse of white, it is very difficult to judge their scale. The first sign of an impending rise occurs when the horizon gradually appears to inch up to the sky. As we start to climb, a biting wind appears from nowhere, howling as only fiercely cold winds do.

The katabatic winds, that are so prevalent in the Antarctic, are driven by gravity, making this precipitous corner of the continent windy as hell. We scuttle up the short step, eager to see what we might find the other side. Far away to the west, we get our first view of the distant Ellsworth Mountains. Now that we have gained a modest amount of altitude and can look down on Hercules Inlet, its true scale becomes apparent. An obvious line marks the divide between the Antarctic landmass and the Ronne Ice Shelf, which is uniformly flat compared to the gently undulating landscape surrounding it. A good ten miles away, a series of long hills marks the far side of the inlet (a gulf would be a more appropriate term), which gradually merge into the mountains of the Antarctic Peninsula behind.

I think I must have eaten too many eggs for breakfast, as by mid-morning I have got terrible stomach pains that refuse to go away. Paul doesn't seem entirely comfortable either, and is burping a lot. I get my minidisk working for the first time, although after just ten minutes it decides to pack up in the middle of Michael Jackson's 'Billie Jean'. I assume it doesn't like the cold – or the music.

After three hours, we stop for our second pit stop of the day. Paul pulls out the GPS and reveals that we have already covered a very encouraging five miles. Given the terrain, this is further than we had anticipated, but Paul warns us that this is a two-month expedition, we are by no means at full fitness yet, we need to acclimatise further to the conditions, and it would be sensible to slow things down a bit.

Later. The childish excitement of the morning begins to catch up with us and we are now paying the price as we continue to climb. The flat sections are just about tolerable and I find I can get into a rhythm quite easily. But the steps are now hard toil. Furthermore, the terrain has changed from smooth hard-packed snow to a mixture of blue ice and sastrugi. The slopes would barely pass for a beginners' piste in a ski resort but it requires a Herculean effort to drag our fully laden sleds up them. The full weight of our sleds is accentuated by the gradient – if we were to unclip ourselves from our chest harnesses, the sleds would accelerate down the slippery slopes and off to the coast. 'The other group must have had it so easy with their empty sleds!' exclaims Pat as we try skiing side by side.

Worried about getting too cold, I'm foolishly wearing far too many layers today and the heat is adding to my discomfort. To make things harder still, our skis do not give us enough purchase on the ice so we are now walking on foot. This is gruelling, sweaty work.

We reach the crest of the next step expecting the going to become more straightforward, only to find the route ahead crisscrossed with crevasses, glinting in the sun. They are all bridged with wind-blown snow of varying depth and are easy to distinguish against the slippery blue ice either side. Paul drives his ski pole into the snow of the first crevasse to test its strength. He assures us it is safe to cross. I nervously follow him as quickly as possible, breathing a huge sigh of relief once I have made it to the other side.

Over the next two hours, we have to negotiate a further 20 or 30 of these icy chasms. Whilst some are no more than a couple of feet in width and can be crossed with ease, a large number are between eight and twelve feet wide and present much more of a challenge.

Our group is pretty strung out now, with everyone trying to find their own route through the maze of crevasses. There is a technique to crossing them. When we reach the lip of an impending crevasse, we pull our sleds alongside us. After prodding the snow bridge that spans the black hole below, it is relatively straightforward to scuttle across without the drag of the sled to slow us down. It still feels like a game of Russian roulette though, and my heart is in my mouth until I have reached the other side.

A little later, just as I'm starting to feel some confidence that these snow bridges are strong enough to support my body weight, I test a relatively narrow one with a ski pole, only for the whole structure to collapse and disappear into the darkness below. It terrifies me how little pressure is required for it to give way. I tentatively peer down into the inky void. The deep blue sides of the crevasse are beautifully smooth, representing thousands of years of Antarctic snowfall that have compacted into ice over time. I can't see the bottom, so goodness knows how deep this monster is – a good 300 or 400 feet maybe. This is certainly no place to hang about and I turn around to look for a new crossing point.

Ever since my first encounter with a crevasse in the Alps nearly seven years ago, the things have scared the living daylights out of me. The idea of being gobbled up by the ice and then gradually digested over time has given me sleepless nights during previous trips to the mountains, and I rank it up there with being eaten by sharks as my least preferred way to go.

Just as our first day is drawing to a close and we are looking for a place to set up camp, I skilfully plant one of my big size twelves right through the middle of a crevasse. My heart skips a beat. Incredibly, the rest of the snow bridge doesn't give way and only a leg disappears through the surface, dangling precariously over the abyss. In a split second, a sort of adrenalin-induced autopilot takes over, and before I realise what's really happened, I have miraculously hauled myself out of danger and onto solid ground the other side. Phew.

'Bloody hell, Tom, you alright?' asks Pat, still the wrong side of the crevasse.

'Should be. You might want to look for another place to cross,' I reply helpfully.

He does and we are soon on our way again. I am amazingly fortunate. Had I fallen right through, I would have been in more than a spot of bother. We are carrying a 160-foot rope with us, but had I gone in, the chances are that I would have been unconscious, wedged between the walls of ice where the crevasse starts to narrow and far out of reach of the rope. It doesn't bear thinking about.

It might seem strange that we do not travel across this hazardous landscape roped together. There are good reasons for this. Fiddling around with ropes and harnesses in this biting wind would lead to frostbite in seconds. Furthermore, if someone were to fall down a hole, because of the slippery nature of the blue ice either side, the rest of the team would not get enough grip from the surface to hold the fall and would be dragged in as well. Better to lose one man than the whole team. Losing nobody would be better still. In normal circumstances I would be absolutely terrified by what had just happened, so I presume it must be the sheer fatigue that is numbing my emotions. Only later in the comfort of the tent will I be able to appreciate fully what nearly happened out there. Other than wounded pride, there is no damage done but it serves as a serious warning of the hidden dangers of this place.

During Mawson's fateful *Aurora* Expedition, the unfortunately-named British soldier Belgrave Ninnis disappeared down an apparently bottomless crevasse in Wilkes Land on the east of the continent with a team of dogs, much of the expedition food and their tent. When his two colleagues, Mawson and Mertz, shouted down to him, only the whimpering of a wounded dog could be heard, deep inside the bowels of the ice.

It comes as a huge relief when Paul signals the day's end. Camp is erected in just under an hour – we will have to become far more efficient at this over the days ahead. It takes me a good five minutes to take off my jacket. All that sweat has frozen on the inside of my outer layers of clothing and it takes for ever to brush away the ice enough for me to undo the zip. I'm shivering when I finally crawl into the tent after six and a half hours of the hardest exercise of my life. Andrew and Pat sit there in total silence, shattered and clearly in a state of shock. If it's like this every day for the next 60, there is no way I'm going to make it as far as halfway, let alone to the Pole. From the vacant looks on my friends' faces, I think I speak for us all.

Pat points out a black streak on each of my cheeks. On closer inspection in the small mirror in my medical kit, I am horrified to discover these warpaint-like marks are the first tell-tale signs of frost damage, which has set in unnoticed thanks to the wind. The wind must have somehow found a way through the protective layers of my fur-lined hood, balaclava, neck gaiter, goggles and facemask. Livid with myself for not having taken more care to cover every bit of exposed skin during the day. Andrew seems to have suffered too, and the pair of us look more like Red Indians than polar explorers. The bottoms of his earlobes have also succumbed to minor frostbite, as his hat is too small to cover the whole of his head.

The three Londoners are pretty useless this evening and leave Paul to dinner duty. Whilst he makes hot chocolate for us all, Pat is in a major panic, unable to find his mug and bowl. 'I think I've left them at Patriot Hills,' he says, frantically searching under sleeping bags and jackets. After half an hour's stressing, Paul asks: 'Are you sure they aren't in your sled?' Pat goes outside to have one final look, and sure enough there they are lying at the bottom of his sled.

I'm not at all hungry and it's a struggle to finish my bowl of pasta carbonara. Today is the birthday of a good friend back in London and I call Alasdair on the sat phone to wish him well. He asks me what the temperature is and seems surprised that it's as warm as $-7°C$. 'Sounds like a piece of piss!' he jokes. If only he knew what we have endured today. Although we have climbed a whopping 1,500 feet, we have covered only 9.25 miles. The gradient should start to level out during the coming days, but tonight the next step looms high above our tents. Our mood is deflated further when just before bedtime, Pat knocks over his water bottle, spilling the best part of a litre of precious warm drinking water over the inside of the tent.

The South Pole feels a very long way away tonight.

DAY 2: THURSDAY 14 NOVEMBER   604.2 MILES TO GO

Things get off to an atrocious start. At 6.15 am on the dot, Pat and I are woken by Paul, unzipping the tent door. We've overslept. Last night he told us to have everything cleared away for his morning arrival so that he could begin his breakfast duties on time. But we haven't and the tent is like a bombsite. In our semi-conscious state and still in our sleeping bags, we desperately try to clear some sort of space for him. Everything from food bags and fleeces to inner boots and smelly socks litters the tent floor and we desperately try to limit the damage. But it's all too late and from the stern look on Paul's face as he crawls in, it's clear that he's far from impressed. He rightly gives us a roasting.

Goody-goody Andrew follows Paul in moments later after a night alone in the gunner's tent. Even though the expedition is very much in its early phases, it's vital that we get into some sort of routine as quickly as possible and become much more efficient in everything we do. Whilst Paul gets the stove going, Pat and I sheepishly do our best to get the place ship-shape, feeling as though we have just been disciplined by the headmaster.

Over breakfast, I cover the marks on my cheeks with tape and pray that today the cold doesn't penetrate through the many protective layers around my face. Much to our surprise, we discover that almost all the clothing that we hung up last night has thawed and dried out completely. This is excellent news and provides a tremendous fillip after yesterday's horrors. Even our inner boots have dried out in the warmth of the tent. Sweat and ice build-up are going to be a real problem if we're not careful. Wearing damp clothing in cold climates is not recommended. On contact with the cold outside, any moisture in gloves or socks quickly freezes, leading to instant discomfort and subsequent frostbite.

Scott supplied his men with a large amount of special dried grass from Norway to help keep their feet dry. Although warm, their cumbersome finnesko (reindeer fur boots) readily collected moisture during a long day's march that would then freeze overnight. To counter this, strands of grass were stuffed between sock and boot every morning to absorb the sweat from the foot. At the end of the day, the grass would be removed from the boot and left outside to freeze, when the sweat would congeal in the form of frost. The following morning, the frost could be simply brushed off, enabling the grass to be used again. I can't even bear to think how uncomfortable it would be to have strands of soggy hay sloshing about at the bottom of my boots. But I guess in those days, having never encountered the modern-day wonders of vapour barrier socks and neoprene-insulated boots, explorers would have been none the wiser.

Our first effort at packing up the tents takes some time, and we set off behind schedule. I'm very stiff after yesterday's exertions. Luckily Paul's initial pace is fairly gentle, which is just as well as the day begins with a series of steep climbs on mixed ground similar to yesterday's. It feels much colder today, and there's still a biting wind that buffets us relentlessly.

With skis securely fastened to the outside of our sleds, we spend the morning travelling on foot, laboriously making our way through the complex maze of sastrugi, blue ice and crevasses. Although it means we can travel faster over the constantly changing terrain, it makes these damned crevasses much more of a hazard – the laws of physics mean that a boot exerts far more pressure on the surface, making the snow bridge far less likely to hold a man.

This is demonstrated as I prove yesterday's mishap was no fluke by going in twice again this morning. I'm sure that any day now, my luck is going to run out and I'll end up falling hundreds of feet into the jaws of one of these monsters. At the moment I'm just counting my lucky stars. Although I let out a petrified wail each time I feel myself accelerating downwards, my overriding feeling is one of irate frustration.

Once a crevasse has been safely dealt with, I turn around, grab hold of the rope that connects the fibreglass sled to my harness and start pulling it across the snow bridge. The surface is nothing like as smooth as the polished blue ice either side, and it's a real strain to pull what is effectively a 13-stone bathtub over the sticky expanse of snow. The far side of the widest crevasses is guarded by a short, but steep, lip of hard blue ice that requires a final heave to haul the sleds over. I catch my breath, turn to the south again and continue on my way. Pat and Andrew are not immune to the danger either, and they too have several crevasse scares early on. It's all quite sobering.

By midday it seems that the worst of the climb is over, and we can now clearly make out the Patriot Hills off to the west. Whilst a dramatic sight in their own right, they are mere foot-hills to the more imposing bulk of the jagged spires of the Ellsworth Mountains behind. The gradient is easing and the blue ice and crevasses are gradually petering out. There is still a fair bit of sastrugi around, but less concentrated than before and therefore easier to negotiate. I am becoming aware of some bruising across the top of my right foot that is giving a fair amount of pain. I'm trying to grin and bear it for now and I just hope that it doesn't get any worse as we move south.

In order to counter the problem of my minidisk freezing up, I have rigged up a container for it, which I am most proud of, using a ziploc bag, some gaffer tape and a length of thin prusik rope. Supported round my neck, it lives under my jacket where it should be warm enough to continue playing the tunes. However, I make the error of trying to listen to Phil Collins's Greatest Hits this afternoon, and it's not long before the cockney crooner's soppy ballads start irritating me. I kick myself for not recording more uplifting music before I left home. To my immense relief, just as I'm scanning the horizon for a gaping crevasse into which I can throw Phil and his band, the battery conks out.

We are now definitely on the flat and have at last completed the climb onto the Antarctic Ice Cap proper. According to the map, the terrain should start to improve from here, and with our sleds becoming lighter as we get through our food and fuel supplies, our speed should gradually begin to pick up. We have climbed to 2,600 feet above sea level in a day and a half and I am as spent as a man can be. But it is a wonderful feeling to know that even though we still have a further 7,000 feet to climb to reach the Pole itself, any further gains in elevation are unlikely to be as abrupt.

Off to the southwest, I notice three identical hillocks protruding through the flat ice. I wave my ski pole in their general direction in an effort to point them out to Pat, who is skiing behind me. He doesn't seem very interested. We had first seen the Three Sails, as they are known in these parts, when we touched down at Patriot Hills four days ago, and the straightforward beauty of these giant white dunes captivated me straight away. It's good to see them again, a familiar landmark in very unfamiliar surroundings.

After six hours Paul asks us if we want to camp or continue for another hour. Feeling somewhat revitalised now that the climb is behind us, I'm very keen that we should push on in the improving conditions. Just as I'm about to suggest we do the extra hour, Pat pipes up and beats me to it. I'm a little peeved for not getting in there first, as I've been quiet all day and eager to show that despite the pain in my foot, I'm coping as well as anyone.

The final hour turns out to be the best of the day, with sastrugi few and far between. The skies are clear, the strength of the wind has receded and the going is flat as far ahead as we can see. I spend most of this time glancing across to my right, mesmerised by the vista of the Three Sails.

Camp is pitched on a polished area of firm snow. The wind still has some punch to it. It would not be difficult for a gust to whisk away a tent, so all hands are on deck to ensure that each one is erected and firmly secured to the ground.

Once we've settled into the big tent, we check our position on the GPS and to our great disappointment we discover we have clocked a paltry 9.21 miles in seven hours. We can't understand why. Despite travelling for half an hour longer today, with slightly lighter sleds and with a shorter climb, our mileage is actually less than yesterday's. Paul laughs at our dejected reaction to the GPS reading. 'Guys, relax! We're just two days into a sixty-day expedition. We're doing great. Just be patient!'

Any frustration quickly recedes when we hear on the radio that Matty's team are still at Patriot Hills and not leaving until tomorrow morning. Even though we are eight miles further east, our GPS position puts us a mile closer to the Pole than the Patriot Hills camp and therefore the other group. 'We can't let them get ahead of us!' says Andrew.

My neck is quite stiff this evening – I think I've spent too many hours staring down at my ski tips. The two black marks on my cheeks haven't got any worse and the bruising on my foot doesn't feel as bad as it looks, but I slap on some anti-bruising Arnica cream all the same. Back home, this is Mum's panacea for every condition under the sun from operations to jetlag so I hope it does the job.

My major health concern at the moment is that I have yet to go to the loo since leaving Patriot Hills, home of the comfy wooden-seated toilets. I think it might have something to do with the army-ration biscuits we are eating every day. The last time I ate these inconceivably bland biscuits (which come in a tough green foil pack of six, with the mouth-watering name 'BISCUITS BROWN' emblazoned in big black lettering on the front) was when on night exercise with the school army corps in a muddy forest in Hampshire. The primary function of the biscuit seemed to be to prevent a soldier being distracted during a combat situation, as none of our platoon had to nip off to the bog in the middle of the night. A more effective version of the Biscuits Brown, and more commonplace on longer exercises, was the even less appetising 'BISCUITS AB', which we swore stood for 'anal blocker', thanks to their extraordinary ability to constipate an army cadet for days on end. I've therefore decided to give my Biscuits Brown ration a miss tomorrow.

We are all sore and tired this evening but smiles are gradually returning and there is some good banter in the tent over dinner. We are very pleased with our decision three days ago not to go through Patriot Hills camp as we head south. Although travelling through that horrible terrain above Hercules Inlet with near-empty sleds would have been far less exhausting, I think I would have felt a bit of a fraud stopping off for freshly baked bread, a few glasses of wine and a warm bed just two days into my first polar expedition. It feels as though we are very much under way now. I just pray that Paul is right and that the toughest part of the journey between here and the Thiel Mountains is over.

Don't want to see another crevasse for a very long time.

Things have obviously moved during the night, and my first thought this morning is that I need to find a loo. Pat is also doing this for the first time and, halfway through breakfast, disappears into the cold to use the outdoor facilities, armed with a shovel and some pre-folded loo roll. The three of us continue sipping our tea, eagerly awaiting his return. Just three minutes later and he's back. 'Wow, what the hell happened out there?' asks Paul. 'You look terrified!'

'That was the coldest, most unpleasant experience of my life,' replies Pat, shivering uncontrollably.

I am now filled with trepidation. Faced with the predicament of having to expose my bottom to the polar winds, I need to find an alternative method quickly. The vestibule[2] will have to do, and as soon as Paul and Andrew have packed away their breakfast things and are outside, I am straight in there. To say that the vestibule is cramped would be a gross understatement, and having dug myself a small pit in the snow where the stove had been, there is barely enough room for me to squat. Being properly house-trained I have zipped up the vestibule door, which does at least afford some privacy, although the fabric is so thin that I'm sure Pat can easily make out my silhouette. He is sitting no more than two feet away from me, so this would not be a very clever time to suffer the indignity of bog fright. Through the canvas partition, we try having a polite con-

[2] The area opposite the entrance between the flysheet and the main tent that serves as our kitchen.

versation about the weather before Pat cracks up with laughter at the absurdity of it all, which in turn sets me off.

Once I have finished my business, I cover up the pit with snow and dive back into the main part of the tent. What a performance. It brings a whole new meaning to the phrase 'shitting on your own doorstep', but at least I have avoided freezing my undercarriage.

As we clamber out of the tent to begin a new day, I pan around at the view. To the west, the Patriot Hills are bathed in early morning sunshine, with a pure expanse of white stretching in every other direction. The sun kisses a multitude of ice crystals on the surface, making them sparkle like jewels. The only blemish to this pristine beauty is the curly brown heap lying in the snow, no more than a few yards from the tent. It's pretty obvious what it is, but who left it there is another question altogether. My first assumption is that a giant penguin must have wandered past camp in the night, marking out his territory on his way through. 'Ah, that will be mine,' confesses Pat. 'I was so cold that I didn't have the time to dig a hole for it.'

The day begins with a two-hour march. Now with new batteries, the Pet Shop Boys provide a welcome change from Collins, who has been relegated to the very bottom of my sled. I glance across at our friends the Three Sails and see that a grey haze shrouds their base. Over the next ten minutes, this strange mist gradually extends right across the southern horizon and appears to be getting closer.

Then suddenly it hits us, a harsh wind belting straight out of the south at 20 to 25 knots. It sounds like a jet engine, primed for takeoff. I stop to make sure I've covered up every exposed bit of flesh around my face, put my head down and grind on. All around us the snow has been whipped up into a frenzy, completely obscuring from view the solitary humps of the Three Sails. For the rest of the morning I am mesmerised by the snow as it slaloms its way around clumps of sastrugi, the flakes whirling like dervishes round my legs and on towards the coast.

I have always been quite tolerant of the cold, and even in the depths of winter I will happily sleep with my bedroom window wide open. One of the reasons I prefer being in cold climates is that if I don't feel warm enough, I can just throw on another fleece or an extra pair of socks. But for the first time on an expedition, the cold is getting to me. Whilst the rest of my body feels warm enough, in the ten minutes after each of today's pit stops, my fingers go completely numb. There then follows an intense period of chilblain-induced pain when the fingers slowly start coming back to life. The trick with gloves is to ensure that one has a system that keeps the hands warm but not so warm as to make them sweat. Any sweat will soon cool and cause dainty digits to freeze. Frostbite is one of our most serious concerns, and we are all agreed that it's not even worth sacrificing a finger to reach the South Pole.

Terrified of never being able to grip a golf club again, I have brought along various glove combinations. Today I am wearing a pair of thin polypropylene gloves, which wick any sweat away from the hands, a thicker set of fleece gloves for warmth, and some windproof Gore-Tex overgloves, providing further insulation and protection from the elements. Even though the windchill must make the temperature around −40°C today, I wonder if I'm wearing too many layers, because not long before our final break the fingers in my right hand go completely numb. No matter how much I wave my arms around in windmills, they refuse to thaw out. Panicking, I take off my skis and run to the back of my sled, pull off both the Gore-Tex and fleece gloves and replace them with my snug goosedown-filled mitts. I am shocked to find a thick layer of ice between the two sets of discarded gloves, formed as sweat became chilled by this ferocious wind. No wonder my fingers had frozen solid. Thankfully the feeling soon returns. This is a potentially serious problem that I'm going to have to sort out quickly – particularly as the temperatures will continue to fall the further south we go.

It surprises me that despite all the advances in polar clothing since Scott and Shackleton first set foot in Antarctica with their felt finger gloves and wolfskin mitts, hands still get cold and explorers continue to get frostbite. During the various sledging journeys of the *Discovery* Expedition, the men often grumbled that despite hanging up their thick fur mitts in the roof of the tent at night, they refused to dry out, leading to ice build-up the following day. Shackleton was one of those who suffered from frostbite, although he didn't have any lasting damage. Those men must have been incredibly hardy to tolerate such appalling levels of discomfort.

The first three days have been a real shock to the system for us all, and far tougher than we ever could have imagined. My body hurts and I am completely shattered. Although the bruising on my foot has eased, the first ominous signs of blistering have appeared on the heels. We always knew it would be a tough beginning but we never expected things to be so physically draining, the terrain so awful or this relentless wind so piercing.

Only three nights ago, I was extremely worried whether I had done enough physical training to get me through this whole ordeal but I have comfortably managed to achieve my aim of sticking to the group pace since we left Hercules Inlet. I now feel much more confident in my own physical condition. With the exception of the superhuman Paul, our natural travelling speeds seem to be almost identical, which is terrific news. Hopefully we can now start looking beyond simply surviving the next day.

I still can't get my head round the fact that we still have nearly 600 miles ahead of us before we reach the South Pole. This incomprehensible task is so depressing I would rather not think about it. So rather than focusing on a target far far away, we are concentrating our efforts on reaching the next line of latitude, the 81st Parallel, just 31 miles away. These invisible lines, which circle the Earth parallel to the Equator, were drawn up by medieval astrologers as a navigation aid to mariners and are still used to this day. Conveniently spaced exactly 60 miles apart, ten degrees of latitude lie between Hercules Inlet and the Pole itself. I hope that by breaking up the main goal into more manageable chunks, it should have a much more positive effect on my state of mind.

Must have a wash soon.

DAY 4: SATURDAY 16 NOVEMBER   585.5 MILES TO GO

Nothing but time changes in our uniform polar world. The white landscape is barren and unbroken, the cold wind relentless, and there is no difference between night and day. Only the sun, which completes a full revolution above our heads every 24 hours, reminds us that we are not completely frozen in time. To stop us from going barking mad in the conditions and to keep us motivated for the long march south, we must maintain a disciplined routine. We have to be strict on ourselves and keep an eye on the clock at all times. A few minutes lost here and there during the course of the day due to lie-ins or mistimed loo breaks may only reduce our daily mileage by a few hundred yards. But if multiplied by 60 days, that extra yardage can quickly balloon into marathon-esque distances and extra days on the Ice. Given our limited food supplies and the short Antarctic summer, it is vital that we become as punctual as the Swiss railway system.

After the shenanigans of our first full day, our morning routine is showing signs of improvement. Pat has no alarm on his watch so to make sure at least one of us wakes up, my alarm is primed to go off at 6, 6.01 and 6.02 am. My watch is tied to a small loop just inches above my head so there can be no excuses. At some point between 6 and 6.01 am, Paul lets out a cheery 'good morning' from his tent. He will repeat this call until he gets a response from both tents. If the wind is too strong for voices to be heard, we can expect a succession of snowballs to land on or around the tent until he can be sure we are up. More often than not, Pat manages to sleep through all of this, so I give him a good shake. Whilst he moans in a dazed half-sleep, I unzip the vestibule and light the stove in preparation for breakfast. It will be a while before the pan of slushy water starts to boil, so I lie down again and don't move for five minutes.

Paul is ruthless and predictable. He crawls into the big tent at 6.15 am sharp, not a moment later. The pressure is on, as there's a fair amount that needs sorting before Paul and Andrew's arrival, and it's all pretty stressful. In that short period, Pat and I manage to get semi-dressed, pack up sleeping bags, nip out and back for a pee and adjust our inflatable thermarest mattresses from large cumbersome sleeping mats into compact chairs so there is enough room for everyone. It's not long before the water is ready and soon we are all sipping hot chocolate in the comfort of our thermarest chairs. Poor Pat is not his usual jovial self this morning, having spilt his all over the tent floor.

I am used to expedition breakfasts being somewhat rushed affairs. In the mountains, we get kitted up at a ludicrously unsocial hour like 1 am. This is so we can start climbing well before first light when the terrain is frozen solid and thus more stable. There's barely enough time to wolf down a biscuit and a cup of sugary tea, before bleary-eyed, we stumble out of the tents and set off on our way, using head-torches to light up the path ahead. Polar breakfasts are more drawn-out affairs, and it's a refreshing change.

The reason everything takes so long is simple: water. Because we are sweating so much and the air is so dry, we need to drink vast quantities of the stuff to stay hydrated. There are no mountain streams down here so our water-source is the snow around us. For two hours every morning the stove churns away quietly, melting enough snow to provide each of us with a hot chocolate, a couple of mugs of tea, a litre of piping-hot orange squash (to be drunk during the day) and enough milk for a large bowl of cereal. A panful of powder snow melts down to an eggcup of water, so it's a long, slow and frustrating process. But it does give us the chance to have a good natter and discuss the plan for the day ahead. I have never been much of a morning person, and usually unable to say anything coherent before lunchtime, so this does at least give me time to try to revive myself.

Back home, cereal is a big part of my life, and the kitchen cupboard is permanently stacked with a wide assortment of breakfast treats from Cinnamon Grahams to Honey Nut Cheerios. We have brought a selection of cereals to Antarctica – a delicious honey-roasted granola and a raisin-filled muesli, both complemented with powdered milk (which is surprisingly good) and bucket-loads of sugar. Much to everyone's disgust today is a muesli day. Whilst the granola is hugely popular, the latter is unbearably heavy and bland, with the texture of cold porridge. The large green Argentinian raisins are jaw-breakingly tough and a heaped bowlful is a serious mission to get through.

Rather than waste valuable time and fuel melting snow for washing-up water, mugs and bowls are hygienically licked clean with a finger. By 8.10 am, everyone is dressed, my feet are taped up in preparation for the impending blister onslaught and we are outside loading up the sleds. The tents are then dismantled and the aim is to be under way at 8.30 am sharpish, but we're still not getting away on time. I blame it on the chewy raisins.

The first two hours follow a similar theme to the ground-blizzard we experienced yesterday, which at least serves to blow the morning cobwebs away. There then follows a big improvement. The wind drops and the surface changes to a thin layer of soft powder snow – the ideal surface for travel. The splendour of the Three Sails emerges from the haze and it feels fantastic not to be knocked about by those incessant winds. The US Geological Survey map of this part of the continent we studied closely before leaving Patriot Hills was divided by a dotted line labelled 'limit of compilation', with the area to the south of the Three Sails totally blank. We are now heading off the map and into an unknown world.

I have decided to travel with a much thinner fleece than the one I wore in the opening days and I'm wearing only one layer of thermals under my salopettes to reduce the sweat build-up. Unfortunately, to compensate for the extra heat loss, I make the error of zipping my jacket all the way up, with the result that I exhale directly inside the jacket. As my breath cools it freezes on contact with the inside of the metal zipper, and, unnoticed, forms a thick film of hard ice the full length of the jacket. By the end of the day the jacket has turned to chain-mail and it takes me ten minutes to chip the ice away with a tent peg before I can take it off. To avoid getting ice in the tent, we must do this cold work outside.

Today is the longest of the expedition so far, with the day now seven hours long (plus a further hour for breaks). The terrain has been excellent so we must have sailed past the ten-mile mark, possibly even as far as eleven. The set practice once the tents are pitched is to crank up the GPS. It takes an agonising couple of minutes before the GPS gives us its reading. 'Distance covered 9.88 miles' shows up on the screen. We are devastated. Less than 200 yards separate us from the magical ten-mile mark. Achieving ten miles for the first time would have given us such a psychological lift but to fall just short is heart-wrenching. Just as Andrew is about to smash the machine to pieces with the shovel, Paul crawls in and says to the three long faces: 'It's another record day. You should be pleased!'

With all the modern advances in expedition equipment, it's easy to become blasé about the latest navigation gizmos. 100 years ago it was just as important for Scott to know exactly where he was on the map as it is for us, but of course he had no GPS to help him. Latitude and longitude readings were taken at midday every day during the Southern Journey, when the sun is precisely due north and at its highest position in the sky. To calculate his daily distances, Scott used a theodolite. This heavy piece of equipment consisted of a telescopic sextant mounted on a three-foot-high tripod. Once the tripod legs had been precisely levelled off using an inbuilt spirit level, a sequence of sun sightings would be taken over a period of 20 minutes either side of local noon to give a precise reading for the maximum angle of the sun in the sky on that day. Scott would then determine their latitude by comparing his results with the many pages of latitude tables in the navigation almanac. Longitude would be calculated at the same time, using the theodolite readings, two watches and more tables.

Over a sumptuous dinner of chilli con carne, we're given an insight into Paul's somewhat extreme views of British polar exploration. Hopefully not including us in his judgement, he tells us: 'Ever since the days of Scott, you guys have been ill-prepared and poorly trained, with the arrogance and naivety that stiff upper lip and British pluck will get you through. The Norwegians have always been the real pros and their achievements reflect this.'

Nobody is let off from Sir Wally Herbert to our patron, Sir Ranulph Fiennes. His outspoken remarks come as a bit of a surprise so early in the expedition, and Pat and I do our best to defend our childhood heroes. Andrew doesn't seem that bothered, he being South Africa's first-ever polar adventurer. Paul does make some valid points but I'm sure the debate will continue over the coming days and weeks.

I have my first wash tonight by dunking a flannel into a few drops of tepid water saved from dinner in a basin consisting of no more than a ziploc bag. I'm not sure how effective the technique is but I do at least feel refreshed. The wind has now died down so it should be much warmer in the tent tonight.

Let's try to knock off ten miles tomorrow.

DAY 5: SUNDAY 17 NOVEMBER   575.6 MILES TO GO

'Mate, can you empty this whilst you're out there?' asks Pat, as I nip out for a pre-breakfast pee. Whereas my bladder has managed to hold off all night, Pat's floodgates opened a while back and he has managed to fill his one-litre pee bottle almost to the brim. It's still warm as he passes it to me. All those romantic preconceptions I had of skiing across Antarctica with close friends were blown out of the window a long time ago, and I am quickly discovering that these unglamorous incidents are the norm on a long polar journey.

The subject of Andrew Cooney comes up in conversation with Paul over breakfast. Paul tells us that just before we left Chile, Cooney told Matty that it was her responsibility to ensure their team reached the Pole before us. Apparently he's concerned that our young team might steal all the publicity if we get there first. I don't really know why he's getting so worked up about it all because it's highly unlikely that there would be any media interest in either expedition in the first place.

According to Paul, Matty feels pretty aggrieved that one of her team should try to influence the whole group's strategy solely for the sake of publicity, particularly as reaching the Pole is going to require such a strong team effort.

Many of the great names in global exploration have been drawn to the polar regions by the lure of public recognition. Several years before he became the first man to reach the North Pole in 1909, the American explorer Robert Peary wrote: 'I must have fame, and I cannot reconcile to years of commonplace drudgery and a name late in life when I see an opportunity to gain it now and sip the delicious draught while yet I have youth and strength and capacity to enjoy it to the utmost ... I want my fame now.' Scott's motives were very different. When *Discovery* set sail from England in 1901, large crowds lined the waterside cheering the ship and her crew. Despite all this adulation, Scott was quite a reserved man when it came to self-promotion. Whilst he may have been ambitious, he hoped that success on the expedition would help further his career within the Royal Navy. He could never have imagined that one day he would become one of the most recognised names in the Western world.

A couple of things distract me from the grind of our first major climb for three days. Firstly a giant nunatak[3] appears out of nowhere, 30 miles off to our right, like a distant ship on the horizon. Paul identifies the rocky sentinel as Mount Godwin. Only the very top is visible and I wonder just how big it might be.

The second distraction is a little closer to hand. I always eat my slices of cheese and salami at the first break of the day, as by the afternoon they have frozen solid, rendering them totally inedible. The salami is delicious, with a real tang to it. It is also particularly stringy, and I manage to get three strands of Chile's finest salami lodged between my teeth. Over the course of the next hour I try desperately to dislodge the irritating morsels with my tongue. By the time the final piece has been weeded

---

[3] Inuit for a solitary craggy peak protruding through the ice cap.

out and swallowed, it is devoid of any taste whatsoever, but the whole exercise has kept me occupied for ages.

Andrew leads the second 45-minute stint after lunch and really burns up the ground. I can feel myself starting to sweat profusely, so I take my foot off the pedal, eventually arriving at the next break five minutes behind the others. Paul tells Andrew that his stint was the fastest of the expedition so far and there's no need to overdo it. Considering this is his first expedition, Andrew has been absolutely brilliant since the whole trip began, but my one concern is that he might burn us all out before we've really got anywhere. More than the rest of us, he seems hell-bent on beating Team Cooney and I just hope it doesn't distract him from the bigger picture. We've got to pace ourselves.

Having given Andrew a ticking-off, Paul puts his minidisk on and promptly scampers off into the distance like a man possessed. By the time we finally catch up with him, he apologises and confesses that when he listens to the Rolling Stones on the Ice he 'totally zones' and has no concept of what speed he is going. Andrew grins wryly and says: 'Landry, that was way faster than my lead!'

A quick final half-hour means that at last we have cause to celebrate our first ten-mile day. Coupled with the fact that the gale has blown itself out and our second-hand Fischer skis are holding up admirably, we are all chuffed to bits.

Once the tents have been erected, we sit outside in the sun for about 20 minutes, sipping whisky and thinking that maybe this polar travel malarkey isn't so bad after all. On the rare occasions when the mercury drops below freezing back home, the whole country seems to grind to a halt. But thanks to this evening's benign conditions this is the first time I've felt the warmth of the sun's rays on my face since we arrived in Antarctica. Paul rigs up the solar panels outside his tent to charge up the sat phone and video camera. I take a few moments to soak up the breathtaking spectacle of the saw-like peaks of the Ellsworth Mountains behind us, knowing that in the next couple of days they will go the way of the Three Sails, slip over the horizon and disappear from view. Other than our voices, there is not a sound. All is blissfully quiet.

Following a piping hot bowl of Pasta al Fredo, Pat and I set about defacing the inside of the tent by drawing the beginnings of a Dungeons & Dragons-style map of our route to the South Pole. The 81st Parallel lies just 10.4 miles from our tents tonight and is marked up optimistically in thick blue biro. It would be great if we reached it tomorrow.

DAY 6: MONDAY 18 NOVEMBER   564.9 MILES TO GO

What a stifling night. With not a breath of wind, we've had the tent door and vents wide open to stop the place turning into a furnace. Thanks to the 24-hour daylight, the tent warms up in much the same way as a greenhouse in these calm conditions. Whilst it may be around −15°C outside, the thermometer on my watch shows a temperature of +19°C inside the tent. Provided the wind and clouds stay away, we can expect things to hot up at night as we approach the southern hemisphere's summer solstice on 21 December when the sun will be higher in the sky.

I'm up before the alarm and go for a short stroll wearing only my boxer shorts, goose down tent booties[4] and a thin thermal vest. It's hard to imagine that this land of such serenity is the same as the one that pummelled us for the first few days with howling gales and spindrift. The tiniest hint of breeze right now would chill me to the core, but the strength of the sun's rays is such that I can stay outside for a good ten minutes. I even manage to pluck up the courage to use the outdoor facilities for the very first time. Squatting in the cramped quarters of the vestibule has thus far been a pretty uncomfortable (and antisocial) business, and I was beginning to believe Geoff Somers's comment to us back in London that going to the loo is the worst part of polar travel. But I find there's something strangely satisfying about digging a pit in the snow, doing what

[4] Booties are a sort of polar slipper and typically worn in the tent.

you have to do and covering everything up again. I doubt there is a better view from a WC anywhere on the planet.

The terrain remains good for the first few miles before we come to quite a steep climb in the middle of my first lead. I find my sled keeps getting stuck behind lumps of sastrugi, requiring an extra push with the ski poles, a thrust of the hips and a grunt to pull it over. Pat gets the video camera out to film us struggling through the creased terrain.

Later, both Mount Godwin and the Ellsworths vanish from the horizon, and it appears that we've stumbled upon some giant depression. It gives us our first textbook view of Antarctica – nothing but an endless sea of white stretching out in every direction with a vast sky of vivid blue overhead. Antarctica is one big empty place. In fact, with an area twice the size of Australia, it is the fifth largest continent on the planet. By the end of the austral winter, its area effectively doubles to twelve million square miles with sea ice extending a further 600 miles from the actual coastline. The mountains that have temporarily disappeared from view this afternoon are part of a great chain that stretches almost continuously from the Antarctic Peninsula to Victoria Land, dividing the continent into East and West Antarctica.

But this place is known for its ice. Satellite images have shown that as much as 99.6 per cent of the continent is covered in the stuff, with only the highest mountains poking through. As we push deeper into the vast emptiness of East Antarctica's interior, there will be many more views like this one and I'm not particularly relishing the thought. I wonder if I shall go totally insane with nothing to look at for days on end but snow, sky and the back of the sled in front of me.

At the day's third pit-stop Andrew draws his sled alongside mine, pulls down his hood and brashly exclaims: 'I've been doing the maths and if we keep this pace up, we could be at the Pole before New Year's Eve.'

'But we've only just started!' I point out, slightly taken aback by his optimism. I'm not sure if his self-belief is genuine or if it's just his way of showing us that he is coping with his first experience of expedition life. As we found during our New Zealand training, the South African will always be the last to show that he's struggling. But Andrew's remarks reflect our increased confidence in our own abilities and the fact that we are looking beyond just trying to battle through each day unscathed.

I try to put Andrew's big shout to the back of my mind during the last session but instead find myself imagining a wild New Year's Eve party at the American South Pole station, with line dancing, folk music and topless Californian scientists dancing on the tables.

Everyone seems to have increased their speeds today, Paul and Andrew in particular, so there's no surprise to find we have crossed the 81st Parallel by the day's end. We're a tenth of the way there. It's depressing when put like that, but we've made it past the first hurdle and everyone leaps for joy and shakes hands when the GPS reading is read out. It really feels as though we are well on our way now.

This evening we agree that Andrew shouldn't have to spend the entire expedition in the solitude of the gunner's tent and Pat is happy to swap places with him for the next six days. I'm looking forward to sharing with Andrew. Not only is he much tidier than Pat, but he's not the sort of guy who would ask me to empty his pee bottle every morning. It's less than nine months since I first met Andrew and whilst I'll miss re-enacting endless Monty Python scenes with Pat, I hope that the next six days will give me the chance to strengthen my bond with our South African companion.

We may have 70 per cent of the world's fresh water at our feet, but getting at it is far from straightforward. So this evening Paul introduces us to the pleasures of the snow bath. As the name suggests, a snow bath involves jumping in the snow with not many clothes on and is the most effective way of maintaining a reasonable level of cleanliness on a polar expedition, without having to burn valuable fuel supplies to make warm water. 'Come on guys, we do this all the time in Canada!' says Paul, looking more excited than ever. Everyone else looks unconvinced, laughing nervously. But now seems as good a time as any to go through this ordeal – the weather conditions are tolerable and six days of continuous exercise have passed without a wash. We're really starting to smell.

We all emerge from our respective tents wearing nothing but boxer shorts. Paul, of course, isn't even wearing those. Straight away I feel my body heat draining through my feet and into the snow. I've got to get this over and done with as quickly as possible, so I grab a handful of powdery snow and start scrubbing away like a madman. The snow feels like sandpaper and refuses to melt on contact with my body.

The next 60 seconds are a blur of arms and snow, accompanied by the occasional high-pitched squeal when a particularly sensitive spot comes into contact with snow. Bizarrely, it's the armpits that feel it the most. I can't take any more of this and I dive back into the tent before I freeze solid. My new tentmate is already there, shivering uncontrollably, desperately trying to put on a thermal top. Fortunately we aren't that wet, which is just as well as we didn't bring towels to Antarctica. There is silence for a few moments whilst Andrew and I struggle to get dressed, a task made all the more challenging with numb fingers. We ignore the whimpering coming from next door and concentrate on the job in hand. This is surely the most sadistic way of keeping clean ever devised.

Ten minutes later and we have just about recovered. We are dressed, my fingers are coming back to life and I'm actually feeling wonderfully refreshed. Paul is smiling as he comes into the tent for dinner. 'That wasn't so bad, was it? What a great way to celebrate crossing our first degree!'

Not even the likes of Captain Scott would have put himself through that ghastly experience. During the Southern Journey, the men washed regularly with a sponge and a mug of tepid water, and whilst they did use snow towards the end of the journey, this was typically done in the comfort of the tent. There is no evidence to suggest the Southern Party's degree celebrations were anything more than a slap on the back.

One of the highlights of the evenings, and the thing I look

forward to most during the final few hours march into camp, is checking our satellite phone for text messages. Before we left the UK, we gave our number out to everyone we knew, not really expecting to hear from anybody, as our phone has no facility to reply to a message. When we were in Punta Arenas, Steve (ANI's radio operator) said that, if we were interested, he could send out a bulk email every day we are on the ice with the transcript of our daily radio call to Patriot Hills, including our latitude and longitude coordinates. A similar message and position report from Matty's group is on the same email, so that everyone back home knows exactly where we are, how we are coping and how we are getting on compared to the other team. Stories of crevasse falls and frostbite are likely to alarm the parents, so we try to keep our daily message fairly light-hearted and succinct.

Whilst Paul stirs the tomato and noodle soup, I fire up the satellite phone and wait for the telltale bleeps. One, two, three … nine, ten … 19 messages! Most of them are for Andrew (his mother seems to have mastered the concept of the text message far quicker than Pat's or mine), although we all get some 'post'. Every text message is read out aloud, often more than once. Irrespective of their content, the messages always make us smile and are our only form of contact with the outside world. 'Boys, I'm bored. I'm coming to see you. Look out for a parachute in the sky. Angus' is typical of the sort of stuff we get this evening, but it puts us in wonderful spirits to know that we are in the thoughts of the people who mean so much to us back home.

The degree celebrations continue after dinner with the sickly combination of marshmallows and a bar of dark Swiss chocolate that Paul had squirrelled away in the bottom of his sled. As I take another swig of malt whisky, I know we have still got a mountain to climb. I hope we will get there, but right now it feels like we are only in the foothills.

Day 7: Tuesday 19 November 553.6 miles to go

Over our morning cuppa, Paul tells us he spoke to Matty on the sat phone last night and like us, they are camped at exactly 81°S, though about eight miles further west. They covered an impressive 13.5 miles yesterday in order to make their first degree, which surprises us as we had thought with their varying degrees of fitness, their speeds would be less than our own. Recent text messages have said things like 'Go on lads, the others are flaking! Love, Jacko' or 'Keep going! Show 'em who's boss. Russ'. They have led us to believe we were gradually pulling ahead. Maybe we're just not as strong as we think. Anyhow, at least it keeps this 'race' very much alive, which should help to keep us focused over the days ahead.

After the success of yesterday's trip to the open-air Gents, I've decided that unless the most almighty blizzard comes our way, I shall refrain from using the vestibule again for all non-culinary activities. I couldn't have chosen a better time to sneak in a quick outdoor visit this morning, because no sooner have I returned to the tent to get kitted up for the day ahead than a full-on gale is raging around camp, blowing snow so high that the sun is partially obscured. As a result, we take extra care when dismantling the tents for fear that one might blow away. Thanks to the combined effects of cooking and breathing in the tents, the flysheets have developed a thick coating of ice. We don't want to be carrying any extra weight, so most of it is removed with a good old-fashioned shake in the wind. Ever since my first school camping trip to the uncharted woodlands of the Sussex Weald, I have struggled to squeeze a nicely folded tent into the tiny stuffsack that comes with it (why do they always make them so small?) so it's a joy that the practice in Antarctica is to roll the tent loosely into a large sausage before stuffing it into the airy insides of the sled.

In less than a week, the expedition has metamorphosed from a shambolic rabble of beginners into quite a well-oiled machine. Our daily procedure has developed almost military time-keeping, with every day following the same rigid pattern. We are getting so slick that the time is more like 8.25 am when we set off. Paul deserves most of the credit for this transformation. We like and respect him enormously and want to prove to him that whilst we will never be polar machines in the way that he is, we are very much up for the challenge and will give our all to making the expedition a success.

Having said that, not for the first time I'm late out of camp after making some final alterations to my hat/neck gaiter/ goggles combination in a fruitless quest for comfort and end up having to sprint to catch up with the others. Fortunately Paul always sets an easy pace for the first hour, before handing over the reins to Pat.

I find that no matter what the weather, those first two hours of the day fly by. Even though the wind today is straight in our faces and gusting up to 30 knots, I'm all snug under the cocoon of my big fur hood, still half asleep and not thinking about very much at all. The wind is fairly angry though and it could pose a problem if it is still this strong when we have to put up the tents later on. It would be disastrous for a tent to be ripped, or worse, lost in the wind, but I try not to worry about it too much for now and keep plodding on. In much the same way as a family of elephants crosses the savannah holding each other's tails in their trunks, we ski along in single file, ski strides completely in sync, with only a couple of feet separating ski tips from the sled in front. Just like the elephants, we do this so we don't get lost, the lead person can provide the group with some shelter from the elements, only one person has to make fresh tracks in the soft surface and we don't waste any time waiting for a straggler to catch up. But quite why we have to be this close with all this space around us is beyond me.

The 10.30 am break always comes much earlier than I expect and is marked by Pat planting both his ski poles deep into the snow. As is customary at a break, we all pull our sleds alongside one another's, take off skis and walk to the back of our sleds. Because our bladders are still full of breakfast's tea and hot chocolate, we always take this opportunity to go for a pee. With the sled's short towrope still attached to our harness, it's not as if we can walk much further than the sleds themselves, and we do well to keep the sleds, and each other, out of the line of fire. I sit myself down facing the sun with my back to the wind, and reach into my sled for my bottle of orange squash for a few gulps of hot juice and my lunch bag. Inside this most precious of tuckboxes are the daytime meals that will get me through the next few days, all carefully divided up into ziploc bags.

The slices of salami and cheese do me a power of good. They consist primarily of animal fat, and release their energy to the body slowly throughout the day at a much steadier rate than the more instant energy rush of a chocolate bar. Because I'm always lost in my early morning dream world, I never listen to music during the first two hours, so my final task of break one is to get the tunes pumping. But all this fiddling with ziploc bags, bottle tops and flies has quickly turned my fingers numb. With no feeling in my hands, feeding the earphones under my neck gaiter and into my ears is complex work and can take anything from a few seconds to several minutes. I get even more stressed when trying to press the tiny 'PLAY' button with clumsy gloved hands.

For the first ten minutes of Andrew's lead I try desperately to defrost my hands by shaking them, wriggling them or rubbing them. If all else fails I will stop in my tracks and swing my arms round and round in giant windmills to try to get the blood flowing back to my fingers. I am not alone in this strange pursuit, and up ahead I can see both Paul and Andrew furiously whirling their arms about like a pair of demented ten-pin bowlers.

The shifts in the middle of the day are 45 minutes apiece, and it is with great pride that I take over the reins at 11.30 am. Having been in the pack all day, it is now my responsibility to break the trail for the team and to select the best course through the sastrugi. With our route winding its way inexorably through the snows ahead, it's such a thrill to be out in front.

'Lunch' is taken at 12.15 pm and consists of a slice of flapjack, a packet of my old pals Biscuits Brown, and another few swigs of (now tepid) squash. The strength of the wind makes conversing with the boys pretty impractical because everyone still has their hoods up and goggles on. I turn towards Pat to ask how he's feeling and find him attempting to post a biscuit through the narrow letterbox gap between his jacket and face-mask. Any attempt at dialogue is a pointless exercise. On windy days like this, it is common for not a single word to be uttered between us, though there will be a sporadic thumbs up to say 'All's well' or tapping at watches to indicate someone's slacking. Paul then leads from 12.30 pm to 1.15 pm and Pat until 2 pm.

'Teatime' is my favourite break of the day and I am salivating for most of Pat's shift in anticipation of the treats that await. I delve into the bag of chocolate chunks and pull out an assort-ment of goodies from bits of Double Decker to Yorkie bars to Boosts to crumbly Snow Flakes. Andrew ate his chocolate ration much earlier in the day, and as I line the pieces up on my leg, he glances across with envy. These breaks are supposed to last 15 minutes, but it's more like 2.10 pm when Andrew starts getting ready for his second lead of the day.

Despite being able to take a few precious moments to rest our sore bodies and to relieve the groans in our empty bellies, these breaks are actually pretty unpleasant affairs. No sooner have we sat down than we start getting very cold, particularly if there is a strong wind like today. Worryingly, Andrew's fingers are showing a markedly low tolerance to the cold and he can only survive ten minutes before having to get moving again. I hope for his sake that they don't get any worse during our journey south.

I take over from Andrew at 3 pm and lead until the final stop of the day at 3.45 pm. Having begun the day piping hot, my orange squash has steadily chilled, so now it resembles a slush puppy, the icy chunks stinging the back of my parched throat as I gulp it down. The food selection is pretty miserable at the fourth break and I scour my dried fruit supplies in the hope of finding one last pineapple chunk or apricot slice amongst the unappetising collection of green raisins and unidentifiable chewy orange things.

Paul leads the final shift from 4 until 5 pm, which he has inappropriately christened 'Happy Hour'. The only happy thing about it is that it is our last. It drags on interminably. The enthusiasm of the morning vanished a long time ago, and whilst Paul ploughs on relentlessly ahead, we are now desperate for it all to end. The music in my minidisk has run out and I need all my powers of determination just to stick with the group pace. The one thing that's keeping me going is the knowledge that this misery will all end at 5 pm on Paul's watch, and not a second later.

Just as I'm contemplating collapsing in a feeble heap in the snow, Paul veers off to one side to look for a flat area of firm ground on which to pitch the tents. We've survived another day. Thankfully, the wind is not as strong as earlier, and setting up camp is straightforward enough. We are all smiling again and it's not long before we're enjoying a brew in the warmth of the main tent. This has been our first $7\frac{1}{2}$-hour day (excluding breaks), and unless we get a kiting day we shall stick with this regime at least until the Thiel Mountains.

The Southern Party's typical travel day would last between ten and twelve hours but followed a very different pattern from our own. Because they could only calculate their position at midday, the men took this opportunity to take an extended lunch break. The whole procedure of setting up the theodolite and taking sun readings took well over an hour, so whilst Scott was carrying out the necessary measurements, Wilson and Shackleton would set up the tent and prepare lunch. For the remainder of the day they would take no further breaks before camping for the night.

Today is particularly exciting as it's my first boxer short change in 71 miles.

DAY 8: WEDNESDAY 20 NOVEMBER (PAT'S BIRTHDAY)   542 MILES TO GO

Why does a change in the weather always coincide with my trips to the loo? It was sunny and calm when I strolled over from the tent, mug of tea in hand, but just as I am getting down to business a wind springs up out of nowhere, tickling my behind with a cruel blast of spindrift. Then, shortly after we set off high clouds roll in from nowhere, totally filling the sky. The old adage of the Antarctic weather changing in a split-second is holding true, and it's going to make navigation extremely difficult for the rest of the day.

Up until now, all that we have needed to plot our way south has been the sun and a wristwatch, a simple technique adapted by mariners to chart their course over the high seas. Ever since the ancient cartographers started drawing maps of the Earth over 2,000 years ago, latitude and longitude meridians have crisscrossed the Earth in a grid of imaginary lines. The latitudes wrap themselves round the Earth from the Equator to the Poles in a series of ever-shrinking parallel lines, whilst the lines of longitude circle the globe in giant rings, all of them converging as they pass through both the North and South Poles.

Because it takes 24 hours for the Earth to complete a full 360° revolution, 15 degrees of longitude translate to an hour of time. This will be reflected in an apparent movement of the sun across the skies of 15 degrees per hour. Since we are travelling due south down the 80th meridian and our clocks are five hours behind GMT, local midday will always be at precisely 12.20 pm, day after day. Provided we don't stray off course, at local midday when the sun is due north, our shadows will point directly at the South Pole. Because we have all been doing the same shifts since we left Hercules Inlet, we now recognise where our shadows should be for a southerly course to be plotted during the day. For example, when Paul leads us off at 8.30 am every morning, his shadow should be at an angle of $57\frac{1}{2}°$ to the right of his skis, which gradually reduces to $42\frac{1}{2}°$ when Pat takes over an hour later. Of course, we are just estimating these angles with the naked eye, but having had a week to get used to the position of our shadows during our respective shifts, it's amazing how accurate due south can be calculated with dead reckoning.

But for now the shadows have vanished and we shall have

to resort to navigating by compass. This poses problems. The compass only gives an accurate reading when held horizontally, meaning we are going to be continuously looking up and down to take an accurate bearing, wasting valuable time. Also, because we are so close to the South Magnetic Pole,[5] instead of the compass needle pointing straight at the North Pole, it actually veers way off to the east. The compass deviation is currently 41°, which will rise to nearer 60° by the time we reach the Pole itself. We are able to calibrate the compass to allow for magnetic variations, but it's an added complication.

Halfway through his lead, Andrew pulls over to say he can't see a thing. At first he thought it might be due to the grey light, but he takes off his goggles to reveal a thin layer of ice which has built up on the inside of the lens, clouding his vision completely. We'll have a proper look at them in the tent tonight, but for the moment he has to stay at the back of the line, trying to follow the blurred outline of the orange sled in front. Having got used to blue skies day after day, I'm actually quite enjoying this change in conditions. Everything is dark, the wind has dropped altogether and the surface is quite powdery, making a satisfying crunch with each stride. The occasional snowflake falls out of the monochrome sky, and for the first time on the trip it feels really wintry. This is how I always imagined Antarctica to be.

It's my turn to lead. I fix the compass due south (technically speaking, 41° east thanks to the magnetic variation) and pick out a lump of snow on a southerly bearing about 50 yards ahead. I head straight for it. I cannot let it out of my sight, a task that requires all my powers of concentration in the pea soup. Once the lump has been reached, I take a new bearing and look ahead for my next target. This process is repeated a dozen times before I am forced to stop in my tracks. The light has gone so flat that every topographical feature is obscured

[5] The South Magnetic Pole is the point where the Earth's magnetic field is vertical. A compass needle will try to point straight down here. Unlike the Geographic Pole the position of the South Magnetic Pole moves about ten miles a year. In 1902 it was located in Victoria Land. Today it is found 200 miles off the Antarctic coast in the Southern Ocean – over 1,500 miles from the Geographic South Pole.

and I'm unable to find a new marker. In every direction, the surface appears grey and featureless. This is what the inside of a ping-pong ball must be like. I know the ground is far from flat, because I keep tripping up over hidden pockets of sastrugi. I look ahead in the hope of finding a snowy mound on the horizon which I can aim for but the dull light has removed all definition between land and sky. Everything is eerily still and silent in this strange murky world.

I press on, but this time I am having to look down at the compass around my neck every couple of strides to make sure we are going the right way. All sense of direction and perspective is long gone and I'm sure I'm drifting off to the left. By the time I come to the end of my 45-minute shift, I am disorientated, seasick and fed up.

It's now very unlikely that we will see any sign of Antarctica's wildlife during our journey to the Pole. The Antarctic interior may be lifeless but its coastline is teeming with remarkable creatures. The nutrient-rich waters surrounding the continent provide the perfect habitat for immense populations of krill. This shrimp-like organism is the major component of the Antarctic food chain and forms the staple food of most whales, seals, fish, penguins and other seabirds in the Southern Ocean. A few hundred miles to the north of us, on the edge of the Ronne Ice Shelf, Weddell seals and emperor penguins have gathered in large breeding colonies. Emperors are renowned for going walkabout and vagrants have been spotted as much as 60 miles inland. The only animal we might see this far south is the skua. The onboard homing system on these large brown gull-like scavengers often malfunctions, and skuas are regularly sighted at the Pole itself – 800 miles from their nesting grounds. Antarctica is not the best place to get lost.

Despite the overcast conditions, we rack up a new personal best of 12.1 miles, which puts us on course to reach the 82nd Parallel by Saturday evening. We've got our camp-pitching time down to less than 30 minutes, which gives us enough time to get out of our wet clothes, hang up gloves, socks, jackets and inner boots to dry and get the place looking shipshape before

Paul and Pat come in for supper. We have a bit of a scare when Andrew notices that one of the fuel canisters in his sled has leaked onto his sleeping bag. Thankfully, further inspection reveals not a huge amount has been lost, and as long as Andrew avoids setting his sleeping bag, or himself, on fire, it should evaporate overnight.

Pat was very quiet this afternoon and has clearly had one of those days. Whether it's because of the difficult conditions or the fact that he turned 27 today is unclear, but he quickly cheers up when the sat phone bursts into life with a bevy of birthday text messages.

Paul is very much in charge at mealtimes. Our early offers to help in the kitchen were politely declined and so now we just leave him to it. 'I enjoy cooking and I'm far more efficient with fuel than you guys will ever be.' I'm starting to feel less guilty about leaving Paul to do everything because he genuinely looks very happy melting snow and dishing out meals. Pat pulls a collection of paper hats, balloons and whistles from his dinner bag that he has been saving for festive occasions such as this. I don't think our rendition of 'Happy Birthday' will be winning any pop idol competition. The evenings have been our chance to unwind from the rigours of the expedition and after today's struggles, tonight feels particularly relaxing. Everyone is in excellent spirits, Pat is back to his old chirpy self and Paul is taking the mickey out of my woeful facial hair, which is pretty negligible considering ten days have passed since my last shave.

We've got quite a feast to get through this evening. As well as the standard three-course gourmet spread of soup, a calorie-packed freeze-dried main course (Pat has chosen couscous tonight – a curious selection) and a slice of shortbread, Pat has generously offered to share the birthday presents that he has just opened, all of which are edible, with the rest of the team. As I delve into the pick 'n' mix bowl in the centre of the tent, wondering whether to pluck out a chunk of Yorkie Bar, some South African biltong, a Lucozade energy sweet, or if I'm being really greedy, an extra large Canadian dry roasted peanut, I wonder if there can be a more happening party on the entire continent.

DAY 9: THURSDAY 21 NOVEMBER   529.9 MILES TO GO

Paul arrives at our tent one minute ahead of schedule this morning. This is a catastrophe. Those critical 60 seconds are usually a very productive time, when I'm able to stuff my sleeping bag into its stuffsack and clear all my clobber out of his way. The last thing Paul wants to do is hang around outside in the cold whilst I am faffing about inside, frantically trying to make the place look orderly. I try to distract Paul to pinch a handful of crucial seconds. 'How's the weather looking out there? Any sign of the other group? Describe in no less than a hundred words the view in front of you.' He knows exactly what I'm up to and promptly barges into the tent with a grin on his face.

'Avery, get your shit together.' Luckily I've caught him in a good mood.

As usual Andrew begins his first shift shortly before 10.45 am and sets a good steady pace. Knowing that I'm due to take over the reins at 11.30 am, I stop for a pee about five minutes before the end of his stint. I don't want to hold up the group by stopping for a pee break halfway through my lead and the five minutes will give me enough time to catch up with the pack before I take over at 11.30 am. No sooner have I zipped up to begin my quick dash to the back of the pack, than Andrew stops, planting his ski poles in the snow. To my horror, everyone else follows suit and then in complete harmony they all look back to find me about 50 yards behind. 'But it's only 11.27,' I shout out, knowing that nobody can hear. All wrapped up in their hoods, goggles and facemasks and looking like angry jet fighter pilots, their stare holds for an eternity. I am fuming myself, knowing they will be getting cold and no doubt blaming me for being slow. My skis are a blur as I sprint towards them. Nobody says anything as I ski straight past them to the front. I yell at Andrew: 'You stopped three minutes early.'

119

'I did my 45 minutes.'

'I don't care, you keep going till 11.30 ON THE DOT, like we agreed.' I grab his arm to look at his watch and see that it is three minutes faster than mine, which I synchronised to Pat's when we were back at Patriot Hills.

My 45-minute shift, sorry 48-minute shift, flies by as I curse Andrew and his poor timekeeping, knowing that this little scene that would seem trivial back home is just as much my fault as Andrew's. I've never been a confrontational guy, and I think my outburst was just as much of a surprise to Andrew as it was to me. My temper calms down during the day, which turns into one of our best so far, with light winds and a good surface. Off to the right, the sinister summit of Mt Godwin plays a teasing game of hide and seek as it continually disappears and reappears all afternoon long.

This evening everyone has a chortle about my strop. I manage to persuade Andrew to calibrate his watch with everyone else's, prompting Pat to have a dig at how Swiss I am becoming with my timekeeping: 'Tommy, when did you start becoming so anal!' I hope Paul is impressed with our professionalism, but he doesn't seem to be able to take us seriously any more, laughing at most things we say. Unlike many modern polar expeditions that seem to be plagued by continuous bickering and infighting, any friction amongst our team is extremely rare and evaporates as soon as the day is over.

With nothing else to divert our attention from the daily monotony of skiing across a very big piece of snow, it is hardly surprising that seemingly insignificant issues like someone's watch being a few minutes fast can get out of all proportion. On an expedition I find it much better to have a good shout at someone or something as the best way of relieving the tension. Fortunately, we are good friends here and nothing is taken too personally.

I'm not the first man in Antarctica to take my frustrations out on a fellow team member. Much has been made of an altercation between the members of the Southern Journey. One morning Shackleton and Wilson were packing the sleds up when Scott called to them: 'Come here you bloody fools.' As they walked over towards their leader, Wilson asked: 'Were you speaking to me?' Scott failed to answer, supposedly prompting Shackleton to say: 'Right, you are the worst bloody fool of the lot, and every time that you dare to speak to me like that you will get it back.' The reality is that Shackleton had probably just got out the wrong side of bed that morning, and misinterpreted Scott's light-hearted comments to mean something far more antagonistic.

I'm turning in for the night. The time is exactly 10.52 pm and 23 seconds.

DAY 10: FRIDAY 22 NOVEMBER   517.5 MILES TO GO

I am awake at 4 am and cannot get back to sleep. It's windy, very windy, and everything is shaking like crazy. Most of the clothes have fallen off the drying lines and are lying about on the tent floor or on top of our sleeping bags. My inner boots remain attached and jump about like hyperactive disco dancers as the tent is subjected to a sustained attack from the wind. It hasn't blown like this since those terrific storms we witnessed at Patriot Hills and I'd be surprised if it's safe enough to travel. Andrew is still fast asleep, mouth wide open, blissfully unaware of the gale around us. Staring up at a row of crusty socks above me, half expecting one to land on my face, I start planning how I'm going to spend my day if our travel plans are called off. Food, sleep, a bit of reading, food, sleep, maybe a game of cards before supper, or a phone call home and then back to bed. I nip out to the bathroom at 6 am, and despite the Saharan-like dunes of snow that have built up against the tent, it's almost a bit of a disappointment to find the wind isn't quite as bad as it sounded in the tent. It looks like there won't be a day off after all.

Whilst unzipping the vestibule to put the stove on I notice that snow has drifted into the kitchen through a tiny gap under the snow valances.[6] A major clear-up operation is launched as

---

[6] Flaps of material around the base of the tent which are covered in blocks of snow to stop the tent blowing away in the wind.

everything from the stove to the open kitchen box is smothered in a large heap of spindrift. The stove in particular needs special attention, but instead of roaring into life as usual, it splutters a bit before dying a sorry death. Luckily we've got two spares. The tents take an extra long time to excavate after breakfast, delaying our departure further, and despite our clock-synching last night it's nearer 8.45 am by the time we are on our way.

Over breakfast, a text message on our clever little satellite phone showed us that England had reached 298–4 on Day 1 of the second Ashes test against the Australians, with Michael Vaughan scoring a majestic 177. Conditions this morning couldn't be less conducive to cricket, with a keen headwind, a plethora of sastrugi about the place and a temperature that would have even the hardiest of Yorkshiremen dashing to the pavilion for extra sweaters. Nevertheless, the Adelaide Oval isn't all that far away, and I'm soon deep in fantasy land, imagining how England are going to capitalise on their strong position to level the series at 1–1. Surely not even England can throw the match away from here.

Much of the going this morning is uphill and I can really feel it in the calves. At the moment I've got just the one blister on my little toe, which is so insignificant I feel ashamed to mention it. Considering we never even had the chance to wear our boots in at all, our feet have so far got off very lightly.

The day we arrive at the South Pole still seems an eternity away. It's all very well breaking up the colossal distance ahead of us into more manageable morsels of 60 miles, but even the degrees seem to drag on for ever. Being surrounded by all this snow, it's hardly surprising that I have spent so much time dreaming about the Swiss ski resort of Verbier, the place I like to think of as my second home. I was last there in April and drove all the way from London in a day, including making a detour via my parents' house in Sussex. The journey in my Volkswagen Golf was exactly 700 statute miles door to door, which at just over 600 nautical miles is the same distance as walking from Hercules Inlet to the South Pole. It is a route I know well, and so I have decided to plot our southern progress across a mental map of Western Europe and imagine I am walking all the way from London to Verbier. A quick calculation reveals that depressingly we are still in England. But the M20 has begun its descent through a valley of gorse and fields of sheep, and in the distance I can see a fleet of ferries moored in the walled harbour of Dover. Maybe it's the first sign that I'm losing my marbles, but it's my little way of breaking up the vast distance that remains between us and the bottom of the world.

For once, Happy Hour lives up to its billing. There is seldom a chance for privacy on an expedition like this, and after the final break I purposefully wait for the others to get ahead so I can do some filming, take photographs and have some quality 'Tommy time'. It is frightening how small three people appear in this vast land with a head start of just ten minutes, and once or twice I lose sight of them altogether in the undulating terrain. I am eager to take this unique opportunity to savour the moment of being completely alone, and sit on my sled, trying to take everything in. The only noise is the relentless whine of the polar breeze, gradually covering my skis in a light coating of spindrift. Looking around, I can now appreciate the solitude that the likes of Borge Ousland and Erling Kagge experienced during their epic solo journeys across the Antarctic. The tracks of my fellow adventurers have been wiped out by the wind, and all I can see in this featureless landscape is snow and sky and the distant sugar loaf of Mt Godwin. I can't believe it's still in view. This mountain has been doing its very best to tease us up all day, peeking over the western horizon from time to time, stubbornly refusing to slip behind us. Either it's a long way away, or it's very big, or we aren't travelling that quickly.

Paul is not his usual chatty self in the tent this evening and tells us that he has really struggled today. It wasn't so much that the conditions were testing, more that he was in a bad state of mind, constantly thinking of home and wishing he was with his wife and children. Paul's not normally one to show his emotions but I am surprised that this man-mountain has had such a tough day. Maybe the mental battle of the expedition is slightly easier for us because this is our first trip to the polar regions and everything is so novel. The same must have applied to Scott, Wilson and Shackleton in 1902 as they pushed southwards into the unknown, with little idea of what to expect from one day to the next. It's got to be doubly tough for Paul because his wife is only a few miles away but he knows he won't see her for weeks. 'This will be the last major expedition I do without my family,' he says as he dishes out everyone's chicken and rice soup. It's disconcerting to see Paul down like this, and we all do our best to cheer him up.

We are eating well on this expedition, and the daily intake of over 6,000 calories is more than enough to satisfy our healthy appetites. The saying goes, 'An army marches on its stomach,' and it's true to say that the key ingredient to maintaining team morale is a well-planned diet. It makes such a difference to have such a varied menu. As well as a wide selection of soups, we have six different main courses that are rotated every six-day food cycle. Although subject to change in the event of birthdays or somebody pulling the wrong bag out of the sled in the evening, the dinner cycle typically goes:

1. Bountiful pasta carbonara
2. Sweet and sour pork
3. Spaghetti bolognaise
4. Couscous
5. Pasta al fredo (my favourite)
6. Chicken pilau rice

The Southern Party did not have this luxury and ate the same food day after day. Their meagre diet consisted of:

Breakfast:
    Chopped-up bacon fried with pounded biscuit
    2 biscuits
    2 large mugs of tea
Lunch:
    2 biscuits
    2 cups of hot chocolate

Supper:

2 large cups of soup, boiled with peas, bacon powder, powdered cheese, pounded-up biscuit and pemmican[7]

1 large cup of hot chocolate, brewed with the delightful-
sounding plasmon[8]

Just like us, once dinner was over, bowls, mugs and all kitchen
utensils were licked clean to make use of every calorie that's
going.

Later, we receive a confusing text message from an army
captain informing us that Prince Charles is trying to contact us.
As I read out the message, Andrew roars with laughter, 'It has
to be a prank!' Unlike normal mobile phones, there is no way
to trace the sender's number on a sat phone, because all messages are sent via Iridium's website. Although we are raising
funds for the Prince's Trust and have received several letters of
support from HRH, I would be surprised if he had the time to
try to send a text message to the Antarctic. We debate this long
into the night and, largely as a result of Paul's excitement at the
idea of receiving a royal text message, we decide to sit tight and
wait for more information.

Thanks to our late start this morning, the climb and the wind,
we haven't covered twelve miles today, but barring a disaster
we should pass 82°S tomorrow. We have now clocked up a total
of over 100 miles and, more importantly, I'm waving goodbye
to the White Cliffs of Dover from the deck of a ferry.

DAY 11: SATURDAY 23 NOVEMBER   505.7 MILES TO GO

The shocking news from Adelaide takes away all enjoyment
from my bowl of granola this morning. 'England collapse to
342, Australia 242–2. Sorry. Alasdair' reads the message.

The winds are even stronger this morning and Paul asks if

---

[7] Nutritious, but unappetising cake made by mixing pounded dried beef with beef
fat.
[8] A jelly-like protein additive.

we want to take a day off, having been on the go for ten continuous days. Everyone says they are feeling fit and strong and eager to keep going so we unanimously agree to carry on until the conditions really deteriorate.

During Pat's lead, Andrew pulls out his compass to check on the bearing and discovers that Pat has been skiing a full 20 degrees off course. When he stops to point him in the right direction, Pat looks at the compass incredulously, and, shaking his head, mutters 'For fuck's sake'. He dutifully alters his bearings and continues on his way, legs pumping faster than normal. I know how he must be feeling. During every hour of every day, the thing that dominates our thoughts more than anything else is our progress southwards and what we can do to make the group's journey as fast and efficient as possible. Something as trivial as having to temporarily alter course to ski around a lump of sastrugi or stopping for ten seconds to rearrange an uncomfortable piece of clothing may only cost a handful of yards, but is enormously frustrating. Luckily, Andrew spotted him veering off course quite early on but Pat is clearly livid with himself that his simple mistake has cost the team valuable time.

The rest of the day passes without incident, and when we have found a good area of flat hard snow on which to camp, Paul pulls out his GPS to make absolutely sure we've crossed 82°S. He pauses, before punching his fist in the air, 'Two down, eight to go, guys!' It turns out the 82nd Parallel is about 180 yards behind us. Once the tents are up, I look back at an area of snow no more than a well-hit six iron away. Of course, there's no thick red line there, as one might expect from looking at a map of Antarctica, but it's an important psychological barrier nevertheless, and I just hope I am not speaking too soon by saying that a fifth of the way in, things aren't looking too bad. But we're under no illusion that the toughest part of the expedition lies ahead.

Now that Mount Godwin has at last vanished altogether, this is our first campsite without a single mountain in view and it feels more remote than anywhere I have ever spent a night. To the south we now have an uninterrupted ocean of brilliant whiteness to navigate before the Thiel Mountains should eventually come into view, nearly 150 miles and two weeks away.

Once the three tents have been erected and secured to the ground with piles of snow on the flysheet's valances, we take all the essentials out of our sleds that we will need for the next 15 hours – sleeping bags, food bags, thermarests, water bottles, wash bags and 'eveningwear'. This evening the dry thermals that we will wear during tomorrow's march double up as pyjamas, whilst a fleece, dry hat and a pair of down booties keep us warm at dinnertime. The kitchen box also has to be pulled out, along with all the food and fuel we will need for supper and breakfast. By the time all of this has been thrown indoors, there's just about enough room for the four of us to sit in comfort. Skis and poles are tucked under the flysheet so they don't blow away in the night, and the half-empty sleds are wedged against, and tied to, the windward side of the tent, giving the tents extra protection from the wind. No sooner has everything been hung up to dry inside the tents, than everyone is running about in the snow with very few clothes on, screaming like children. The degree celebrations go on well into the evening, with whisky, jelly babies and extra chocolate sending us to bed with not a care in the world.

The days of endless whiteness are drifting by.

DAY 12: SUNDAY 24 NOVEMBER   493.5 MILES TO GO

The wind, no more than a slight breeze twelve hours ago, has gathered pace overnight to the point that a full-on gale is now roaring uncontrollably around us. Andrew and I have had a dreadful night's sleep. The incessant howling has been going on for some time now, coupled with a deafening tapping noise as snow shrapnel is blasted against our vulnerable little home. The muffled humming noise outside can only be the guy lines moaning their displeasure. I carefully unzip the tent entrance to gain a better picture of the conditions outside, to be met with a blinding wall of powder snow. It's getting on for six in the morning so I shout out to Paul at the top of my voice. His tent is barely ten feet from ours but I can't see it through the blizzard. There's no answer. I hope he hasn't been blown away in the night.

Finally, after three attempts, a voice calls out from the gloom: 'The wind is way too strong. Go back to bed.' This is sweet music to our ears. I pass on the good news to Pat, coming to the end of his stint in the gunner's tent next door, and dive back inside. Eleven days after leaving Hercules Inlet, we are going to get our first day off.

Things have calmed down enough by 10.30 am for Pat and Paul to pluck up the courage to make the short dash across to the main tent for a bite to eat and a natter. Paul reckons that at its peak, the wind was gusting at over 40 knots (46 mph), whilst at Patriot Hills, we hear on the radio from Jason that the weather beacon by the runway recorded a gust of 82 knots (94 mph) during the night. Paul calls Matty on the sat phone to see how her team is faring and learns that they are just 800 yards short of the 82nd Parallel, four miles to the west of us. Apparently the wind arrived as they were setting up camp yesterday evening and was strong enough to snap two of their tent poles clean in half. It sounds like the katabatics are unleashing their full fury across the whole of this part of Antarctica. It's a good time to be indoors.

A lazy day is spent catching up on lost sleep, playing cards, chatting and eating – a pastime that Andrew seems to be doing more and more of. I'm sure he has worms. I have at last started reading my book. I brought along Dava Sobel's highly entertaining *Longitude* for the journey, but until now I just haven't had the time to read a single page. The evening banter, which has been such a great release after a long day on the ice, typically continues well beyond dinner and by the time I've scribbled the day's events into my diary it's usually nearly 11 pm and time for bed. Given the nature of polar travel, where map coordinates and compass bearings have far greater relevance than the geography of the land, *Longitude* seems a wholly appropriate read and should provide valuable mental stimulation as we traverse the Earth's invisible gridlines. It was a wise decision to leave *Lord of the Rings* at home, which I think would have almost doubled the weight of my sled. Almost exactly 100 years ago to the day, the Southern Party were not faring much better and they too were forced to sit out a blizzard. On 26 November 1902, Wilson spent the day 'darning and mending ... read a chapter of Darwin's *Origin of Species'*.

The conversation after lunch gets onto global warming. I'm soon in my element and gibbering away about my university dissertation – which happened to be about the effects of global warming on Antarctica. 'Oh no,' says Pat, making a beeline for the tent door. 'I've heard so many of Tom's geography lessons over the years. I'm out of here!' Paul quickly follows. Anyway, Andrew seems keen to hear more so I go on to tell him that Antarctica consists of two ice sheets, imaginatively named East Antarctica (which we have been crossing) and West Antarctica. The mountains that we have been following since leaving Hercules Inlet mark the boundary between these two great ice masses. The West Antarctic Ice Sheet differs from its much larger neighbour because its base lies below sea level, and it is this that makes it very susceptible to the effects of global warming. Were it to melt, there is enough water locked up in West Antarctica to cause sea levels everywhere to rise by 20 feet.

Rarely a month goes by without a news headline about Antarctica's melting ice shelves, with the doom-mongers warning us that London and New York will soon be under water. The good news is that this has no direct effect on sea level and, much in the same way as a snake sheds it's skin, the process is all part of Antarctica's natural cycle of renewal and has been going on for millions of years. And just as with cubes of ice in a gin and tonic, the level in the glass will not increase when the ice cubes melt because they are already afloat. The floating Ronne and Ross ice shelves are effectively very large ice cubes that fringe the continental ice of West Antarctica, protecting it from the ocean. The bad news is that these giant ice dams, each the size of France, would melt in a warmer world. If this happened, seawater would come flooding in beneath West Antarctica, causing it to disintegrate and sea levels to rise. There's no need to book tickets on the Ark just yet, but leading scientists believe that if global temperatures continue to increase at today's levels, this catastrophe could occur sometime within the next 200 years.

Later, Andrew and I set about giving the main tent its first proper spring-clean. As well as the large amount of snow that has found its way inside after all this morning's comings and goings, the tent floor is also littered with sleeping bag feathers, Biscuit Brown crumbs and hair. There is hair everywhere. It sticks to socks, fleeces, hats and longjohns and has multiplied to plague proportions.

With all the detritus eventually brushed outside and surplus clothing packed away, I telephone home. It's Sunday evening in Sussex so the folks should be in. Due to the astronomical costs of using the sat phone and its potential to devalue the whole wilderness experience for everyone, we are careful to limit the number of calls we make and I have been looking forward to this moment for days. 'Hi Dad, it's me!'

Possibly forgetting where I am, he asks: 'You couldn't call back in ten minutes could you? We're in the middle of supper.'

Despite being in a storm in one of the most remote corners of the world, the line is frighteningly clear, which might be adding to the confusion. Not wanting to interrupt one of Mother's famous roasts, I call back later and speak to everyone in turn, including Jessica and Leo who have been down for the weekend for a bit of parental pampering. With Andrew sitting right beside me, it's not the most private phone call I have ever made, but they all seem on great form and keenly following our progress on the internet. I know they are worried about their boy but they don't let on. Mum says she got a bit carried away the other day and telephoned Radio 2's Children in Need appeal to request the Bee Gees' 'Stayin' Alive' for us. Brilliant. I'm not very surprised to hear from Dad that England lost the second Ashes test by an innings, but my mood is lifted (and

Andrew's soured) with the fantastic news that earlier today England trounced South Africa 53–3 at Twickenham.

After supper, Pat stays in our tent to join Andrew and me for a team shave. It's our first since leaving Punta Arenas and I am embarrassed to say that my 'beard' has only managed to develop into a feeble collection of blond whiskers around the chin. Pat's facial hair has a habit of turning ginger after a few days' growth, a source of much ridicule, and he seems particularly keen to remove it. Despite being strangely unable to grow a moustache, in barely two weeks Andrew has nonetheless developed a thick Amish beard and he's still hacking away at it with our only disposable razor long after Pat and I have turned in for the night.

During the early stages of the Southern Journey, Scott, Shackleton and Wilson clipped their beards about once a week with a small set of scissors. After a while they tired of this, and as their beards were left to grow, Shackleton's in particular became bleached by the sun.

Shaving in these conditions is not a pleasant affair. Despite my meagre excuse for facial hair, I am someone who prefers the creature comforts of hot water, shaving foam and a decent razor and I will probably make this my last shave until we return to civilisation.

Let's hope for kinder conditions in the morning. Today has at least given us the chance to rest our bodies, but with food and fuel supplies strictly rationed, another storm day would really set us back.

The wind is still screaming wildly this evening – it's set to be another rough night.

Chapter Five

COLD PLAY

As I peer tentatively through the flysheet this morning, it looks as though the storm has passed. The day is going to be clear and settled, if a bit colder than we have been used to of late. Large drifts surround the tents and Pat's sled is nowhere to be seen. A mass of snow several feet deep has piled up against the tent entrance and I need to clear it out of the way with one of our two aluminium shovels just to get outside. The great news is that another day will not be wasted and we will soon be on the move again. There's just the small matter of digging out the tents and sleds before we can get going.

The sleds are becoming noticeably lighter. We're getting through over two pounds of food and fuel per man per day, which has helped to reduce sled weights to 150 pounds. However tempting it may be to bury our rubbish in the snow and reduce the load still further, we carry every piece of litter with us. At the end of the expedition we will take it back to Punta Arenas, where it can be carefully disposed of. Nothing degrades in Antarctica's bitter climate and we are all conscious of our responsibilities to preserve this unique place. The *Discovery* Expedition was not the most environmentally friendly of trips, and Scott, Shackleton and Wilson left a trail of debris all along the route of the Southern Journey, which has since been buried by the Antarctic snows.

Some recent expeditions have gone to extraordinary lengths to minimise their impact on the pristine Antarctic environment by collecting all human waste, carrying it in their sleds for weeks on end before disposing of it once they have returned to civilisation. This may appear to be very good for the environment, but removing it from Antarctica just takes the problem elsewhere. The reality is that the environmental impact of burying our own effluent in the middle of the ice cap is non-existent. Provided it is well buried, any stool is likely to be crushed by the processes of snow accumulation and glaciation so that by the time it emerges at the coast after an epic journey of tens of thousands of years, it is the size of a pea and a welcome snack for a passing fish.

Human and industrial waste is a far more serious environmental concern at the continent's scientific research stations, because they are fixed in place. There is a very real danger that over time it can accumulate in the same spot – the consequences of which would be catastrophic for the local ecology. This is why ANI is so concerned to limit any pollution at their Patriot Hills base.

Scientific activity is responsible for over 99 per cent of all Antarctic pollution. A few miles off the Antarctic Peninsula, King George Island has been the focus of a major environmental clear-up operation in recent years, led by the British polar explorer Robert Swan. Since 1999 his 'Mission Antarctica' organisation has removed 1,000 tonnes of scrap metal and a further 30 tonnes of oil and paint from Russia's decrepit Bellingshausen base. Penguins, seals and other wildlife have returned to the area but many other bases continue to show precious little regard for Antarctica's sensitive ecology.

I'm having a sip of hot orange at our midday break when I'm distracted by a dark object running across the snow at great speed. It's one of Pat's Gore-Tex mitts. The breeze is too strong to catch it and before we've realised what's happened, the mitt has disappeared. Antarctic scientists have been known to lose whole hands to frostbite after a brief moment of carelessness with a mitt. Luckily, Pat has a spare in his sled, but it serves as a severe warning of how we must look after our gear in this harsh environment.

By 5 pm we've smashed our daily distance record by a full mile and are now 13.4 miles closer to the Pole. This means I've made it across the Channel on my long trek to Verbier and am taking my first few steps through the French countryside the other side of Calais.

Tonight is my first away from the main tent and I feel a little left out hearing Pat and Andrew chatting and laughing away next door.

DAY 14: TUESDAY 26 NOVEMBER   480.1 MILES TO GO

Today marks an important day for the expedition. Even though we are travelling across the opposite side of the Antarctic continent from our illustrious predecessors, we have not lost sight of the fact that we are celebrating the achievements of the *Discovery* Expedition, and in particular the Southern Journey, which reached a farthest south similar to our own current latitude.

The Southern Party of Robert Scott, Ernest Shackleton and Edward Wilson departed McMurdo Sound with 19 dogs on 2 November 1902 to the cheers of *Discovery*'s flag-waving crew. The flat surface of the Ross Ice Shelf (dramatically termed the Great Ice Barrier by the early explorers) stretched interminably to the south. It remained unclear whether the mountains of Victoria Land to the west and southwest were merely islands protruding through the immense floating Ross Ice Shelf, or if they formed the ramparts of Ptolemy's great southern continent. Scott hoped to uncover Antarctica's great secret by reaching at least as far south as 85°S, and possibly further. Wilson wrote that he hoped to push 'as far south in a straight line on the Barrier as we can go, reach the Pole if possible, or find some new land'.

Reaching the Pole itself was of secondary importance for Scott and his team – they were also here to discover new land. Their excellent initial progress, during which time the dogs covered 67 miles in just over five days, must have raised their hopes of going the whole way. With one man at the front finding the route and the other two either side of the sled train, the men often had to run to keep up with the animals. They soon caught up with Michael Barne's support party, which had set out on foot from *Discovery* a few days earlier with supplies for the Southern Party. From then on they were constantly waiting for Barne's foot party to catch up.

Ecstatic at the performance of the dogs but frustrated by all the delays, Scott decided to send Barne's team back to McMurdo much earlier than planned on 14 November. After transferring a fully laden sled from Barne's train, the loads increased from 94 pounds to 121 pounds per dog. To put this into perspective, when Amundsen reached the Pole nine years later, his dogs pulled just 64 pounds each. Although Barne's team's early return might seem understandable given the dogs' early success, if only they had remained with Scott then the extra support would have undoubtedly enabled him to push deeper into the south and reveal that Antarctica was indeed a continent.

Scott, Shackleton and Wilson were now alone, and farther south than man had ever been. But as soon as Barne's party disappeared over the northern horizon, the going became tough and progress ground to a crawl. The dogs had quickly lost their energy, and by the end of 15 November they had made just $2\frac{1}{2}$ miles. As well as having to pull greater loads, the dogs' work rate deteriorated because the men who had fed and exercised them throughout the winter had now gone. They were left with three relative strangers and were far less willing to work for them.

Unlike the fresh seal meat that they had been fed during the winter, the dogs' diet now consisted of dried codfish, which inexplicably began gradually to sap their strength. The men's confidence must have suffered a great blow at the sudden lack of pace and it would have been understandable had they turned around. But in a display of extraordinary mental drive and steadfast devotion to the cause that was to set the benchmark for future British exploration in Antarctica, they vowed to push on as far as they could go. Unable to get the dogs to pull six fully laden sleds any more, the men resorted to relaying the supplies in two shuttles, meaning that for every five miles of southern progress, they actually had to travel 15 miles. Knowing how much it frustrates me to lose yardage after veering off course, I find the concept of having to backtrack quite appalling.

All hope of reaching the Pole had vanished, but Scott's men continued to push southwards across the floating mass of ice. When land was sighted to the southwest on 21 November, the men altered their course and headed straight for it. By late November the dogs were weak with dysentery and starting to pass blood. As green mould began to appear on the dried codfish, Scott concluded that the dog food must have partially rotted during *Discovery*'s passage through the tropics.

As their condition deteriorated, the men began killing the weakest dogs and feeding them to the strongest. Although they had hoped that it would never come to this, detailed plans had been drawn up the previous winter for a dog-eat-dog system, should such an eventuality arise. By now the men had developed a strong bond with the animals, so having to butcher them, one by one, must have been truly awful. The remaining dogs had to be beaten to make any progress. After Wilson had killed two dogs with a scalpel to the heart, Scott wrote: 'I think we all could have wept ... I scarcely like to write of it.' The slaughter of their dogs left an indelible scar on the men and they vowed never to take dog teams on subsequent polar expeditions. This decision would have serious implications for future British exploration in Antarctica.

After four long weeks of mind-numbing to-ing and fro-ing that yielded just 90 miles of southerly gain, they were at last within a mile of land. A depot could be safely left for the return journey, and to everyone's relief, the sleds could be pulled without having to relay. The men hoped to collect rock samples for analysis back in London but were prevented from reaching the land by a treacherous expanse of unstable ice and deep crevasses.

The surviving dogs were getting weaker with every passing day, and soon the men were pulling everything themselves. They wanted to continue their push into the unknown as far as they could, and rations were cut to dangerously low levels. A conveyor-belt of rocky outcrops and colossal mountains kept appearing on the southwest horizon as Antarctica slowly revealed her most precious secrets. Wilson was a talented artist and recorded the new lands in great detail. The men were slowly starving and increasingly fatigued, but seeing this land unfolding in front of them, never before seen by human eyes, must have been enormously uplifting. On 28 December, a distant 14,000-foot twin-peaked mountain came into view, which Scott referred to as 'a giant among pigmies' and named Mt Markham after the father of the expedition, Sir Clements Markham.

That evening, the exhausted little party camped just short of the mouth of a ten-mile-wide inlet, flanked by giant headlands. Were these merely islands or did they mark the coastline of the unknown continent? With dense fog preventing them from moving on the 29th, they continued towards the inlet on the 30th. They hoped to see sufficiently far up the inlet to establish whether the gap was a strait between two islands or the mouth of a vast glacier, spilling down from a continental ice cap. Unfortunately, the weather was not on their side, fog preventing them from seeing as far as they had hoped. Unbeknown to them, had it not been cruelly shrouded in mist, the plunging icefall of a continental glacier (now called the Nimrod Glacier) less than 40 miles up the inlet would have revealed the continuity of the land. They had everything bar the ace.

Amid increasing numbers of crevasses, they pitched camp and made the decision to turn north. On the off chance that the weather might clear, that afternoon Scott and Wilson continued to 82°17'S.[1] Wilson wrote: 'The Captain and I went for a ski

[1] The theodolite reading at midday on 30 December gave Scott a latitude of 82°15' for the final camp, and by adding his and Wilson's extra 'mile or two' of southerly gain would have produced a farthest south of approximately 82°17'. However, recent photographic evidence now suggests that Scott and Wilson's farthest south was in fact no more than 82°11'. This minor error can be attributed to the conditions that day. The expedition log shows the temperature on 30 December was an almost tropical +9°C, with a gentle northerly wind, and it is highly likely that after the theodolite had been levelled, one of the tripod legs sank fractionally into the softening snow. This would have affected the instrument's reading of the angle to the sun, thereby producing an inaccurate latitude reading that day.

run this afternoon to the south, but saw nothing and were compelled to return when we had gone a mile or two, as we were afraid of losing our camp, the weather was so thick.' With food supplies for the return journey depleting and Shackleton showing early signs of scurvy, they decided to head for home. They had not travelled nearly as far as they had hoped, but this was more than made up for by their discovery of over 300 miles of virgin coastline. For the time being, the mystery of Terra Incognita would have to remain unsolved.

Paul pulls out the GPS at 10.30 am to find that we are still 500 yards short of the Southern Party's farthest south. I insist we carry on for a further ten minutes to the exact latitude at which they turned round (this is after all one of the main aims of the expedition), but Andrew says this is close enough. He has already taken off his skis but I tell him: 'Gerbs, we're going on. If you feel that strongly about it, you can take your break here and catch us up later.'

Reluctantly, he chooses to stay with us, and at exactly 82°17'S according to the GPS, we stop for the first break of the day. The whisky is pulled out and I propose a toast to the memory of Scott, Shackleton and Wilson. When one considers that no previous expedition had journeyed more than 20 miles from the Antarctic coast, and that all three men were polar novices, the march of Scott, Shackleton and Wilson across the Ross Ice Shelf 100 years ago stands as one of the most impressive in the history of Antarctic exploration.

Several polar historians have suggested that Scott and Shackleton never saw eye to eye, and that the reason Shackleton was left behind on that final afternoon was so that Scott could claim the farthest south record for himself and his close friend Edward Wilson. The reality is that somebody had to stay behind to look after the dogs, and Shackleton, who was starting to suffer from the effects of scurvy, most likely volunteered. Weakened as the animals were, the men could not afford to lose any more dogs in fights over food. It would have been impractical to harness up the dogs all over again for a round trip of just an hour or two. The fact that he named the two most prominent landmarks in the vicinity of their farthest south 'Shackleton Inlet' and 'Cape Wilson' is a testament to the equally high regard in which he held both his teammates. Paul's view of the Heroic Age of Antarctic exploration has been shaped by Roland Huntford's bestseller *The Last Place on Earth*, which 25 years ago set out to discredit Scott as an incompetent imperialist failure, a reckless, panicky individual who was totally unsuitable for leading a polar expedition. 'Whilst I'm happy to have a drink for Shackleton, I'm afraid I don't particularly feel like toasting Scott and Wilson,' he jests, knowing it will wind me up.

Later. For the past 15 minutes Paul has been steering the wrong course and I'm sure he's following a bearing a good 20° too far to the east. I make numerous checks with my own compass to ensure I'm not making a grave error before finally mustering up the courage to correct him. Last night in *Longitude*, I read that on one foggy night in 1707 a sailor aboard an English vessel called *Association* approached his admiral to warn that they were sailing in the wrong direction and heading straight for rocks. For a subordinate to question the admiral's navigation was deemed as mutiny in the Royal Navy, and he was promptly hanged on the spot. For the record, Admiral Sir Clowdisley Shovell's fleet proceeded to run aground off the Scilly Isles, with the loss of over 2,000 men. The admiral was one of only two survivors. Fortunately, when I point out his mistake, Paul just smiles back. 'Sorry guys, I've been so into my Led Zeppelin minidisc today that I haven't really been paying attention to where we're supposed to be heading.' You just can't get the polar guides these days.

Pat comes up with the inspired suggestion that the loser of tonight's card game should carry the rubbish the following day. We've collected a fair amount of garbage in the two weeks since we left Hercules Inlet and we're all determined to avoid the indignity of having to take the trash bag. After a particularly vindictive game of 'Shithead', it falls on me to be the trash man tomorrow. I return to my tent to the taunts of 'Tommy's been taken down, taken down to Chinatown'.

DAY 15: WEDNESDAY 27 NOVEMBER   467.5 MILES TO GO

We have been blessed with another calm, clear morning. I plant the shovel in the snow and assume the position over my freshly dug snow pit. Before setting about my business, I place the loo roll on the snow. This is a mistake. Moments later, I watch in horror as, mid-squat, a gust of wind springs out of nowhere, knocking the roll on its side and out of reach. It's picking up speed. 20 feet on and the loo roll snags a small piece of sastrugi, promptly proceeding to unravel Andrex puppy dog style. Desperate situations require desperate solutions, and with long-johns round my ankles I set off in pursuit across the snow looking like someone from the Ministry of Silly Walks. To my great relief, I rescue it before it blows away again.

The tents are packed up and I am just zipping up my sled cover when Pat comes over towards me and says: 'Mate, I think you've forgotten something.' Grinning from ear to ear, he passes me the expedition rubbish bag in ceremonial fashion.

The day begins with a short, steep climb, strewn with big sastrugi. At one point, my sled gets jammed behind a clump of ice, almost sending me A over T. Eyes focused on the horizon, I heave away for ages, trying to get the damn thing moving again. I turn around to find my sled has actually capsized on the uneven terrain. Throughout the day, everyone suffers from the same problem, and on one occasion Pat's sled flips so awkwardly into a narrow fissure in the hard snow that it requires both Andrew and me to right it.

Today I am listening to Pat's four-hour Monty Python compilation minidisk, comprising the cult classics – *The Meaning of Life*, *The Holy Grail* and *The Life of Brian*. It helps to know most of the lines off by heart and I'm often laughing long before the punch line is delivered. Classic sketches like 'The knights who say Ni' and 'There's a mess in here, but no messiah' have been re-enacted countless times with Jessy and Leo and I'm in fits of giggles throughout the day. There's no better feeling than having a chuckle on the move.

Everyone is going super fast today. I am not too sure why,

although the latest update is that we are one mile behind the other group. I'm starting to sweat a bit and I can feel the onset of what must be a kind of nappy rash – an embarrassing condition I don't think I've had since my third birthday when I spent too long on the bouncy castle. Oh the glamour of polar travel.

The cloud descends during the afternoon so it's back to the chore of navigating by compass.

Andrew has absolutely no food discipline. He has developed a fetish for Biscuits Brown and even though we are only halfway through the latest six-day cycle, he has already consumed his full quota. He proceeds to polish off his entire chocolate ration before supper and now has less than half his lunch quota remaining. Andrew's extraordinary appetite provides a constant source of amusement to us, but as we continue to climb, he could end up with serious problems when the temperatures drop further. On the high Polar Plateau, we can expect to use up more energy keeping warm in the colder conditions, but our intake of 6,000 calories per man per day will remain unchanged.

15 days across Antarctica and we are a quarter of the way there. After Paul leaves the tent for the evening, the three of us discuss our strategy for the coming days, buoyed by the news that we've clocked up our first 14-mile day. Unaware of what I might be letting myself in for, I point out that if we average 13.9 miles per day we can reach our depot at the Thiel Mountains eleven days from now. 'Mate, that's a ballsy shout,' replies Pat.

The log from Paul's expedition last year shows that the winds blew from a southerly quarter when they reached the 86th Parallel, making the prospect of having a kiting day before we reach the Thiels unlikely. Reaching our depot in just eleven days would mean no further rest days. I think we can manage this on our current performance, especially as the sleds are getting appreciably lighter every day. Andrew suggests upping the day by 30 minutes or even an hour so we can get ahead of Matty's team. 'Lads, it would be so sweet if we got there before them,' he says, tucking into a bag of dried fruit.

And they said this was not supposed to be a race! Pat and I aren't quite so enthusiastic. Comparing our progress with that of the other group is something we have all found productive. They are the yardstick by which we can check our own progress. Whilst things would certainly be spiced up by a race, there's more to this trip than beating Andrew Cooney to the Pole.

It's Pat's turn to be the trash man tomorrow. He's not amused.

DAY 16: THURSDAY 28 NOVEMBER   453.4 MILES TO GO

The first few hours of the day pass without incident. Early on in Andrew's morning shift, I am skiing along in his tracks, minding my own business, when I notice a couple of metal shards in the snow. I just assume it's a bit of debris from his sled so I ignore it and carry on. 30 yards on, I stop to pick up a metal screw. I look ahead to find Andrew standing still and looking down at his boots. What on earth is he doing? I pull alongside him and notice that one of his bindings has completely shattered along the plastic base. We have encountered more sastrugi over recent days than at any time on the expedition and the uneven surface has no doubt increased the pressure on the bindings. It's a major worry that one has failed after only 160 miles, especially as they have been designed specifically for long polar journeys.

Andrew hands over the lead to me and swaps the faulty ski with one of his kiting skis. These differ from our everyday skis because they have not been fitted with skins, thus providing very little in the way of traction. Incredibly Andrew manages to keep up despite having one semi-redundant ski.

I lead for the next hour and a half in rapidly deteriorating visibility. Soon I can't see a thing. It's my worst nightmare – nothing but grey, grey, grey. I have to keep checking the compass – without it I would be lost. With no horizon to aim for, keeping my balance is a real struggle. We could be travelling over a freshly hosed ice rink or a treacherous crevasse field for all I know. I strain my eyes in the hope of trying to find the way. Crunch. My skis crash to an abrupt halt as I slam straight into a solid lump of ice. I pause for a minute to make sure I'm on the right bearing. Moments later, I slip down the side of another lump and hit the deck hard. The sastrugi are everywhere but the gloom makes them impossible to pick out. It is more straightforward for the others to follow as they can see where my skis are going. I have absolutely no idea what lies in front of me.

Scott suffered exactly the same problem when the light was bad. His solution was to switch to travelling at night. With the sun much lower in the sky, there would be more in the way of shadows, making the pockets of sastrugi easier to pick out. The men used a compass very similar to our own, but because the exact position of the South Magnetic Pole hadn't yet been established,[2] the compasses were not accurately adjusted to allow for the magnetic variation. As well as simplifying navigation in overcast conditions, the dogs were happier pulling the sledges at night as the temperatures were slightly colder and the animals wouldn't overheat under the blaze of the midday sun.

Any changes in wind direction in Antarctica occur very gradually. The Southern Party used this to their advantage by setting up a wind vane on one of the sleds. The convoy could travel in a straight line if the direction of the wind vane remained unchanged. Wilson wrote: 'Complete absence of anything to look at or steer by. Made progress all the same using a little tuft of wool on a bamboo cane as a wind vane to steer by.'

I have developed my own method for keeping a straight course in the murk. By kicking my ski into the snow, a cloud of spindrift is flicked up and taken away by the wind. Every 50 yards or so, I give the ground another kick and note the direction the puff of snow is blown. As long as I can make sure the spindrift is blown at the same angle relative to my skis, I know I'm going the right way. Unfortunately nothing can be done to make the sastrugi more visible, so all I can do is put my head

---

[2] This was one of the aims of the scientific work being carried out back at McMurdo Sound.

down and hope for the best. The winds continue to blow from the south – goodness knows when we're ever going to be able to use these kites that we have been lugging in our sleds all this time.

Whilst Scott's idea made route-finding easier when it was overcast, navigating when the sun returned was much trickier. The midnight sun lies in the southern quarter of the sky, so as the men marched straight into the blinding sun, unless they turned round the whole time, they could no longer get an approximate bearing from the angle of their shadow. Scott was an ingenious man and had already thought of this scenario during the long winter in McMurdo Sound. The unknown magnetic variation made compass navigation a bit of a lottery, so he devised a 'sun compass'. It had a simple design and looked like any normal compass. The difference was that instead of having a metal arrow in the centre, there was a vertical wooden pin. Around the dial of his sun compass, Scott had marked the 360 degrees of a compass and a 24-hour clock face. By lining up the shadow of the pin to the hour at the current time, the compass fell automatically into place.

After nearly an hour of hell, I am given hope by a thin blue strip of sky on the horizon, slowly inching our way. I desperately hope that this drunken stumbling about will come to an end soon. By the second break, the gloom has lifted and Paul can see enough to sort out Andrew's broken binding. He does a remarkable job. In less than ten minutes, Paul removes the old binding with a knife and screwdriver, replacing it with one of the two spares that we are carrying. This is really fiddly stuff and my hands feel cold just watching him at work. With only basic tools and a windchill touching −30°C, it's a very impressive pit stop. The Ferrari Formula 1 mechanics couldn't have done much better.

Today's pace has been much more sensible than yesterday's. That is until Happy Hour, when Paul decides to put his foot on the pedal like a man possessed. By the end of the 2.2-mile sprint, I am sweating like a polar bear in a sauna. I think Paul's trying to test us because he seems quite surprised when he turns around at 5 pm to find us right on his tail. 'You can't shake us off that easily, Landry!' jokes Pat.

This evening I call Jessy from the privacy of the gunner's tent. Whenever the family is together there is always lots of laughter, with Jessy always at the heart of things. Despite being three years younger than me, she is my closest friend and confidante. 'Are you smelly?', 'Are your toes cold?' are the first things she asks. I tell her that I'm still wearing her power bracelet, and despite being ridiculed by my fellow adventurers for wearing jewellery, it is my talisman and I will wear it to the end of the expedition. I miss her a lot.

It turns out that last week's text message from the Palace was no prank after all and we have been informed by a member of the Royal Household to await further instructions.

DAY 17: FRIDAY 29 NOVEMBER   440.1 MILES TO GO

My morning visits to the loo have been revolutionised. Andrew has introduced me to the delights of the 'snow wedgie', a chunk of snow which is used instead of toilet paper. The snow wedgie technique is far more hygienic, better for the environment, and, because everything can be done wearing gloves, one's not going to freeze one's fingers off trying to fold up pieces of loo roll in the wind. And shoving a piece of snow up one's bottom is not nearly as painful as might be expected – no more than a cold tickle. As Andrew points out, 'Antarctica is basically one large piece of bog paper.' Instructions for going to the bathroom are as follows:

1. Find suitable location to build a pit – ideally in soft snow behind a lump of sastrugi.
2. Dig a pit twelve inches deep with aluminium shovel.
3. Select a few snow wedgies from the fresh pile of snow that are not too crumbly or jagged. They must be large enough to use with mitts on.
4. Just behind the pit, drive shovel deep into the snow at an angle of 45°.

5. Face wind, locate poo-flap zipper at back of salopettes and unzip.
6. Squat, pulling poo flap aside with one hand, the other resting on the shovel handle.
7. Let rip, aiming into centre of pit. May need to adjust aim to take account of the wind.
8. Using gentle strokes, wipe with snow wedgies.
9. Dispose of snow wedgies in pit.
10. Step away from pit, zip up quickly and carefully.
11. Cover up pit with snow.

I spend the morning thinking about the progress of the other team. They have been gaining over a mile on us every day for the best part of a week now and, according to the email updates, are aiming to arrive at the Thiel Mountains as early as 7 December. Are they going very fast or are we just slowing up?

To everyone's horror, just after lunch Andrew breaks another binding. Rather than wasting more time repairing the thing, he decides to take both skis off and walk. Luckily the surface is hard and he easily keeps up with the rest of us.

Half an hour after the 2 pm break I get my first real bout of hunger, gnawing away deep inside my belly like some living creature. Despite wolfing down several handfuls of peanuts and cashews, the stomach cramps persist for the rest of the day. For Andrew in particular, the resupply can't come soon enough. A fortnight ago, I was struggling to find room for the ample food rations, but now there's always a hole crying out to be filled.

It's another record day and we are now well beyond 83°S. Despite the broken bindings, confidence has never been higher, and we hope to reach the Thiel Mountains by 8 December. I still try not to think about the Pole, but there's now serious consideration being given to getting there before the New Year. We bring Andrew's unusable ski into the main tent to replace the damaged binding before dinner.

One of this evening's text messages tells me that at the end of the first day's play in the Perth test, England were bowled out for 189, with Australia on 140–2. The Ashes will be lost by Sunday. Why are we English so hopeless at the sports we invented? This is seriously bad for my morale. It drives me insane that none of my companions shares my passion for sport. There is the potential for hours of in-depth debates about a multitude of subjects from the greatest England XI of all time or Tim Henman's prospects at Wimbledon this year, but nobody else could care less.

After a welcome dinner of sweet and sour pork, Andrew recounts the story of the Zulu Wars and the battle for Rorke's Drift. He is a brilliant storyteller and has a natural talent for bringing episodes of African history alive. This is a huge improvement on the usual banter, which has recently degenerated to heated discussions about our favourite Bond girl or Kylie Minogue's rear end.

It's just before bedtime and Pat is in a panic, desperately rummaging around the tent. 'Has anyone seen my Gore-Tex mitts? I can't remember bringing them inside.' Following Paul's lead, we have all become meticulously organised in the tents, to the point of being neurotic. Everything is packed away or hung up to dry in exactly the same place day after day. It is all part of the polar routine and is designed to prevent scenes such as this.

Ten minutes later and after turning the tent inside out, there's still no sign of the mitts. I bid the lads goodnight and retire to my tent. As I zip the flysheet on my way out, I notice Pat's gloves resting on top of his ski poles, exactly where he left them when we arrived into camp this afternoon. I call out: 'Mate, your mitts are still out here. And you've left your sled wide open, you great pillock!' It's not too windy this evening, and even though some snow has drifted into his sled, nothing appears to have blown away. He's a very lucky guy.

DAY 18: SATURDAY 30 NOVEMBER   425.6 MILES TO GO

It's my turn to be the camp fool this morning. Last night was my last in the gunner's tent and I have slept well, too well.

After yelling his head off incessantly and still with no sign of life, Andrew's patience has run out and he crawls out of the main tent to wake me up. 'Get out of bed you lazy git,' he says, clearly unamused, 'it's six thirty.'

As a rule, I try to avoid skiing in the middle of the pack. I dislike intensely the sensation of being boxed in and usually make sure I'm the last in the procession, a yard or two behind the third sled. At least this way, if I need to stop for a pee, or to take a photograph, I can do so without disrupting the others and quickly rejoin the back of the queue. But I'm second in the line this morning, plodding along in metronomic fashion deep in thought, eyes fixed onto the orange canvas of Pat's sled in front of me.

Suddenly, Pat stops to signal it's time for the day's first break. I'm skiing far too close and before I realise what's going on, I ski straight into the back of his sled, rather camply falling on my side. Andrew crashes into the back of my sled, just about managing to stay upright. Paul, bringing up the rear, avoids the pile-up altogether and bursts into uncontrollable laughter. It seems quite ridiculous that here we are in this huge expanse of nothing, the only people for many miles, and yet we still manage to trip up over each other.

I would have been a pretty unpopular member of the Southern Journey had I been doing this 100 years ago. When Scott, Shackleton and Wilson turned for home at the mouth of Shackleton Inlet, they were pulling the sleds themselves because the few surviving dogs were too weak to pull any weight. All excess equipment was jettisoned so that they could travel as lightly as possible for the long march back to *Discovery*. But unlike us, the men did not have individual sleds. They managed to pack everything onto two sleds, which were dragged along in a train with all three men harnessed up to the leading sled. If anybody were to pause to have an itch or a pee, they would all have had to stop. This would have been incredibly frustrating. As they were travelling three abreast, they would all have had to make fresh tracks in the snow, further draining their already limited strength. The beauty of our 'family of elephants' system is that everybody takes it in turn to plough the route ahead. Once someone has finished their stint, they can return to the pack where the surface has already been compacted by those in front, making life much easier.

News of our broken bindings has filtered back home, because this evening's text messages poke fun at Andrew's misfortune.

'Gerbs if you can't ski properly, then you should go to ski school! Toby.'

'Gerber lose some weight! Mike.'

He takes it all very well but the bindings are becoming a concern. During this evening's sat phone call Jason gives us the news we've been waiting for: our ski bag, complete with a box of spare bindings, has made it as far as Patriot Hills after a protracted journey via the Colombian jungle, Buenos Aires and Punta Arenas. Pretty impressive work from DHL. It will be waiting for us at our depot at the Thiel Mountains but that's still well over 100 miles away. For now, we're fresh out of spares.

It's good to be back in the main tent again. Pat asks me if I have broken anything on the trip. 'Touch wood, nothing,' I reply. During an expedition I'm quite superstitious and it bothers me that I can't find a piece of wood to touch anywhere in the tent. I hope it's not an omen.

DAY 19: SUNDAY 1 DECEMBER   411.4 MILES TO GO

I like December. December is the month of mulled wine, my birthday, Christmas parties, canoodling under the mistletoe and the start of the ski season. And now that we have altered our plan to arrive at the Pole on New Year's Eve, it's great to think we might reach our goal later this month.

After the first break, I can't get my left boot to clip back into the ski binding. I pick up the ski to remove a bit of ice build-up and see that two screws have sheared off and the binding's plastic base has cracked in two. This is serious. Following his previous mishaps, Andrew has used up both our spare bindings, so we've got to pray we can find and reuse the necessary pieces from his broken ones this evening. With skis strapped to the outside of my sled, I continue on foot. The snow is good and hard, enabling me to make reasonable progress, although I'm reduced to a snail's pace when we occasionally come across an area of powdery snow.

To begin with, the Southern Party were somewhat reluctant about using their skis. Because of the lack of funding to organise a proper training trip, the men had never used their skis before they arrived in Antarctica. On 5 January 1902, *Discovery* became trapped in thick pack ice during its passage from New Zealand to McMurdo Sound, and Scott signalled that a day off should be taken to test the skis on the flat surface. Armitage, Koettlitz and Bernacchi were the only three members of the entire expedition party of 48 who had skied before, and they oversaw what must have been a hilarious ski lesson with men on their backsides most of the time. Wilson commented: 'Officers, staff and men staggering about in all directions, everyone thoroughly enjoying it.'

Their skis were very different from our own – much wider and weighing 20 pounds a pair. The bases of the skis weren't fitted with skins in those days, so the skier would have had to rely on the natural grain of the wood to provide some sort of purchase. It wouldn't be unkind to describe their skis as planks. To complicate matters further, they had to master the technique of using just the one ski pole – a seven-foot long stick that would be grasped with both hands in much the same way as a resident of Cambridge might punt down the River Cam. The concept of using two shorter ski poles like our carbon fibre ones, which would have generated more pulling power, was completely unknown to them.

Further ski trials followed in the autumn and spring, and although one awkward tumble over a ridge of sastrugi put Scott's leg in a splint for a few days, by the time he and his fellow sledgers set off on their Southern Journey, they were fairly competent. For the first few days of the journey however, the men travelled on foot, despite an excellent surface for skiing. The problem lay not in the skis but in the boots. The men each took two pairs of boots – the warm reindeer fur 'finnesko' boots and a set of leather ski boots, which could be fixed to the toe-strap ski bindings. The ski boots were made from a thick leather that froze solid in low temperatures, making every stride both painful and cold. Often they were so stiff that the boots could not be worn. Having been ice-skating myself in old leather skating boots, I can imagine how uncomfortable and painful it must have been.

After their earlier problems, the men travelled on skis for the next few weeks and whilst not as comfortable, the going was much easier.[3] When the men turned round on 30 December 1902 to begin their return journey, the situation changed for the worse. Because the men were now having to manhaul, they found that the skinless skis did not provide the necessary purchase in the snow and they were sliding all over the place. After a time, two pairs of skis were dumped, leaving one pair for Shackleton. His health was now deteriorating rapidly as he suffered from the effects of scurvy, sometimes leaving him unable to pull his share of the load. So whilst the others hauled the sledge train in their boots, the invalided Shackleton skied unharnessed alongside them.

Scott based the design of his sleds on the models the legendary Norwegian explorer Fridtjof Nansen used during his Arctic journeys at the end of the nineteenth century. The wooden sleds were between nine and eleven feet long, with wide runners. With a large area of sled coming into direct contact with the snow, the sleds would have generated significant amounts of resistance. Knowing how tough it is to pull our lightweight fibreglass sleds along the surface, I find it hard to imagine what gruelling work those men put themselves through.

There is a peculiar sensation in my fingers. The cold has really got to them and it feels as if I've been stung by a thousand nettles. Despite my best efforts to keep my gloves dry and my

---

[3] It is likely that after the first two days, the ski boots were thawed out over the stove each morning before they got going. Scott would learn his lesson in 1911 and designed a special lightweight ski binding for his journey to the South Pole that enabled finnesko to be used with skis. Two ski poles were also used.

fingers warm, my hands go through the freeze-thaw process several times a day. And it's happening more regularly.

The sastrugi are getting increasingly spectacular and give the impression that we are afloat on a vast restless sea. Big ocean rollers, complete with gravity-defying licks of snow, swell up around us, frozen in time at the point of breaking. They are everywhere and it's impossible to avoid them all. Struggling up the gently sloping seaward side of each wave requires a real pull from the waist with ski poles providing extra thrust. When the crest is reached, the sled careers down the steeper side of the wave under its own momentum, often gliding right past me. This wonderful release of tension around my lower back provides only a temporary respite before the grind starts again.

We're now averaging two miles an hour thanks to our first 15-mile day and this seems a good enough reason to share a cheeky dram of Talisker in the tent.

After dinner, everything is cleared away as the tent is turned into a ski workshop. The problem is that my bindings have been superglued to the skis, which then need brute force to be removed. Paul and Andrew do a sterling job not only in salvaging good parts from Andrew's two broken bindings, but also in replacing the whole binding. Clearly relishing the challenge, Andrew proves himself to be a master of the complex intricacies of the ski binding and toils away with his screwdriver, making sure every little part is in full working order. It's as if he's been playing around with the things all his life. On big expeditions, equipment has a habit of breaking, and it's vital to be able to carry out a repair with the limited resources on hand. An hour later and I have myself a pair of fully functioning bindings.

My worst fears have been realised – England have lost the Ashes.

DAY 20: MONDAY 2 DECEMBER   396.4 MILES TO GO

We're packed up and just about to set off when Pat comes up to me, anxiously shaking his head. 'I can't find my goggles anywhere. The only place I can think where they might be is still inside the tent.' For the next few minutes, the others wait around as Pat and I take off our skis and harnesses to unpack the tent from my sled. Fortunately the goggles are still inside, but more time has been wasted.

10.30 am. It's a cold, drab morning. For the past two hours my crown jewels have been perishing and it frightens me to think that the first signs of frostbite could be just around the corner in the place I want it least. There is no way something like this would ever happen to Pat. Whilst he may mislay his gear from time to time, his nether regions have been a constant focus of attention since we touched down in Antarctica, and he has gone to extraordinary lengths to ensure they are fully protected from the cold. A few weeks before we left the UK, Pat tracked down a woman up in Glasgow who had the distinction of being the only specialist Gore-Tex haberdasher in the UK. He gave her detailed instructions of the appendage he wanted her to attach to the bottom of his Antarctic jacket to safeguard his undercarriage from the worst of the polar weather. Money was no object. Unfortunately for him, in the elaborate plans for his 'snow skirt', he forgot that he would need a couple of slits in the material to allow his legs to move freely. Rather than put a slit either side, the seamstress cut a single slit right down the front, with the result that any headwind would be funnelled directly towards his groin.

Not to be defeated, when we were in Punta Arenas Pat managed to get hold of some Velcro, a few strips of fleece-like material and some windstopper fabric from Maria. At Patriot Hills, he spent the best part of an afternoon constructing a detachable wind-proof 'willy warmer' which he was able to fix to the inside of his salopettes for extra protection from the cold. It is a work of great ingenuity and even comes complete with a custom-made slot for peeing. I really think he should give serious consideration to producing them commercially. They would sell like hotcakes.

Envious of Pat's willy warmer, I reach down to make sure everything is in order and to my horror find that my flies have been wide open since we left camp. We've been skiing straight into a steady headwind all morning. I immediately zip up and pray to God that it all thaws out down there.

Later. We have found ourselves in mega sastrugi country. Some of them are well over seven feet high from peak to trough. I had no idea Antarctica would be this lumpy, and the sleds continue to capsize as we pick our way through the uneven terrain. The snow is rock solid and the intricate banks of sastrugi so close together that it is easier to walk on foot, rather than weaving awkwardly on skis through the icy obstacles. I find I can go much faster like this and it is not nearly as tiring on the arms. When leading, finding a path through the maze of ice chunks does at least provide a welcome distraction from the monotonous grind of manhauling. When Andrew takes the lead, he typically heads due south, irrespective of what hurdles lie in his path. Even if there is a wall of ice directly in front of him, he bulldozes his way straight through the middle, instead of taking the line of least resistance. Rather than panting and sweating ourselves silly, the rest of us will often leave him to it and find our own way through the icy labyrinth.

The sun returns this afternoon, its rays reflecting off the numerous jagged edges in a dazzling luminescent display. I find it a constant source of wonder that these spectacular natural sculptures have been crafted by the wind. Reports from previous expeditions suggested we could expect to encounter a major sastrugi field at our present latitude but we never imagined things would be this severe. It's putting a tremendous strain on our backs. All we can do is hope that the surface will flatten out before we're totally crippled.

Towards the end of the day, one of Pat's bindings packs in. With no more spare parts, we will have to resort to removing the skin from his redundant ski and attaching it to a kiting ski. This of course means abandoning all kiting plans before the

Thiel Mountains. It also means further repair work in the tent tonight.

I'm tired and hungry by the time we pull into camp. The frostbite marks on my face have returned with a vengeance. Looking forward to our resupply now.

DAY 21: TUESDAY 3 DECEMBER   381.1 MILES TO GO

Conversation over breakfast turns to what each of us thinks about during the day. Paul's daily thoughts revolve around his family and how great it would be if they could all do an expedition like this together one day. He also tells us that, apart from his journey to the North Pole in 2001 with his great friend Paul Crowley, this is the most fun he has had on all his many expeditions. Paul has two tickets to see a Rolling Stones concert in Montreal on 7 January but up until recently didn't expect that he would get back in time. But now that we're making such good headway, he is hellbent on getting to the Pole and back to Canada as fast as possible so that he can take his daughter Sarah to see 'Mick and the boys' performing live.

Pat confesses to spending the hours conjuring up fantastic ideas that he could transform into documentary programmes for television. Andrew is so preoccupied fantasising about lavish feasts that he finds listening to music an unwanted distraction. When not thinking of food, thoughts turn to his brother Mawande, ski holidays and, strangely, solving complex mathematical brainteasers.

I have a library of around a dozen daydreams that I can retreat into with no trouble at all. I think about my family a lot and wonder what they all might be doing right now. Friends back home are never far from my thoughts either, particularly those who have been sending text messages. Hours have been spent meticulously designing a fantasy ski chalet in Switzerland with an amazing swimming pool that is both indoor and outdoor. Cricket and golf also feature in a major way. In fact, I spent most of yesterday at the Augusta National Golf Club, where I was playing in the Masters. Having watched this great tounament on television every year since I was twelve, I know the course well and every shot of my final round is replayed over and over in my mind. For the record, I beat Tiger Woods in a play-off. I refuse to get bogged down thinking about what I might do for a career when I get home – I don't need the added stress factor right now.

Since we lost sight of Mount Godwin nearly two weeks ago, our immediate world has been reduced to our ski tips and the back of the sled in front. Daydreaming offers the only escape from the monotony of it all. We are so wonderfully far away from the day-to-day stresses of mobile telephone bills, parking fines and double glazing salesmen, that all the clutter that seems to fill our lives back home can be filtered out with ease. My thoughts have become so streamlined that I can focus much more clearly on the people and things that really matter in my life.

But the most important issue at the forefront of our minds every single day is our southern progress. Whether discussing logistics in the tent or away with our thoughts during the day, we are constantly assessing how things are going and what can be done to improve the group's overall performance. Calculating hypothetical arrival dates at the Pole is a great time-filler, not to mention a serious test of my mental arithmetic. Having been climbing mountains for some years now, I have become used to this blinkered mentality where one's position on the mountain and the journey to the summit and back dominate all thinking. Nothing else merits such importance and we cannot really relax until that goal is reached.

We're not far along our way this morning when the flat rocky top of a nunatak emerges silently off to our right. Temporarily frozen in our tracks and lost for words, we stand transfixed at the outcrop that marks the beginning of the Thiel Mountains. It feels as if land has at last been sighted after a long journey at sea. It's a wonderful sight.

The wind has been dropping all day and conditions are now perfect for travelling. Just as we are thinking how good life is, Andrew breaks his third binding of the expedition, bringing our tally to five in the last six days. I think we must be skiing too aggressively over this gruelling terrain, which is putting excess pressure on the front of the bindings.

Around midday we pick up the footprints and ski tracks of the other group. Until now all signs of human existence and other forms of life have been absent from this sterile world. It has felt as if we have had this entire continent to ourselves. Before embarking on this journey I questioned how I would cope with the isolation, especially coming from a city of eight million people. But over time I have grown used to this profound solitude – to the point where I selfishly didn't want to share this place with anyone else other than my three companions. That's suddenly changed and I'm now excited at the prospect of maybe bumping into our fellow adventurers.

It's extraordinary to think that in an area ten times the size of the UK, we have managed to stumble across some of their tracks. I try to imagine how Scott must have felt in 1912 when he saw the ski tracks and paw prints of Amundsen's party as he was crossing the Polar Plateau and the awful realisation that someone had beaten him to the South Pole finally sank in. We on the other hand are given an enormous lift at having seen that Matty's team passed through here no more than a few hours ago. Like a pack hound that has just picked up the scent of a fox, Andrew takes the lead and sets off in pursuit at a blistering pace. None of us can keep up and soon Andrew is no more than a tiny speck with the rest of us strung out far behind. There's no point in wasting unnecessary energy so I slow down to a more reasonable speed.

It's ridiculous to think that we might be able to catch up with the other group today – for a start we can't even see them. Despite repeated attempts over the last few days to get Andrew to chill out a bit, he seems intent on showing us how fast he is capable of going. He's got to look at the bigger picture. We're not even halfway to the Pole yet and it would be crazy to burn ourselves out by going at this pace.

By 3 pm, he has got so far ahead that, rather than wait for me to take over as normal, he decides to lead my shift as well, carrying on for a further 45 minutes at exactly the same pace. I arrive at the next break just behind the others (and a full 15 minutes after Andrew) to find Pat launching a tirade about Andrew's supersonic pace. It's the first major fracas of the expedition. 'Why the fuck do you need to go so fast? What's the point?' he asks angrily. Andrew answers monosyllabically, muttering an apology.

Interrupting Pat, who looks as though he's about to start bludgeoning him with a ski pole, I tell Andrew, 'I have to say I'm with Pat on this one. Please can you just slow down a bit. We've all been asking you to reduce the pace for a while now but you seem determined to ignore us. When you look back and see the rest of the team, even Paul, strung out behind you, you must realize that you're going too quickly. You've got nothing to prove. We're supposed to be doing this as a team for Christ's sake.'

With precious few outside influences to stimulate our thoughts, any altercation like this, which would seem so petty in a normal environment, smoulders away in the dark recesses of the mind to alarming levels. I suggest to Andrew that the two of us hang back for the last hour to do some filming and take things easy for a change. This should at least give Pat a bit of time to cool off. The day has turned calm, and for the first time on the expedition we are able to have a good natter on the move, skiing along side-by-side. We arrive at camp to find Pat and Paul already setting up the tents.

Despite the earlier squabble, all hard feeling quickly fades away once we are inside the sanctuary of the tent. It's as if nothing happened, and we're soon giving Andrew a ribbing for his ludicrous speed. Because of his dreadful rationing skills, we have put his pace down to the fact that he must be con- suming several hundred calories more than us each day. It means he has more energy and a marginally lighter sled – at least for now. Cockily, he jests: 'Lads, you either go big or you go home!' We all fall about laughing. It's great news that this potential break-up has been sorted and as long as Andrew has learnt his lesson, I hope that it will be the last of the squabbling.

Looking forward to a clean pair of underpants.

DAY 22: WEDNESDAY 4 DECEMBER   365.7 MILES TO GO

'Nottingham Forest 3, Brighton & Hove Albion 2. You're still bottom of the league' reads the depressing text message. It looks like my beloved Seagulls are going to be relegated from Division One well before the end of the season.

The main massif of the Thiel Mountains is still a good 60 miles away but ever so slowly more and more peaks are coming into view. They are the only things that lie between us and the Pole. Very few people have been fortunate enough to see these secret mountains and the sight of land has given us all a tremendous fillip. The sight of new mountain ranges must have had a similar effect on the morale of Scott, Shackleton and Wilson as *Discovery*'s Southern Party pushed southwards.

Unless everyone is well behind me during my lead, I find it very difficult to judge what sort of pace I am setting. I have felt good all day but don't think I have been going any faster than normal, so I am genuinely surprised at the day's final break when Paul says: 'Tom's in the zone today. You've been flying.'

With a large dose of sarcasm, I brag: 'Well if you're finding the pace a bit too much, Landry, let me know and we'll slow things down a bit.'

Foolish move. Without saying anything, Paul smiles and turns away to put on his skis before charging off into the distance. We haven't gone far before I'm breathless and dripping with sweat. It makes Andrew's pace from yesterday seem like a funeral march and I'm sure I can see sparks flying from Paul's skis. We clock up a staggering Happy Hour record of 2.4 miles to give us our first 16-mile day. As we arrive into camp he walks over towards me, puts me in a headlock and says: 'So you think the old boy is struggling?' I have learnt my lesson – don't mess with a former cross-country skiing champion.

Tonight in the tent we discuss our tactics for the weeks ahead. We will pick up our resupply at the Thiel Mountains and take a full rest day. Taking a breather will do us the world of good and means we can then head off with the aim of going straight for the Pole without any further stops. The aim remains to celebrate New Year's Eve at the South Pole. Paul points out that because the South Pole station operates on New Zealand time, or 17 hours ahead of us, we would probably have to arrive there on the 30th if we wanted to join in with the festivities. We would have to average 13.8 miles a day to achieve this. It all seems slightly premature to be talking about the end, but whilst we're still taking things degree by degree, we mustn't lose sight of the overall goal – that tiny speck at the bottom of the planet.

Perhaps I am speaking prematurely, but apart from the headache with the bindings, everything has been going like clockwork in recent days and I'm discovering that polar travel isn't so bad after all. Everyone is in good health, spirits have never been higher and we are constantly exceeding our targets. Before we set out we all had our own idea of what we might expect from this beautiful but dangerous continent. My own expectations were largely shaped by a handful of recent accounts from British explorers who had journeyed to the South Pole in the last few years. Antarctica was portrayed as 'Hell on Earth', where only the bravest men dared to tread. Admittedly, the remarkable achievements of the likes of Ranulph Fiennes and Robert Swan make our own expedition look like a stroll across the South Downs. But the image of a journey to the South Pole that formed in my mind was one of bitter temperatures and howling winds day after day, frostbite, endless crevasses and horrendously uneven terrain. David Hempleman-Adams, who reached the South Pole in 1996 after following the same route as our own, warned of the terrifying prospect of 'fields of crevasses stretching all the way to the Pole'. Luckily for us, we haven't come across any since the first day and a half.

Sitting in the warmth of the tent this evening, we are all agreed that the polar books we have read in the past and the lectures we have listened to paint a picture quite different from our own Antarctic experience so far. Of course, there have been times when we have been very cold, exhausted and downright petrified and this is without doubt the toughest physical challenge of our lives. It's just a great relief that during the weeks we have been here, Antarctica has not been the cruel, forbidding place we had first feared. But it would be foolish to be complacent – accidents, health problems and equipment failures can quickly turn into very serious situations out here, and the next storm could be just around the corner.

It is now almost inevitable that we will arrive at Thiels on the same day as the other team – probably 8 December. This is such good news. Not only will it be great for Paul to see his wife again but we are all really looking forward to seeing the other guys, swapping stories and having a few swigs of whisky together. There is even talk of an England versus the rest of the world cricket match. Our evening banter is starting to get a bit stale now to the point that we regularly finish each other's sentences. Some form of other human contact would be very welcome. And of course there will be those well-travelled skis, clean socks and chocolate bars awaiting our arrival.

During our 6.30 pm call to Patriot Hills Jason tells us that the lovely Amy dropped off all our provisions for the second half of the expedition at the Thiel Mountains depot this afternoon. Paul is dishing up tomato and rice soup when, right on cue, the unmistakable drone of an aeroplane can be heard overhead. Leaving Paul poised with ladle in hand, the three of us dash outside to see the Twin Otter heading straight for us on its way back to Patriot Hills, no more than 50 feet above the ground. We wave like mad and can clearly make out Amy's face animatedly returning the greeting. The sight of three unshaven young men in tight longjohns prancing about in the snow must be truly bizarre after flying across hundreds of miles of featureless terrain.

Man was treated to his first aerial view of Antarctica during the early stages of the *Discovery*'s Expedition. An army observation balloon with a small wicker basket was carried on board, which Scott hoped could be used to gain a view deep into the south to help him plan the team's sledging journeys. Six weeks after setting sail from New Zealand, the ship sailed a full ten miles down a narrow crack within the Ross Ice Shelf, mooring alongside a part of the ice face that was just twelve feet high. Despite having no prior training, Scott insisted on making the first ascent himself. Without really knowing what he was doing, he threw out far too much ballast, sending him shooting up into the sky. Fortunately the balloon's tether was strong enough to stop him rocketing up to the heavens. Shackleton was the next to go up in the balloon, and from a height of 800 feet took the first aerial photographs of Antarctica. But there was very little to see, with the vast unbroken whiteness of the Ross Ice Shelf stretching interminably to the horizon. They realised that the limited views from the balloon could not possibly show them whether or not there was a southern continent. Wilson, possibly in a strop at not having had the chance to go up, called the flights 'an exceedingly dangerous amusement in the hands of such novices'.

By the time Amundsen sailed south nine years later, the crack in the ice shelf had grown to form an enormous bay. Home to numerous spouting minke whales, it was called the Bay of Whales and used by Amundsen as the base for his attempt on the South Pole. In 1929, the American aviator Richard Byrd became the first man to fly an aircraft in Antarctica. Along with two others, Byrd took off from the Bay of Whales in a Fokker tri-motor ski plane hoping to reach the South Pole. 300 pounds of emergency provisions had to be jettisoned to enable them to gain enough altitude, and they narrowly avoided crashing straight into the Transantarctic Mountains. Concerned that the thin air would prevent him from getting off the ground again, he circled over the Pole instead of landing there, throwing the Stars and Stripes onto the snow. Byrd returned home a national hero and showed that the future of Antarctic exploration lay not in lugging heavy sleds across the snow but in the much safer and quicker method of aerial reconnaissance.

Drift to sleep dreaming of female aircraft pilots.

It's 3.30 am and I wake up in a serious amount of pain. What the hell is happening to me? I am writhing about in sheer agony. I want to scream but that would wake up Pat lying next to me and no doubt the other two as well. I bite hard into the fleece that I have been using as a pillow. This excruciating pain is something that can only be fully appreciated by the world's male population. It's as if David Beckham has just drilled one of his trademark free kicks straight into my privates from point-blank range. I swallow a couple of painkillers and try not to move.

I put my hand down to try to find what is causing the pain and find my thermos mug under my sleeping bag. It must have slipped out of the pocket on my side of the tent during the night and its super-strong reinforced handle has caught me right in the bollocks.

Maybe the agony will pass if I just keep still. But instead the pain gets worse and worse until the whole of my lower abdomen feels as though it is being stabbed repeatedly. I can't lie still any longer so I pull on my down booties and stumble outside. I'm promptly violently sick and start shaking uncontrollably. All I can think of doing is rubbing snow where it hurts most to try to freeze the pain. God, this is utterly terrible.

An hour later and things are no better. I make another quick exit into the cold to throw up. Pat stirs and murmurs: 'What the hell are you doing?'

'Oh, just popping out for some fresh air,' I gasp. He thinks nothing of it and goes back to sleep.

Two and a half hours and six painkillers after the free kick and I'm still awake, feeling drowsy but not much better. As I lie there, giving serious consideration to calling up Patriot Hills to request immediate evacuation, I picture the newspaper head-lines: 'Young explorer evacuated from Antarctic with swollen plums'. I would never live it down. For the rest of my life I would be labelled as the guy who crushed his balls on a mug and had to be flown home. It would haunt me for ever and do my marriage prospects no good at all.

I think back to the unfortunate Yorkshire climber Al Hinkes, who was well on his way to becoming the first Brit to climb all 14 of the world's 8,000-metre peaks when disaster struck. Whilst tackling the tenth peak on his list, Nanga Parbat in Pakistan in 1997, he slipped one of the discs in his back after a sprinkling of chapatti flour caused him to have a sneezing fit. He was in such agony that a helicopter had to be scrambled to evacuate him off the mountain. The poor guy was the butt of countless jokes in newspaper columns and magazine articles around the world. So despite being this country's most successful high-altitude mountaineer, he is known more for his encounter with a chapatti than for his phenomenal climbs.

Paul and Andrew come into the tent at 6.15 am for their morning cuppa. I sit motionless in my thermarest chair, unable even to say 'good morning' to them.

'Rough night's sleep, Tommy?' asks Andrew. 'You look like shit.'

'Yeah, something like that.'

By the time we set off I am drugged up to the eyeballs with painkillers. I continue on foot throughout the day, with legs wide apart so as not to aggravate things further. To my immense relief, the pain gradually lessens. I'm still in shock but I think I'm going to be OK.

For much of the day I scan the southwest horizon in the hope of catching a glimpse of the Thiel Mountains, but the cloud base is now so low that one of the most dramatic mountain vistas on the continent might as well be the Hanging Gardens of Babylon. With the other team just three miles ahead of us, it's no great surprise to see their tracks again this afternoon. Even though we are close, there's absolutely no chance of seeing them as the poor light and gigantic sastrugi have reduced the visibility to 200 yards. Just before the day's end, Andrew breaks another binding. This is now getting boring.

Back in camp. Now that I'm beginning to feel more human again, I tell the others about my drama with the mug. The piss-taking and sniggering hardly come as a surprise. Andrew gets things going. 'When I saw you looking knackered at breakfast, I never realised how right I was!' The general ridiculing is unrelenting. I have recovered enough to find the whole episode almost as funny as they do, but I wouldn't wish that kind of torture on anyone.

I check the undercarriage before bed and happily it all looks and feels as it should. Phew. I leave my mug in the tent's vestibule tonight well clear of harm's way.

Cricket boxes should be standard issue on polar expeditions.

DAY 24: FRIDAY 6 DECEMBER   333.7 MILES TO GO

We have been treated to a beautiful morning, not a cloud in the sky, a slight breeze from the south, and on the horizon we can see the tips of giant mountains. According to my mental map of France, I reckon we have successfully negotiated the Pas-de-Calais and Picardie and now find ourselves in Reims, where Joan of Arc witnessed the coronation of her King. Champagne country is just around the corner.

Around midday, the full extent of the Thiel Mountains becomes dramatically apparent. This colossal ice fortress of seemingly impregnable ramparts rises abruptly from the surrounding plains like a giant glacial Ayers Rock. Shelves of ice cling precariously to the fortress's rocky defences, ready to break away at any moment. The flat summit, many miles across, is draped in a thick cloak of ice, pierced by lofty turrets of rock. These are like no mountains I have ever seen before, and it takes a while to come to terms with the awesome scale of rock and ice.

About ten miles to the north of our ice castle is a small collection of alpine-type peaks, and after checking our course with the GPS we pick out a lone summit in the centre of the group and head straight for it. If the coordinates are correct, we should find our depot directly beneath it.

The altimeter on my clever digital watch shows that we have now reached 5,000 feet and half the altitude gain to the Pole is beneath us. It continues to baffle me that this relentless climb can be attributed solely to the gradual build-up of snow over millions of years. Over time, the snow has been compacted to form ice. In fact, if there was no ice here at all, we would be standing no more than a few feet above sea level with the Thiel Mountains towering a further 10,000 feet above us. In some places in Antarctica the ice is over three miles thick (the height of Mont Blanc), and its enormous mass has depressed the underlying land by up to 5,000 feet in places. If both East and West Antarctica were to melt (and they have done before), global sea level would rise by 200 feet. This wouldn't be great for the future of Brighton & Hove Albion.

We make camp for the night just 24 miles from our depot, which we should reach in about a day and a half. I dust the ice off my jacket outside before diving into the tent. Despite our protestations Pat still refuses to do this, with the result that dinner is a constant game of 'dodge the drips' as his jacket slowly thaws out on the drying lines above us.

Since hearing that our resupply has been safely dropped off at the depot, we have allowed ourselves the luxury of breaking into extra rations. In fact, for the last few days we have been eating so well that I haven't felt the hunger cramps for quite a while. Dinners are now complemented with butter, which is either stirred into the main meal or simply eaten raw. There are a cholesterol-tastic eight calories for every gram of butter and we are now consuming 6,200 calories per day. Down here the taste of raw butter is just divine.

Andrew continues to eat more than the rest of us and always seems to have a few chunks of chocolate or a packet of Biscuits Brown to hand. Given that he had all but run out of food supplies a few days ago, the extra rations have come as a godsend to him. All this gratuitous over-indulgence is a far cry from the latter stages of the Southern Journey. Rations were cut to give the men more time to push southwards. By mid-December, they were consuming just 4,000 calories a day – woefully inadequate for manhauling loads similar to ours. The men's cravings for food became so severe that they started hallucinating about lavish banquets. By mealtime their burgeoning appetites had degenerated to serious pangs of hunger. They were effectively starving themselves, each of them losing a stone in weight every three weeks.

This evening Paul telephones Matty, whose group has recently been making excellent progress. She now finds herself in an impossibly difficult position because one of her party does not want the two teams to see each other at the Thiel Mountains depot. Apparently Andrew Cooney wants us to wait for a day or two a few miles north of the depot to give his team time to repack the supplies for the second half of the trip. Having seen his eight-day head start evaporate, he still wants to ensure that he reaches the Pole before us.

Paul's voice starts to break up mid-conversation. I've never seen him like this. He says to his wife in a stern voice: 'Well, you can tell him, we're not waiting anywhere. We all want to see you, and apart from Andrew Cooney your team sound pretty keen to meet up with us. If he feels that strongly, he can sit in his own tent whilst the rest of us get together and have a good time.'

DAY 25: SATURDAY 7 DECEMBER   317.4 MILES TO GO

It's been a ferocious night and I have not slept well. Ever since we turned in, it's been blowing an absolute hooley. Peering outside the tent, I can see that large drifts have once again piled up around our little home. Having to take a storm day now, so close to our resupply, would be very depressing.

We wrap up and set off straight into a biting headwind. For most of the morning I find myself transfixed by a solitary nunatak, no more than a couple of miles to the west of us. Due to the pressure created by the icecap's colossal weight, the ice is constantly on the move during its relentless progress from the continental interior to the coast. I can clearly make out several yawning crevasses as the icecap flows either side of the nunatak's rounded form like wood grain swerving around a knot. At only ten metres per year, the speed of the ice isn't exactly going to break any records, but because of Antarctica's huge mass, this still represents an enormous amount of ice. Once it reaches the coast, the ice floats on the surface of the sea in the form of an ice shelf, the Ronne and the Ross being by far the largest two. Whilst there is some melting along the base of the ice shelves, the majority of ice in Antarctica is released into the Southern Ocean in the form of icebergs.

We are skiing across what could be thought of as a giant iceberg factory, producing tens of thousands of these extraordinary formations every year. Most are no bigger than a large house and called growlers, but occasionally a really large one will break away. In March 2000 an iceberg the size of Cyprus calved off the Ross Ice Shelf and started drifting towards McMurdo Sound. Nicknamed 'Godzilla', this giant ice cube eventually became grounded on the seabed, causing major climate change to the entire Ross Sea region as ocean currents were thrown out of kilter.

The glacial stretch-marks off to our right are the first crevasses we have seen since our second day, but should be far enough away not to pose any problems. Because they spent their entire journey on the flat ice shelf, the Southern Party only encountered crevasses when they were close to land. However, those that they did see terrified the men to the core. Scott wrote: 'The tide crack gradually narrows to a crevasse, which in places is bridged over with snow but in others displays a yawning gulf. We must have crossed it within a few feet of such a gulf ... unconsciously passed within an ace of destruction.'

The last few hours of the day are pure bliss and the wind I was so rude about earlier has virtually died. The pain in my feet has temporarily vanished, I'm no longer hungry, the surface is excellent and my sled seems almost weightless. I turn off my minidisk and float across the snow on a wave of inner calm, thinking what a lucky lad I am to be here. This is polar travel at its absolute best.

Another day has rushed by. We have crossed from 84°S to

85°S, so we are now closer to the Pole than we are to Hercules Inlet. By the time we make camp we are just eight miles away from our depot, as the magnetic pull of the mountains draws us in. As I am unpacking my sled, I spot a couple of tiny yellow specks off to the east. Tents. It is the other team, barely half a mile away.

Tonight we discuss tactics for the second half of the journey. The decision is taken to reduce the weight of the sleds by leaving the gunner's tent behind at the Thiels depot. This will also save us a bit of time pitching and collapsing camp every day. We give the new arrangements a trial run tonight, with Pat, Andrew and me sleeping in the main tent. Our ambitious aim of trying to reach the Pole on New Year's Eve is going to mean covering the second half of the journey in just 22 days at an average of 13.3 miles a day. We plan to spend a day at the Thiel Mountains, going through the new provisions and repacking the sleds. Once we leave the depot, we estimate it should take us four days to cover the remaining 48 miles to 86°S, a further nine days to reach 88°S, and just eight more before we arrive at the Pole itself. We will only take enough supplies to last that amount of time plus a few days of emergency rations. This doesn't leave much margin for error, so we'd better pray that the weather doesn't hold us back. It would be nice to get the kites up as well.

My feet are looking revolting. A couple of large blood blisters have appeared on each heel and a nasty red rash has spread to my ankles. The bottoms of my feet are white and wrinkly as if they've spent all day in the bath. My socks are now so smelly and full of bacteria that I'm half expecting to see them walk out of the tent.

Just before dinner, Paul takes off his own socks and says: 'You think your feet are bad, take a look at these little beauties.' We all wince and turn away. His feet are in a shocking state, with large parts of each ankle badly blistered and going pussy. Each step must be agony for the man. Making me feel ashamed for showing off my minor injuries, he says in that very matter-of-fact way of his: 'I get blisters on all my trips. I've got kinda used to it by now. You've just got to grin and bear it.'

The really bad news is that the whisky has run out.

DAY 26: SUNDAY 8 DECEMBER   301 MILES TO GO

Other than being accidentally kicked in the head by Pat during the night, I have slept well. Having an extra man in the tent is a bit cramped, but as long as we can put up with the extra stench I think we'll get by. The main concern is going to be finding the space to dry everything at night.

The Thiels glisten in all their splendour as we clip into our skis for the final run to the depot. There is no sign of the other group's tents this morning so they must have set off before us. The temperature may be −18°C, but with no wind and the sun beating down, it feels positively tropical. All protective headgear has been stowed in the sleds and we ski along with sunglasses on and our hoods down. Paul looks like a skier from the Eighties today with his big sunglasses, oversized minidisk headphones and wild blond locks flowing behind. His purple all-in-one completes the look.

At the first break, we spot six objects about a mile in front of us, equally spaced and of the same height. Paul thinks they are fuel barrels, but on closer inspection, the barrels are clearly moving – it can only be the other group. In a last-gasp effort to get to the resupply before them, Andrew sets off at a ridiculous speed, leaving the three of us trailing in his wake. He quickly remembers the problems his energy spurts caused the other day, and with Pat and me screaming for him to slow down, he stops to wait for us to catch up.

The four of us ski the final ten minutes into camp side by side, in great spirits and for some reason talking about *Top of the Pops* and one-hit wonders. Pat confesses that the legendary Chesney Hawkes (of 'I am the One and Only' fame) once stayed at his house.

When we arrive at the depot, the other group are there to meet us. Matty, Devon, Graham, Andrew Cooney, Willie and Angél arrived just 20 minutes ago. It's extraordinary that after more than 300 miles of travel, two groups of people travelling across this barren land completely independent of one another should arrive at the same place within minutes of each other. We're halfway there.

Everyone, including Cooney, seems genuinely pleased to see us and there are warm handshakes all round. Theatrical hugs are shared with Willie and Angél, who greet us like long-lost brothers. The Spaniards have grown thick beards, making me very much the loser in any facial hair competition with only a few feeble whiskers to show for two weeks of concentrated effort.

Doug Stern is also here. Two weeks ago, he was dispatched on a solo mission to the Thiel Mountains to give weather reports to ANI's headquarters. This is the peak season for tourist flights to the South Pole and every aircraft making the journey from Patriot Hills to the Pole will stop here to refuel. Doug hasn't seen anyone for days and his watery gaze is even more distant than I remember. It is a wonderful surprise to see him again. Other than his tent (to which Doug has built an igloo-type extension), about 80 drums of aviation fuel, a weather vane and our blue resupply barrels, there is absolutely nothing here. We are still some distance from the foot of the mountains but their bulk is deceptive and they appear much closer than that. The airstrip is marked out with black bin bags filled with snow. Doug tells us that most of his days are spent flattening out the sastrugi on the runway with his big polar boots and a steel shovel. It doesn't sound the most exciting way to pass the time.

There's a very relaxed atmosphere here, and for the next 20 minutes the eleven of us stand around chatting and taking photographs in the calm conditions. With Andrew murmuring something about food, we head over to the barrels and other containers that Amy dropped off four days ago. Everything that we will need for the second half of the journey from teabags to clean sets of thermals to a one-litre bottle of Talisker Malt is checked off against our inventory. Partially buried under a snowdrift, I dig out what looks like a ski bag. Eureka! After an epic journey across three continents, miracle of miracles, our skis and several new sets of bindings have made it to the Thiel Mountains.

We set up camp away from the drums of aviation fuel and far enough away from the other group to give them and us some privacy. Matty helps Paul pitch his tent a good 100 yards from camp. He wants to spend the next two nights with his wife, and they want as much privacy as they can get. Who can blame them.

To my amazement, whilst sifting through our resupply barrels, I come across a tub labelled 'Sticky Toffee Pudding'. I feel like opening it straight away. Further foraging unearths a packet of butterscotch sauce, a pre-cooked chicken curry, some freshly cooked carrots, and a box of Pringles. Mairi and those other great girls at Patriot Hills must have slipped them in before Amy set off in her little plane. The stove is on for the remainder of the afternoon as we cook up our first proper meal in weeks. No banquet ever tasted so good.

After dinner, Matty and Devon come round to the tent for a natter and a game of cards. It's quite a squeeze with six of us crammed inside but great to be with other people again. Devon reveals that the women at the American-run South Pole science base are amongst the most beautiful in the world. Last year he led a team on a 60-mile 'Last Degree' expedition to the Pole and his face lights up as he describes one girl who he took a particular shine to. 'There's this babe from Alaska with fiery red hair who is totally hot. She drives a snow plough and is planning on being there again this year. If you guys get there before me, she's all yours. Her name is Angela.' I'm not sure quite how seriously to take him but I can't think of many better incentives for the second half of the journey than gorgeous maidens awaiting our arrival at the South Pole.

Happiness is ... clean boxer shorts.

DAY 27: MONDAY 9 DECEMBER   293.2 MILES TO GO

Midnight. We're out for the count when a deafening roar shakes us to the bone. At first I think it's an avalanche crashing down from the mountains behind us before Andrew points out that the noise might be explained by the fact that we pitched the tents a mere 30 yards from Doug's well-groomed runway. Forgetting that this is one of the busiest airports on the continent, it should have come as no surprise to see a Twin Otter coming in to land to deliver more barrels of aviation fuel. No sooner does it disappear over the horizon and leave us in peace than the next plane touches down to unload its cargo of fuel. To make matters worse, alarming symptoms of indigestion have started and I'm soon bent over double. Helping myself to a fourth portion of sticky toffee pudding at dinner wasn't such a good idea after all.

It's been a rough night. Bleary-eyed, I crawl outside to see that the Thiel Mountains appear to have vanished. A thick mist has once again descended upon us and we could be anywhere. It's cold and the occasional snowflake drifts down from a steel-grey sky. With zero contrast, it would be a grim day to be travelling, so it's just as well that today has already been set aside as a day of rest.

It may be a day off but there's much to be done. The first big project is packing the food. Much of the work was done whilst we were at Patriot Hills, so it's now a matter of dividing the loads up equally between us. We will take just 25 days of rations for the second half of the journey and reduce our Coleman gas cooking fuel quota from 27 litres to 18 litres. This is cutting things a bit tight on the fuel front – we just can't afford to have any further fuel canister leaks.

As well as saying goodbye to the gunner's tent, we will also be leaving behind a shovel, a solar panel and a fair amount of personal gear. Body odour is not one of my major concerns right now, and in an effort to cut my own sled weight down still further, I shall take just two pairs of boxer shorts and two pairs of outer socks for the second stage. I should also be able to get away with one less hat, one thermal top and a pair of gloves. Even the little things can make a difference in our endeavour to be as lightweight as possible. Tubes of toothpaste and sunblock will now be shared and Richard Branson's weighty autobiography *Losing My Virginity* will have to wait till I get back to England. All leftover supplies and equipment will return to Patriot Hills when the next Twin Otter passes through.

By my calculations, these changes should cut our sled weights by around 20 pounds a man, so hopefully we should be able to travel faster than in the early days of the expedition. Finally acknowledging that he might have an eating disorder, Andrew raids the surplus food box and scavenges six pounds of granola, several packets of Biscuits Brown and extra chocolate bars to boost his daily calorie intake. Andrew's burgeoning appetite continues to be a source of amusement for us and he has acquired the nickname 'The Stomach'. But there's no chance of any of us helping him carry his extra load. If he starts to drop off the pace, then the granola is going straight into the nearest crevasse.

With the sleds now packed up, the next job is to tackle the skis. The two pairs of yellow Fischer skis have stood up to the task admirably but are being replaced with the well-travelled Black Diamonds. The skins that provide grip on the bottom of the skis will have to be transferred to the new skis. But first they must be modified. In much the same way as snow chains help a car grip in snowy conditions, the greater the area the skin covers on the base of each ski, the more purchase it will give us on the snow. But the skins also produce an element of drag, so the decision is made to cut the skins in half so they are just three feet long and little more than an inch wide. These so called 'kicker' skins cover just one quarter of the area of the underside of each ski and should give us more glide as the skis slide forwards. Screwing them into the rock-solid base of the ski is an absolute nightmare with only the screwdriver on my penknife to help. The ability to make running repairs is essential on long expeditions, and for much of the afternoon, Pat, Andrew and I toil away inside the tent. By dinnertime, the tent floor is littered with skin hairs, binding parts, screws and tools and I've had enough.

We haven't had much of a chance to catch up with our fellow

TOP: Leaving the Thiel Mountains behind for the second half of the journey
ABOVE: Blue-ice by the Thiel Mountains – as slippery as an ice-rink. Windy Corner is on the far left

TOP LEFT: Robert Falcon Scott being lowered after Antarctica's first balloon flight

TOP RIGHT: *Discovery*'s Southern Party. From left to right: Ernest Shackleton, Scott and Edward Wilson

ABOVE: Harnessing the dogs in preparation for the Southern Journey

Wilson's watercolour of a parhelion, painted during the Southern Journey

TOP: The Southern Party's Farthest South at Shackleton Inlet. If the plunging icefall of the Nimrod Glacier further up the inlet had not been cruelly shrouded in mist, Scott would surely have solved the mystery of the unknown continent

ABOVE RIGHT: Wilson's water-colour depicting the Southern Party's struggle back to the ship. Mt Markham is the prominent peak in the distance.

One of *Discovery*'s sledging parties using a wind-sail to increase travel speeds

OPPOSITE PAGE:
Polar weather

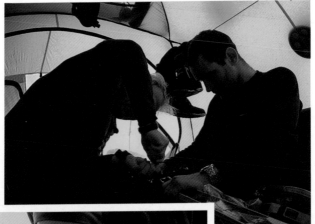

RIGHT:
Paul and Andrew
fixing a broken
binding

BELOW:
Suppositories:
manna from
heaven

ABOVE: Pat trying to
sleep, despite the
glare of the midnight
sun

LEFT: Paul dishing
up dinner. The pile
of snow in the tent's
vestibule will be
melted into drinking
and cooking water

TOP: Everyone kiting in perfect harmony. Polar travel doesn't get much better than this

ABOVE: Andrew kiting beneath a parhelion. This spectacular phenomenon is only seen in the polar regions

TOP: Approaching the South Pole – not exactly the view that Captain Scott would have had 90 years earlier

ABOVE LEFT: The Pole at last. From left to right: Andrew, Paul, Pat and me

ABOVE RIGHT: Scott's party at the Pole in 1912

TOP LEFT: Helping return the South Pole to its correct position
TOP RIGHT: With HRH The Prince of Wales on the expedition's return
TOP: Terra Australis Incognita

Brits, so after a quick spring-clean, Graham and Andrew Cooney are invited round to our tent for a dram of whisky. Despite looking a bit on the gaunt side, Graham is on great form and very proud of his thick polar beard. We are pleasantly surprised that Andrew Cooney comes along, particularly given his earlier wish not to see us. He has brought along a packet of fudge as a peace offering. It's not clear whether one of his teammates has had a quiet word in his ear, but he is clearly making a conscious effort to be nice. We discuss each other's plans and it's only when we explain how we are now aiming to reach the Pole on 31 December, much earlier than their planned arrival date of 4 January, that he becomes uneasy. Nevertheless, after a very amicable half-hour of idle chitchat, he returns to his tent and wishes us the best of luck for the second leg. I'm glad he came along this evening.

Unannounced, Doug arrives at our tent and very kindly offers to cook us dinner. 'What's on the menu?' asks Pat as Doug clambers inside.

'Oh, I've brought along my favourite food in the whole world – boiled conger eel, caught just last month off Punta Arenas.' I try to sound excited but nearly retch as the chunks of eel are thrown into the sizzling pan of butter.

Other than the occasional radio call with Patriot Hills and the Twin Otter pilots, Doug hasn't had the chance to speak to anyone for weeks, and it's not long before the topic of conversation switches to caribou hunting. By the time he turns in for the night it's well past 11 pm.

I find it difficult to nod off tonight. I stare up at the yellow roof of the tent, listening to the gentle patter of light snowfall and wondering what lies ahead for the second half of the journey. Our focus has shifted from skiing to a fuel depot in the middle of nowhere to reaching the South Pole itself. We couldn't have hoped for a much smoother first leg, and for much of the time I've actually enjoyed myself. But now the real work begins. As we continue our inexorable climb to the lofty heights of the Polar Plateau, the temperatures will plummet. The altitude will make the going much tougher, we will be fatigued and the snow conditions will deteriorate. But team morale has never been higher, and with the prospect of favourable kiting conditions further south, I am raring to go. Next stop, the South Pole.

Chapter Six

WINDS IN THE EAST

DAY 28: TUESDAY 10 DECEMBER   **293.2 MILES TO GO**

Great. I have a large blister in the palm of my right hand this morning courtesy of screwing skins into my skis for the best part of two hours yesterday. I ring Amanda in London to wish her a happy birthday and to thank her for somehow managing to get the skis couriered all the way to our depot. 'Just make sure you don't break any of those nice new ski bindings this time,' Amanda says.

She's got a point. The 10,000-foot-high Polar Plateau experiences very cold but stable weather. The absence of katabatic winds up there keeps the snow uncompacted and powdery. Whilst this means far fewer sastrugi to contend with, pulling a sled through light fluffy snow without the help of fully functioning skis would be a backbreaking slog. It would be like wading through an endless sea of mothballs.

We haven't even finished breakfast when we hear the other group setting off. '*Mucho suerte, Españoles*,' I shout out to Willie and Angél, wishing them good luck for their onward journey.

'We are from Basque Region. We are not Spanish. But good luck to you anyway,' comes the slightly abrupt reply.

The most southerly peaks in the Thiels range differ from their more rounded cousins in the main massif, protruding through the ice cap like pyramids in the Sahara. They block our path to the Pole, so we will have to skirt round the edge of the mountains before altering course again and resuming a southerly bearing. In order to avoid running the gauntlet of the dangerous rockfall zone, we will keep a safe distance of a few hundred yards away from the precipitous cliff face. Being struck by a boulder tumbling off one of the unstable mountaintops above us would be a pretty stupid way to go.

It's time to leave the Thiel Mountains. With sleds replenished with provisions for the remainder of the journey and final checks complete, we're ready to go. Doug emerges briefly from his little shelter to bid us an enthusiastic farewell. Things are calm and spirits are high as we set off on the final leg of our journey under a brilliant blue sky.

Straight away the sled feels heavier and the going is noticeably slower than the run-in to our resupply. The encouraging news is that the kicker skins make a noticeable difference and we can glide much further with every stride. Within an hour, the black and green fuel barrels of the depot are out of sight and the landscape before us is littered with sastrugi. It's like trying to ski across a badly ploughed field.

Off to our right, the sharp, rocky summits of the southern Thiel Mountains are utterly breathtaking. A tongue extends from the ice cap behind, splitting the range in two, and we are soon caught up in the crosswinds that funnel through the U-shaped glacial saddle. For 15 minutes we are buffeted by stinging spindrift that has been whipped up into a frenzy by the icy blast. Despite being fully wrapped up against the elements, the tiny snow particles somehow manage to find a way through my protective clothing and down my neck. This is geography on a massive scale, and having been cooped up in the tents for the best part of 48 hours, staggering through Mother Nature's very own wind tunnel feels utterly invigorating.

Midday. After 320 miles of constant climbing the ground up ahead suddenly falls away. Away in the distance we can see the other group – mere pinpricks against the vast expanse of white. The terrain is just steep enough for our sleds to slide without being dragged. Suddenly, a blue and orange object flashes by. It's Pat, using his sled as a toboggan. He's paddling away furiously with both hands in an attempt to propel himself down the slope, letting out loud 'yee haas' as he goes. Any excitement is short-lived and the only downhill slope between the coast and the Pole is over in five minutes.

The terrain is changing all the time. A sea of blue ice now straddles our path, dotted with an archipelago of tiny islands of snow. The bullet-proof ice is pitted with sun cusps that shimmer in the sun like the scales of a fish. When the katabatic winds meet the Thiels massif they are squeezed through its many cols and valleys and accelerate to unimaginable speeds. These hurricane-force winds explain why the surrounding plains have been scoured, so that even when the conditions are benign, only naked ice remains. It's deceptively slippery here, and with the kicker skins offering next to no traction, we're back to travelling on foot. Displaying no grace whatsoever, we flap about across the ice like a family of ducks on a frozen pond, hopping from the relative safety of one snow patch to another. One false move on this lethal terrain and it would be so easy to break a leg or sprain a wrist. With only the tips of our ski poles providing any purchase, it's a slow delicate process.

Discarded rock fragments from the nearby mountains lie strewn haphazardly around. The geologist within me compels me to collect as many samples as possible for analysis in the tent tonight. The others couldn't be less interested and leave me to it. One chunk of granite in particular catches my eye, and as I head towards it, my feet are suddenly swept from beneath me. I'm about to come crashing down on the ice but manage to break my fall by instinctively jamming a ski pole into the hard glassy surface. I cry out in agony as my right shoulder jars awkwardly. Gingerly, I continue towards the others, but I know I'm in trouble.

An hour later, the blue ice gives way to more monstrous sastrugi and we are climbing again. Towering above us, the jagged spires of the southern Thiels fill the western sky. The mountains come in all sorts of shapes and sizes and provide a dramatic backdrop throughout the afternoon. I get a bit carried away trying to record this special place for posterity, and after shooting several minutes of video footage and the best part of two rolls of film, I realise that I have drifted some distance behind the others. As the presence of polished blue ice and sastrugi suggests, we are in the midst of the Thiel Mountains' katabatic wind channel. A ground blizzard quickly ensues, obscuring the guys from view and obliterating their tracks. Visibility shrinks to less than 50 yards. Now I can see why this place is marked on the map as 'Windy Corner'. It takes me a good ten minutes to catch up with the others and they don't look best pleased at having had to hang around.

Shivering with cold, we pitch the tents on a snowy oasis in the middle of another expanse of blue ice. The wind roars down from the mountains with remorseless brutality. 13.2 miles is more than we had planned to travel today, so it has been a promising start to the second half of the journey. The other team are camped a mile behind us. I pull Paul's leg by telling him that I'm planning to take all my rock samples to the Pole.

This has been a unique day. With the raw power of the Antarctic wind machine never far away, the Thiel Mountains have been a truly dramatic place to be today.

A bit worried about my shoulder.

DAY 29: WEDNESDAY 11 DECEMBER   280 MILES TO GO

With an unrelenting katabatic wind howling out of the south, it's been an uncomfortable, sleepless night. The noise has been so bad that we might as well have been camped by the tracks at Clapham Junction.

Before we set off I reluctantly say goodbye to all my lumps of granite. Not only do I not want any extra weight in my sled, but under the Antarctic Treaty I'm not actually allowed to take any souvenirs away with me. The treaty was signed in 1957 by the twelve nations who ran scientific bases in Antarctica at the time. Its aim was very simple – to protect Antartica from exploitation as a natural reserve, with scientific research the top priority. The treaty stipulates that: 'Antarctica should forever be used exclusively for peaceful purposes and not become the scene or object of international discord … in the interests of all mankind.' It prohibits mining, oil drilling, all military activity, the disposal of nuclear waste and commercial fishing south of 60°S. The Antarctic Treaty now has nearly 50 signatories and is chiefly responsible for preserving this icy paradise as God intended. It is widely regarded as one of the most successful international accords ever made.

To get away from Windy Corner, we begin the day on a southeasterly bearing. The sastrugi continue to grow and are becoming a real nuisance. Every time we are forced to cross one of these mounds of concrete snow, we really have to bend our backs just to get the sleds moving forwards. The sleds suffer many capsizes on the uneven terrain. Sometimes our efforts are not enough and we need to call on fellow teammates to help pull the sleds through the polar assault course.

The frustrations of not being able to find my rhythm have put me in a filthy mood. It would be far easier to travel in the same direction as the sastrugi, as opposed to having to cross them broadside on. It feels as if we are beating into a choppy sea.

12.30 pm. We have cleared Windy Corner, and are finally out of the mountains. Our bearing is straightened to 170°. Once we have safely skirted round a crevasse field off to the west, we will alter our course again and head due south. The wind has moderated but there's no let-up in the punishing sastrugi. Not wanting to risk damaging my ski bindings, I walk on foot as we make a series of ascents. The others follow suit. My shoulder is hurting and gives me constant gyp. A stunning ice escarpment that runs south from the Thiel Mountains provides a welcome distraction off to our right, beneath which we can see the six tiny specks of the other team.

Everyone is having a really bad day and tempers are fraying. I decide to take out my pent-up anger on a lump of sastrugi that has just flipped my sled over. Whacking the piece of windblown snow with a ski pole and hurling a torrent of abuse at it goes some way to relieving the tension, until the next obstacle rears its ugly head moments later.

During Happy Hour the clouds roll in from nowhere, and by the time the tents are up, light snow is falling. Despite all the difficulties today, we have managed to rack up 13.7 miles and are already four miles ahead of Matty's team.

A text message from my brother Leo has everyone talking tonight. If he has done his research correctly, a Chilean team travelling along this route from Hercules Inlet in 1995 reached the Pole in just 46 days, thus becoming the fastest team to reach the South Pole from the edge of the Antarctic continent. This means that if we were to arrive some time on 28 December, at an average of nearly 16 miles a day, the record would be ours. Given that our best day so far is 16.4 miles, this is only going to happen if we get the kites up.

Talk of breaking records when we are barely halfway is ridiculous, especially given the difficulty of the conditions since our depot. As Andrew points out, it would be a great thing to aim for, but our focus at the moment must remain reaching the Pole in one piece.

This evening's other exciting news is that Brighton & Hove Albion are off the bottom of Division One for the first time since September.

DAY 30: THURSDAY 12 DECEMBER   266.3 MILES TO GO

A cold night (−1°C in the tent) and nothing has dried. As I slip on my damp, claggy clothing, I find a chunk of ice in my fleece pants. Nice.

Over breakfast, a worried Paul asks me to take a look at his feet. The blisters from a few days ago have completely rubbed away, leaving large areas of bare flesh extending either side of each ankle. Turning away in horror, I know I would have called for a rescue plane a long time ago had I been suffering the same hardship. I give him some of my blister kit and some tape to hold it in place. It's a great compliment that Paul has turned to us for help and shows that he sees us more as fellow expedition companions than simply paid-up clients.

Our morning can be summed up with one word – sastrugi. I am so fed up with these iron-hard bumps and furrows that I just can't face writing about them any more.

The Thiel Mountains and ice escarpment behind us are now beginning to disappear from view, so at least it feels as though we're making progress. We have drawn alongside the symmetrical, almost volcanic-looking Lewis Nunatak – at over 7,000 feet one of the most southerly mountains in the world.

It's hard to imagine that when all these mountains were formed, Antarctica was once joined to Africa, Australia, India, New Zealand and South America as part of the super-continent of Gondwanaland. Over millions of years, tectonic forces deep within the Earth's mantle caused this vast landmass to split and fragment into the continents we know today. Australia was the last chunk to become detached, around 40 million years ago. The clue to this continental break-up is the fact that fossils of a 15-stone dinosaur-like lizard called Lystrosaurus have been found in rocks of similar age in such diverse places as South Africa, India, Australia, and in the Transantarctic Mountains, just 300 miles from the South Pole. The only way our scaly friend could have evolved in all four continents at the same time was if they had once been joined together.

But the Antarctica of 200 million years ago, when Lystrosaurus was roaming about, would have looked very different from the way it does today. This part of Gondwanaland would have been completely ice free. Lystrosaurus lived in temperate swamplands at a time when the climate was much warmer. During his pioneering journey up the Beardmore Glacier in 1908, Shackleton uncovered further evidence of Antarctica's warmer past with the discovery of ancient coal seams just 200 miles from the South Pole. These could only have been formed by the decomposition of extensive vegetation. But once Australia separated from Antarctica, an ocean began to fill the area in between, causing moisture levels to increase and temperatures to fall. Antarctica settled in its current location 15 million years ago.

The planet's polar regions are so cold because the low angle of the sun in the sky means they receive very little of its warmth. This lack of solar radiation, coupled with the climatic changes caused by the formation of the Southern Ocean, were ideal conditions for a steady accumulation of snow and the evolution of the great Antarctic ice sheets. Scientists believe that

Antarctica has looked the way it does today for less than three million years. Only the highest peaks, such as the Lewis Nunatak, remain uncovered by the ice.

After the first break I pack up my sled as normal, put on my mitts and slide my goggles over my face – only to find they have completely fogged up. Disaster. I pull out my lens cover and give them a quick wipe. It's too late. The mist has already turned to ice and they are next to useless. Squinting in the deceptively bright light, I see the others are now well on their way and out of earshot. It's unlikely that they will look back before my next lead in 45 minutes' time. I start to panic.

Travelling without eye protection, even in cloudy conditions, can lead to snow blindness in a very short while. This debilitating condition can cause long-term eye damage and has been the bane of polar travellers for centuries. Wilson suffered dreadful snow blindness as the Southern Party approached their furthest south, brought on after making detailed sketches of the unfolding vistas without wearing goggles. It became so bad that for three days he was forced to ski completely blindfolded, following the others on a leash. The pain in his eyes became so unbearable that he was forced to break into the emergency supply of cocaine for some instant relief. When this failed to produce the desired effect, he had no choice but to inject himself with morphine.

Even though it's an overcast morning, the danger of snow blindness is very real, and these virtually useless goggles are my only pair. There is a small gap in the mist at the very top of the lens. By angling my head towards the ground, I can just pick out three slow-moving dark objects in front of me. My hands have gone numb so I set off as fast as I can, to all intents and purposes completely blind. There is no hope of spotting the sastrugi so I just go in a straight line and hope for the best. Within seconds I'm on my backside.

For the next ten minutes, my stuttering progress is halted by countless falls. I can't take any more of this so I stop and rip off the goggles, carefully aiming two bits of spit where each eye should be. I rub the two areas like mad with the lens cover. To my great relief, two small portholes defrost just enough for me to see. It's not ideal but it will do. The others are so far ahead now that I can't tell who's who. I speed off after them. It's over an hour before I finally catch up and can at last replace my obsolete goggles with the spare pair in Pat's sled.

The sastrugi and climbs continue. My sled behaves like a poorly disciplined dog all afternoon, incapable of following in my tracks and constantly disappearing down little hollows. I turn around to curse the disobedient piece of fibreglass at the top of my voice. Think I'm starting to lose my marbles. The pain in my shoulder is unrelenting. Good God, this is back-breaking toil.

Our toughest day so far – over 400 feet of vertical gain and another 13.7 miles in the bank. Despite the gruelling slog, I haven't been able to get the idea of this speed record out of my head all day. I raise the subject with Pat and Andrew before bedtime and they've been thinking about it too. We decide that it's pointless thinking about records unless we're able to kite.

Everyone is dead tired tonight.

DAY 31: FRIDAY 13 DECEMBER   252.6 MILES TO GO

Wake up in darkness having wriggled down to the very bottom of my goose-down sleeping bag during the night. Being on the lanky side, I brought myself an extra-long bag for the expedition. The trouble is that it's far too long and I keep getting lost inside.

Even after their decision not to take a more lightweight three-man bag, Scott, Wilson and Shackleton must have been utterly miserable in their reindeer skin sleeping bags. The fur would have trapped any perspiration whilst they slept, before freezing solid on the back of the sled during the day. With the sleeping bags' very poor insulation properties, the men would have then had to crawl into their cold, rock-solid bags at night wearing almost all their clothing from the day's march to keep warm. I know our own body odour is nothing to write home about, but those men must have reeked to high heaven.

Friday the thirteenth. I hope that's not an omen. With still conditions, it promises to be an easier day.

Under way by 8.17 am – a new record. The bearing is finally set for 180° – the South Pole. Our target is now clear and simple and that one precise point on the Earth's surface will continue to dominate our thoughts over the coming weeks.

There is yet another big climb to contend with early on, too steep for skis so it's back to travelling on foot. I'm feeling pretty downhearted. Everything is uncomfortable. My eye ducts have frozen, locking my eyes in a semi-closed position, and my runny nose has turned to ice. I am sweating a lot but at least it feels as though the going is faster. I can see this half of the journey being more a battle of the mind than of the conditions. Finding it increasingly difficult to slip into daydream mode. My pool of happy thoughts is becoming more and more difficult to retreat into. Instead my mind is occupied with negative thoughts about hunger and the incessant pain in my shoulder.

After six hours the sastrugi numbers are decreasing, and as we approach 86°S, Paul is talking about snow baths and whisky again. But the clouds roll in during Happy Hour, lowering everyone's mood. Under a mottled sky of cotton wool-like stratus clouds, we take our quickest degree snow bath of the journey so far – more ceremonial than a proper wash. The Lewis Nunatak has disappeared from view for ever, leaving us alone in the empty heart of Antarctica. Every mountain that lies between here and the South Pole has been completely buried by the ice cap, which is now almost 6,000 feet thick. The next topographical feature we shall see will be the American science base at the Pole.

Before turning in for the night, I see the wind has swung round to the east for the very first time . . .

DAY 32: SATURDAY 14 DECEMBER   238.7 MILES TO GO

Wake to the faint tapping of snowflakes on the tent canvas. I quickly get dressed and clamber over Pat to see how much snow fell overnight – maybe only an inch or so, but it's the biggest snowfall of the expedition. Off to the east, the sun tries desperately to peek through the thin haze and the combination is spectacular. The undulating terrain of the last few days stretches away behind us like a bleached desert. All around the ground sparkles as only fresh snowfall does and all is perfectly quiet.

Early on, Pat's goggles ice up and I take over his lead. This is the best surface since our resupply and the sastrugi have all but vanished. On days like this, it's a joy to be out in front. Definitely going insane, because I'm convinced a series of subtle blemishes in the powdery surface are animal tracks. Most of the smaller ridges in the surface have been buried and our sleds gouge out two satisfying parallel furrows in the snow.

At the first break Paul pulls out the digital wind gauge and spends a while looking up at the sky to see which direction the clouds are moving, before announcing: 'I'm going to try my kite.'

We sit back on our sleds, enjoying the extended break as Paul readies himself. 'There's bugger all wind,' says Andrew. 'There's no way he'll get that thing in the air.'

It may be completely still at ground level, but there are obviously a few knots of easterly wind aloft, because before too long we look across to see Paul skiing back and forth, initially on his own and then towing his sled. To our amazement and utter delight, the kite powers him along much faster than we have been pulling our sleds. The kite works, it bloody works! Dragging 15 pounds of kiting equipment all this way may have been worth the extra effort after all. Not wanting to waste a precious moment, we frantically dig our yellow kite bags out from the depths of the sled before carefully laying the kites themselves out on the snow at 30-yard intervals. We can't wipe the grins from our faces.

Ten minutes later, we're all harnessed up, clipped to our sleds and wearing the smooth-bottomed kiting skis that are making their long-awaited debut. With everyone lined up and raring to go, Paul turns to us and says in a stern voice: 'The winds are light so this might well not work. Be patient and don't get disappointed if we don't go very far.'

Like the chief marshal at the start of the Grand National, Paul then drops his arm to signal the all clear. We're off. As I lift my kite into the sky, I immediately pick up speed. Before I've had a chance to think of what I'm supposed to do next, the slack in the sled's towrope runs out and a sharp yank around my waist sends me falling backwards.

I pull myself up and try again. This time, I'm properly away and following along in Paul's slipstream, heading due south. But the joy of not having to manhaul is only short-lived. After about 200 yards, a lull in the breeze sends my kite gradually drifting down to earth in a sorry bundle. I glance back at the others. Pat seems to be having problems getting his kite airborne, whilst Andrew is going along at great guns but for some reason is heading west in completely the wrong direction. 30 minutes later and we haven't made any further progress. My kite ruffles apologetically as I tug at the kite lines as hard as I can. Paul and I agree there is no point in wasting time for the wind to return, and we start packing away the kites and wait for the others to catch up.

'Well, that was a bit of a flop,' says Andrew. Paul doesn't respond. The kites are returned to the bottom of the sleds, and with heavy hearts we resume pulling our heavy loads.

At the next break Paul is unusually quiet and looking dejected. I ask him what the matter is. 'When I saw everyone's reaction when we began packing away the kites back there, I felt kinda guilty for suggesting getting them out in the first place,' he says with a despondent sigh.

'Absolute nonsense,' I tell him. 'This little kiting exercise may have cost us two miles or so but we have gained valuable experience.'

'I'm just confused about the team's aim. Do we want to get to the Pole by New Year's Eve or do we want to go for this record?'

'I think we should stick to our initial target of New Year's Eve but if the winds return, we could still arrive on the 28th. But Paul, nobody is blaming you for getting the kites out earlier. I'm very glad we did it.'

It's agreed that a token half an hour should be added on to the end of the day to make up some of the lost time. It's slow going again, with the sleds getting held up by patches of soft, sticky snow. Nevertheless, I'm in a positive frame of mind, buoyed up at having seen the exciting potential of the kites. What would it be like if we could have a day of perfect kiting conditions, as opposed to just a few minutes? We would be able to go for miles.

We're treated to a stunning late afternoon sky, with the giant ring of a full-blown parhelion circling the sun like a complete 360° rainbow. This extraordinary phenomenon is unique to the polar regions and formed by the sun shining through tiny ice particles in the lower atmosphere. This one's very special, because at the bottom of the multicoloured orb we can clearly see a mini refracted sun, shining brightly. The Southern Party were equally impressed by the spectacle in 1902. Wilson wrote, 'We saw a very wonderful exhibition of mock suns, parhelia and circles of light in the sky, with showers of ice crystals flying about.'

The frost damage in my cheeks has started to go pussy beneath the skin, so before bed, I drain the two areas with the tip of my penknife, making sure to clean them up with antiseptic wipes and cream. I'll cover them with tape in the morning.

Very tired this evening – a little worrying because it has not been a difficult day. The constant effort of doing this day after day is taking its toll. Just hope I'm not burning out. The days are becoming more of a chore and whereas I got a buzz from pulling my sled across the snow during the first half of the journey, I now find myself desperate for the end of the day. But at least I am with friends and I can't think of anywhere else I would rather be. The idea of doing this solo is completely mad – you've got to be a bit of a recluse or an oddball to get a kick out of doing this on your own. Those who have set off across the polar snows by themselves have my full admiration. But it's not my bag at all.

Andrew has been in a miserable mood all evening, distraught that one of the extra 200-gram chocolate bars he took from the resupply barrels at the Thiel Mountains has vanished. After two hours of agonising searches, he goes outside to check his sled for the third time and is euphoric when he finds it buried beneath a fuel canister. He polishes it off in one.

DAY 33: SUNDAY 15 DECEMBER   226.3 MILES TO GO

An utterly foul morning. Spindrift is being blown about by a keen wind and the windchill is in the minus forties. Paul makes the dash across to our tent for breakfast and emerges at the door, plastered in snow.

'I think we should try the kites again.'

We all laugh out loud. Expressionless, Paul replies: 'I'm being serious.'

'It's blowing a gale out there and you can't see shit,' says Pat.

'The winds are coming from the east again and the visibility is not as bad as you might think – it's probably at least a hundred yards. Plus there's a light covering of fresh snow which should make things easier and safer.'

We don't need much more convincing. We haven't dragged these kites, harnesses and extra skis halfway across this frozen continent for nothing, and at last, on the 33rd day of the expedition, it seems that they will come into their own. It's inevitable that there will be lots of standing around, so everyone wraps up with extra layers of clothing. Before heading out into the maelstrom, harnesses are slipped on and we have a brief strategy talk. It's decided that Paul will go first with the three of us following along in a straight line behind.

Paul's final words cause the hairs on the back of my neck to stand on end. 'If we separate, the expedition is over.' With only two satellite phones and two GPS's between us, it would be impossible to find a missing person in the murk. Paul and I are the only ones carrying tents and Andrew has all the cooking equipment. Survival times with no shelter or fuel would only be a matter of hours. Even if we were able to send a distress message to Patriot Hills, there would be no way of landing a Twin Otter in these appalling conditions, even if the place wasn't strewn with six-foot sastrugi. It's a terrifying and sobering prospect.

8.30 am. Paul is the first to launch his kite and heads south at a terrific speed. I'm next. Butterflies fill my stomach. This is going to be very different from yesterday's gentle trial run. Poised on the snow 30 yards in front of me, my kite flaps around wildly at the end of the main lines like some untamed animal waiting to be let off its leash. I tentatively pull on the handles. The kite soars into the air and I shoot off behind it. Paul is already becoming difficult to see so I turn my skis to the left in hot pursuit. My kite follows obligingly. We're away. Whizzing along like the clappers, adrenalin pumping. Absolutely bricking myself. Completely out of control, I'm hurtling through a world of uniform grey, devoid of any horizon. Chances of spotting any bump in the surface are minimal. Seeing the yellow and blue kite arcing gracefully through the air as I work the handles back and forth is quite breathtaking.

Five minutes later Paul and I have already covered half a mile. Have a quick glance back to see how the others are getting on – stupid mistake. Taking my eyes off the kite for a split second, I lose what little control I had, causing the kite to accelerate into the most powerful quarter of the wind. I'm pulled off my feet and promptly bite the dust. Moments later, the twelve-stone sled, which has been bouncing along noisily behind me, torpedoes straight into my back. Winded by the force of the impact. Extremely sore. Must carry on.

Both Andrew and Pat are on their backsides some way behind. Up ahead, Paul has stopped and is waiting for us to catch up. Gasping for air, I try to pull myself upright – not an easy task without ski poles for support. The kite has become badly twisted in the fall. By the time I've sorted out the tangle, Pat and Andrew have caught up. Haven't learnt from yesterday's mistake, and no sooner have I set off again than the slack in the towrope runs out, and the sled yanks me backwards. All three of us are now lying in an undignified heap in the snow.

For the next two hours, this exhausting process continues. A few hundred yards might be gained before the next big wipeout dramatically halts our progress. I'm amazed when Paul tells us we've covered as much as 2.4 miles during the opening session.

The bridle lines at the top of Pat's kite have become badly twisted in a fall. Paul unclips from his skis and sled and walks over to see if he can help Pat untangle the knot. Shortly after takeoff, the kite makes a beeline for the most powerful part of the wind. Without the ballast of a sled to hold him back, Paul is lifted off the ground, legs flailing behind. I stare in horror as the kite threatens to carry him away. After a few yards, Paul comes crashing down to earth, still frantically wrestling with the kiting lines. Seeing the super-experienced Paul being whisked off his feet with such alarming ease sends shivers down my spine.

To prove that this was no fluke, Paul's next two attempts to fly the kite produce similar outcomes. The kites are making fools of us. But at least it looks as if the twist in Pat's kite has become unravelled.

What makes this totally insane sport particularly tricky is that unlike normal ski bindings that are fixed solidly to the ski, ours are only fixed at the toe. So given the slightest loss of balance, it is very easy to fall forwards. Shortly before midday, one especially nasty fall sends me flying over my ski tips, in the process wrenching a binding almost clean off. Paul, who by now must be despairing at our kiting inabilities, replaces it in next to no time. During the unscheduled pit-stop, the new binding somehow becomes iced up, making it impossible to clip my boot back in. Another ten minutes are wasted trying to extract the ice from the binding with my penknife.

I'm unable to repeat my half-mile dash from the beginning of the day as the tumbles continue. This coincides with Andrew and Pat gradually gaining some basic level of kiting proficiency. Rather than be pleased for them, I'm resentful and cheesed off. Another fall. There's no let-up. All the stressful relaunches and falls are tiring me out. I'm having an absolute kite-mare. The final nail in the coffin comes when a spectacular wipe-out leaves me spread-eagled on the deck, legs and skis contorted awkwardly underneath my sled. Unable to pull the fibreglass sled off my back, I wave an arm in the air in a desperate plea for help. Andrew comes rushing over to my aid, and I crawl gingerly from the wreckage. Sit down to catch my breath. Have a feeling I'm going to be black and blue in the morning. 'Tommy, I think you should take a rest before you have a serious accident,' he says, trying to be as tactful as possible.

Pat then comes up with an ingenious idea. 'What about fixing a rope behind my sled so that Tom can ski along behind me? Paul could then tow Tom's sled. It's worth a go.' We pause for a piece of flapjack and a swig of tepid orange squash before rigging everything up. So that Paul doesn't have to drag an impossibly heavy load, some of the weight is transferred from my sled to Andrew's, so that Paul is towing around 260 pounds and Andrew more like 200.

12 pm and we're off again. The wind is still blowing strong, although there are signs that the visibility is improving. To begin with, this water-skiing along behind another sled is terrifying. I cling on to the two loops in the towrope for dear life whilst the sled in front slews erratically from side to side. Both Pat and I suffer early falls, but soon get a basic grip of what is required to stay on our feet with this new set-up. Pat can now give his full concentration to operating the kite, whilst I shout at the top of my voice to warn of approaching banks of sastrugi. I can also use the rope to divert the sled around the oncoming obstacles. Trying to snow-plough in these primitive skis and boots would end in disaster, and there's a danger that if I pick up too much momentum, I could overtake Pat's sled.

The initial disappointment of not being able to kite quickly evaporates and it is an electrifying dash following Pat and his sled. Up ahead, Paul is making great progress, despite having added an extra trailer to the caravan behind him. I reckon we must be hitting at least ten knots over the quicker stretches. We have covered over seven miles in two hours but it could have been even more.

It's now Andrew's turn to suffer his share of tumbles and we find ourselves regularly waiting for him to catch up. On one occasion, we look back to see him with his bare hand in his mouth. When he finally reaches us he explains that one of the kiting lines had wrapped round his mitt, cutting off the flow of blood to part of his hand. Concerned that they had lost all feeling, he removed the mitt and inner gloves to see that two fingers were sheet white – the telltale early signs of frostbite. Stuffing his fingers into his mouth is not the most conventional cure, but thankfully it works and let's hope there's no lasting damage.

2.30 pm and the sun has started to peek through. We are faced with a steep climb. After a brief respite, the sastrugi have returned with a vengeance. There's not enough wind to drag both Pat and me through the monstrous lumps of ice, so we need a change of plan. I am now desperate to have another go at kiting and we rearrange the sleds back to their former configuration. Just before setting off, Paul offers some words of encouragement: 'Launch the kite straight into the power zone, skis pointing due west. To begin with you will head off in that direction but as soon as the kite is up there, use the edges of your skis to turn to the left (the south) before you catch up with the kite. Never let the kite get behind you. It should be slightly easier now we can see where we're going. Enjoy it!'

Off we go again. What a difference a couple of hours makes. This time I'm in complete control, and my confidence builds with every yard gained. With all of us rocketing along in perfect harmony, it's hard to imagine that there had been all those problems earlier in the day. It would be so difficult to master the art of kiting were we not reasonably proficient downhill skiers – by British standards anyway. Having the confidence to trust our skiing abilities sufficiently to ride out any undulations in the terrain means that we are able to focus our attention on the flight of the kite without worrying about what the skis are up to. It's a magnificent sight to see all four giant coloured butterflies buzzing around against the deep blue Antarctic sky, pulling us along on our merry way. Can't take my eyes off the snow rushing past my skis, thankful that I'm not having to haul my heavy sled across this part of the continent.

Making the most of the 24-hour daylight, we continue well into the evening. By 9 pm the first signs of exhaustion are setting in and I take a series of tumbles. On one occasion, the kite refuses to release from my waist harness. With a life all of its own, it continues to fly, bouncing me over several big sastrugi like a rag doll. As I finally manage to unhook the lines, I watch helplessly as the kite corkscrews round and round in a series of elaborate twists as it returns to earth. As well as adding a few more bruises to the collection, this little escapade has led to the most appalling tangle in the kite lines.

15 minutes later and I am close to unravelling the mess. The others are patiently waiting for me a short distance away. Pat takes off his skis and storms over towards me. He doesn' look happy.

'Tom, you've got to pack up your kite,' says Pat.

Surprised at his abruptness, I say: 'What? Listen, I'm massively sorry for the delay. I'm almost untangled. Just give me a minute, Pat.'

'No. We're getting cold waiting and you're holding us up.'

Before I have a chance to ask him to lend a hand, he turns around and heads back to join Paul and Andrew. We're all feeling tired and scratchy, but I don't remember ever being snapped at by a fellow teammate like that on a previous expedition. He has every right to be frustrated by the delay, which is entirely my fault, but I'm taken aback by the abrasive attitude. I pack everything away and walk over to the others.

We try resuming the water-skiing technique for a bit but our easterly wind is fading and we soon find ourselves drifting too far to the west and hardly moving at all. It's getting on for 10 pm and when Andrew breaks a ski binding, the unanimous decision is made to pitch camp.

We have chalked up an incredible 25.5 miles. We have experienced both heaven and hell today and the day has been a non-stop adrenalin rush. I'm absolutely spent, but thrilled at what we've accomplished. There have been no serious injuries and nobody got lost. All the earlier stresses are laughed off and we make camp for the night. As we sit down to a well-earned dinner of spaghetti bolognaise, we're buzzing with the sheer delight of what has been our most exhilarating day on the Ice. Paul has us in stitches when he says in that deadpan way of his: 'When I was cruising along back there, with two sleds right behind me, I said to myself, Landry, make sure you don't fuck up here.'

What an utterly unique experience today has been. It's been a day so totally different from the daily grind of pulling a sled and the rigid routine that a normal day of Antarctic travel entails. I wonder what our friends have been up to back home – probably Christmas shopping on a drizzly Sunday afternoon in London. Even if the kites stay at the bottom of our sleds for the remainder of the expedition, it has been worth bringing them all this way just for this one golden opportunity. If only Captain Scott could have seen us.

DAY 34: MONDAY 16 DECEMBER   200.8 MILES TO GO

Wake up feeling as though I've just gone twelve rounds with a prizefighter. My legs, back and chest are not a pretty sight and we are all covered in bruises and sores. We enjoy a lie-in and a late breakfast and don't set off until 10.30 am. We are fast approaching 87°S. I feel that if we can just get to 88°S, we will be on the homeward run. The climb to the Polar Plateau will at last be over and we can expect to find a much more even surface and more stable, albeit colder, weather. Our extraordinary day has put us 17 miles ahead of the other team, giving us plenty of breathing space.

After all of yesterday's excitements, today comes as a wonderful anticlimax. With a negligible breeze and clear skies, we dawdle along for only a few hours, thinking back to yesterday's fun and games.

I think back to Scott's early attempts at using wind power during the *Discovery* Expedition. Following Nansen's successful experiments with wind-sails during his crossing of Greenland in 1888, he suggested to Scott that he should try them in Antarctica. Given favourable winds, the tent's square canvas groundsheet was hoisted onto a wooden cross, so the sled closely resembled Thor Heyerdahl's raft *Kon-Tiki*. In the event of a following wind, the apparent weight of the sled would be vastly reduced, enabling the men and dogs to cover much greater distances.

The wind-sail was used on just one day during the Southern Party's outward journey, and twelve during their return to the ship. Whilst the wind-sails certainly helped their progress, they were unable to cover the huge distance that our kiting day provided. In fact, had the men been travelling in the conditions we experienced yesterday, they would not have bothered even deploying their wind-sail. We may have been able to use an easterly wind to our advantage, but due to the inflexibilities of Scott's wind-sail, a crosswind would have been well outside their limited wind range of just 45° in either direction.

Thinking that teaching the others how to play bridge would give us a bit of a change from the endless games of Shithead, the other day I asked Mum to text us the basic rules of bridge. Big mistake. Cryptic messages about opening bids, no trumps and slams are pouring in and we just don't want to know anymore. She has already sent 23 and they're threatening to clog up the sat phone. Will have to find a way of tactfully asking her to hold off.

Andrew is already planning his first meal back in London – a Super Burger with nachos and guacamole from the Texas Lone Star on the Gloucester Road. Sounds pretty good to me.

We all look and feel pretty worn out.

DAY 35: TUESDAY 17 DECEMBER (MY BIRTHDAY!)   190.2 MILES TO GO

It was really hot in the tent overnight – so hot in fact that I ended up sleeping on top of my sleeping bag, wearing only my boxer shorts. My 'bed' hasn't smelt this bad since my student days so I'm sure my sleeping bag is grateful for the night off. With the southern hemisphere's summer solstice just four days away, the sun is now virtually at the highest point it ever reaches in the sky in this part of the world. Despite our efforts to ventilate the tent by leaving the main porch door open, its powerful rays make our little home feel like a furnace.

In 1902 the Southern Party experienced similarly balmy conditions on the Ross Ice Shelf and on calm nights had to tie back the doors of their green canvas tent to keep cool. I still find it extraordinary that despite it being around +30°C inside, just the other side of the flysheet the temperature is nudging −20°C. Nevertheless, it makes living in the Antarctic far more comfortable than I ever expected. Our damp clothes are usually bone-dry after a night hanging up in the tent, it's easy to drag ourselves out of bed in the mornings (Pat being the exception), our daily cheese and salami rations thaw out in no time (although my chunk of Edam is more of a smelly goo today) and we are all in good heart. Spirits are lifted further when Paul comes into the tent for breakfast to tell us that a ten-knot wind is blowing from the east. How sweet it would be to be able to get the kites up on my 27th birthday.

I turn on our satellite phone in the hope of numerous birthday text messages. There's just the one – from Patrick Ward (the freelance PR agent who is working on behalf of Hastings Direct) asking me to call him. Despite being over 8,000 miles away, the line is incredibly clear. 'Tom, there is quite a bit of press interest in your story, principally from *The Times*. But I've been doing some research and ANI's Punta Arenas office has told me that a 25-year-old plumber from Cambridge called Steve Peyton reached the South Pole on ANI's first-ever commercial trip three years ago. Are you sure you will be the youngest Brit?'

I can't believe it. I know I researched this as much as I possibly could – when sending out press releases, it is vital to ensure that all the facts are 100 per cent accurate. I feel that I have misled Hastings Direct. Still, I'm pretty cheesed off that last year when I told Anne Kershaw of my 'record attempt' (if you could call it that), she never mentioned this Peyton fellow. Pat lends his support during breakfast, saying it is not my fault and that Hastings Direct, whilst disappointed, will fully understand. I hope he's right.

I'm in a mixed frame of mind as we set up the kites. I'm insistent that after Sunday's little dramas, I am not going 'water-skiing' on my birthday. Paul says his aim for today would be to hit 16 miles.

Things get off to a terrific start. The conditions are ideal as we set off from camp. The surface is hard and flat, there's not a cloud in the sky, and I'm immediately back in the groove and positively zipping along. This is what it's all about. I make a point of telling myself to remember this moment and just how good it feels. Occasionally, a solitary patch of sastrugi will appear, requiring careful negotiation, but the terrain is predominantly smooth. I'm now confident enough to take my eyes off the kite for a moment and glance across at the others, who are all in a line alongside me. Andrew has a broad grin plastered across his face whilst Pat is hollering like an American basketball fan. Everyone is careering across the icy surface in perfect harmony, sleds rattling along behind.

Then, just as I start to harbour dreams that we're going to nail 50 miles today, we are forced to stop. Andrew is lying on the ground by his sled, waving an arm frantically in the air. By the time Pat and I ski across to him, collapse our kites and secure them to two skis that we've planted vertically in the snow, Paul is already with him. As a result of Andrew's nasty tumble, yet another binding has broken and this one takes a while to repair. It's his sixth binding incident of the expedition and our tenth overall. But we've covered nearly seven miles in an hour and a half – a distance that would normally take four hours to manhaul.

The gradient steepens noticeably and we find we're really having to work the kites to generate any forward motion at all. This is complicated by an increase in the sastrugi population. The clouds begin to close in around us, the light goes desperately flat and the horizon vanishes altogether. The sastrugi are now the big problem. When the visibility was good, I could weave my way around these concrete blocks of ice with ease but I'm finding it very difficult to differentiate between the sky and the ground and therefore impossible to know where the obstacles are. I crash into a large mound of sastrugi and fall over. As a result of the extra work, my goggles have started to mist up. I fall again. This time my kiting lines have completely twisted, requiring a good ten minutes to unravel. I can see the others watching me impatiently, itching to get going again. Paul decides this would be a good moment to take a break. Although they have taken the odd fall themselves, Pat and Andrew seem to be coping better with the change in conditions and, more importantly, they are somehow able to unravel their kite lines quicker than me.

Following a break of (now rock-hard) Edam and flapjack, we are on our way again. I take a deep breath, raise the kite off the ground and follow its progress upwards. As I begin to pick up speed, I edge my skis and turn to the left (south) as I had been doing all day. All is going well when, out of nowhere, a large dip appears in the surface. I accelerate downhill before being body-slammed against an invisible wall of ice on the other side. Lie there motionless for a moment making sure nothing is broken before I shake myself down and try again. Cannot see a thing other than the other three who are slowly pulling ahead, and worryingly, still kiting. Take a deep breath and hope that the surface ahead is flat. 'Trust your skis, and focus on the kite,' I mutter to myself.

After about 50 yards, I'm skiing uphill and begin to slow down as the sled tries to slide up the slope with me. However, my body is still leaning way out into the wind just like a windsurfer and I can't correct my balance in time. Just as my skis come to a complete standstill, I topple off the side of the giant sastrugi, landing on my side. My kite is still fully powered up but I find it impossible to release the kiting handles from my harness, which would send the kite back to the ground. All of a sudden I find myself being dragged along on my tummy at great speed back up the side of the sastrugi. I'm making a beeline for my sled and make a last desperate attempt to unhook the kite from my harness. Too late. I crash broadside into the eleven-stone sled, giving myself a nasty dead leg as my right calf takes the brunt of the impact. Only then do I manage to release myself and the kite falls innocently to the ground, flapping away noisily. Very shaken.

Despite being in great discomfort, I'm relieved it's not as serious as a twisted ankle or dislocated shoulder, which could happen so easily out here. Try not to think that injuries such as these can become very serious in Antarctica, particularly as a rescue plane would never be able to land on this terrain. Look at my kite lines to find them completely knotted up again. Confidence fading fast.

For the next hour, I gradually catch up with the others, rarely making more than 200 yards of headway before the next crash halts my progress. As I approach them, Paul, Pat and Andrew are standing by their sleds, making windmills with their arms to keep warm. The metal plate in my right ski binding is completely bent, and when I show it to the guys, it just has the effect of souring everyone's moods further. Having to repair a binding is going to delay us even more, and all three of them look livid with my slow progress. My apologies fall on deaf ears. I explain that as well as finding it difficult to keep my balance in this dreadful visibility, my kite lines have a habit of becoming intertwined, which require lengthy untangling operations – a task made all the more difficult with frozen fingers. Still no reaction. We have been such a cohesive team throughout the expedition, but today I really feel that there are two teams out there – them and me. And it's supposed to be my birthday!

On closer inspection, the damage to the binding does not look as serious as we had first feared and so I am to continue skiing with it on the 'upwind' foot (which takes much less of the strain) until it goes for good. It's agreed that I will take the lead and, after some encouragement from Paul, I am away. All technique is out the window and I ski along like a complete novice – bum out, legs wide apart, elbows jutting out to the side, just waiting for the next battering to my body. I may as well be doing this with my eyes closed. Trying to ski flat out down a steep mogul field in a blizzard without turning is as accurate a comparison as I can make to this suicidal sport.

Five minutes after setting off, I'm on the ground again but

uninjured. I try again. I'm not giving up! These sastrugi are monsters but the trouble is you don't notice them until you've gone over or into them. Again, I go down like a sack of spuds. Pat has already lost patience and sets off ahead of me. Andrew and Paul follow suit. Infuriated, I beat the snow with my fist and yell Fs and Bs at them, at the sastrugi and at my sled. I've had some good tantrums in my time but this one really tops the bill. I cheer up a bit when I see both Pat and Paul (twice) wipe out in quick succession. It's not just me who's finding this difficult.

Just as I'm thinking of throwing in the towel, the light begins to recover and the sastrugi numbers reduce. My kiting skills return and I'm suddenly racing along at a rate of knots again.

My birthday is improving dramatically and those two hours of sheer misery are soon just a fleeting memory. We're really eating up the miles now. Pat stops to take some video footage and as I charge past him, I scream out a loud 'Yee-ha', which I instantly regret.

We carry on all afternoon long with everyone travelling at the same speed again. The winds start to slack off during the early evening and it requires a great deal of effort just to keep the kites airborne.

I'm glad to see I'm not the only one to lose my temper today, and just before we call it a day I catch Pat throwing his kiting handles to the ground in disgust, shrieking expletives and complaining that there isn't enough wind to launch his kite.

It's 6.30 pm when we pitch camp, having clocked up a colossal 23.7 miles in the day and gained 860 feet in altitude. The first thing I do is call home. I've been looking forward to this moment all day so I'm gutted when shortly after hearing 'Happy Birthday', the phone battery dies.

The crumpled party hats are pulled out for the evening celebrations. I've got lots of birthday text messages from friends and family to enjoy and read each one twice. Get to choose my favourite meal from the dinner menu tonight – no surprises when Pasta al fredo is pulled out. It's a popular choice. Paul opens one of his two packs of Turkey Jerky, which he had been saving since the Thiel Mountains, and we finish off his mother's homemade fudge over a dram of whisky. We joke about the day's events and I come in for some stick about my trials through the sastrugi. It is amazing that when you are in the warmth and comfort of the tent, all those difficult times from the day seem so distant and things never appear as bad as they were at the time. I am touched when Paul makes a point of thanking me for my perseverance today. He says that those were by far the toughest conditions he has kited in and most sensible people would have packed away their kites very early. It was my 'British stubbornness', as he called it, which had pulled me through.

Before crawling into bed, I inspect and treat the day's war wounds. I've got a large number of bruises on my arms and shoulders, the one on my right calf is particularly impressive, bulging nicely out to the side. A combination of Deep Heat for the pulled muscle in my back along with Arnica pills and cream for the bruising should do the trick.

Despite the earlier problems, I have decided that kiting beats manhauling by a street. It's such fun and really gets the adrenalin flowing. Because you have to concentrate the whole time, there's no need to worry about finding a daydream to while away the hours. Days like today make it all worthwhile. Team morale is high this evening, we are all talking and laughing again and our hopes of reaching the Pole in less than 46 days are back on track.

Just as I'm dozing off, I remember that we crossed the 87th Parallel today and I never took my customary snow bath. It's not easy dragging myself out of my sleeping bag and into the cold, wearing just boxer shorts.

It's a beautiful evening. The winds are calm so there's not the usual frenzy. I even have the time to wash behind my ears. Mother would be proud.

DAY 36: WEDNESDAY 18 DECEMBER   166.5 MILES TO GO

As expected, there's not enough wind to go kiting today. Paul starts the day off very slowly and his hour flies by. So much has happened in the last 72 hours and my mind is filled with a whole new pool of positive thoughts. Pat then puts in a ridiculously fast hour, and by the first break I find myself very short of breath, beading with sweat and struggling to focus.

During Andrew's lead, the terrain deteriorates rapidly and we're soon amongst the worst sastrugi of the expedition – not dissimilar to the icy jungle we tried kiting through yesterday morning.

It's my turn to lead. Feels like we are going continuously uphill. To make matters worse, visibility has turned to a real pea-souper, making it almost impossible to pick out the effing sastrugi. Leading is a complete nightmare. At the front, one is skiing totally blind. Working out the general lie of the land is impossible. The compass does provide some direction but is unable to help to pick out the bumps.

We're all having a difficult day. At the end of Andrew's second shift, we find that he's been skiing as much as 30° to the west. We were all too tired to bother checking his course. Andrew is not to blame – we think the metallic camera that he keeps tucked away in his jacket pocket led to the distorted compass bearing.

The plan had been to average two miles an hour today, but after $6\frac{1}{2}$ hours the GPS reveals a meagre distance of eleven miles covered. A patch of blue sky way off to the east offers hope of an improvement but it fails to come this way. Just before day's end, Paul breaks his second binding of the journey, blaming the mishap on the hollow screws that hold the binding in place.

The effort is beginning to take its toll. Fair amount of strife from the shoulder and constant reminders from multiple kiting bumps and bruises. My worst day so far.

Trade some walnuts, almonds and dates from my nut bag for a few priceless chunks of white chocolate and peanuts with

Andrew. Weights and measures are stringently calculated and arbitrated.

It's just before bedtime and we are still starving so we break into the medical kit to see what can be pilfered. There's a treasure chest of goodies inside, with a pack of honey-flavoured Strepsils providing a short-lived respite from the hunger.

Even though the sun has hardly touched our faces since we left Chile, we all look sunburnt. My blond beard is turning really horrible – Pat thinks I look like a Swedish porn star.

DAY 37: THURSDAY 19 DECEMBER   153.7 MILES TO GO

Last night was another hot one and I did not sleep well. Am really noticing the altitude and over breakfast find myself having to catch my breath after each mouthful of granola.

As I squat over my snow pit this morning, something just doesn't feel right. Exposing my behind to the elements every day has never been an enjoyable experience, but as I let rip, a sharp pain strikes me right at the business end. I look back into the pit and to my horror I see the pristine snow splattered with blood. Now in extreme agony, I step away from the pit and tentatively try to clean things up with a handful of snow and some loo roll. I am suddenly acutely aware of how it must have felt to be given the red-hot poker treatment in the Tower of London's torture chambers. The prognosis is not great. Further investigation reveals two large grape-like objects precisely where the sun doesn't shine. One of them has ruptured. Haemorrhoids, piles, Farmer Giles, call them what you will, they are not what I need with just one other pair of boxer shorts in my sled and over 150 miles still to go to the Pole.

I am no stranger to this horrendous condition, having been struck down during my Bristol University days. We were all revising hard for the end-of-year exams and the library was crammed with students. One morning I couldn't find anywhere to sit so plonked myself down on a large wrought-iron radiator in the corner until a chair became free, blissfully unaware that sitting on warm radiators is a sure-fire way to get piles. The upshot of my predicament was that I was physically unable to sit down for any length of time, let alone for a three-hour palaeontology exam, because I was in such pain. Having to go to the university medical centre to get official permission to postpone the exam was one of the most humiliating moments of my life, and I have been haunted by images of rubber-gloved doctors ever since. I had to return to Bristol in the middle of the summer holidays to retake the exam and I've kept a safe distance from radiators ever since.

As I shuffle back to the tent, my first thought is, 'Do I tell the others?' From my one previous experience of haemorrhoids, other than slapping on a bit of antiseptic cream, there is very little that can be done to ease the pain but to grin and bear it. It took three weeks for everything to clear up last time. David Hempleman-Adams suffered from piles during his journey to the Pole in 1995–6, gaining immediate relief by shoving tampons up his derrière. Suppositories might relieve some of the discomfort, but having rummaged through the medical supplies, I know we don't have any. We don't even have any tampons. The guys would initially be very sympathetic to the unfortunate state of my bottom but there's nothing else they can do. There's something about piles that people find absolutely hilarious, and having been there before, I know that I would never hear the end of it. Anyway, I have made up my mind and shall spend the next couple of weeks in my own private world of suffering.

I'm incredibly anxious before we set off and make sure I am at the back of the line so I can rearrange undergarments as and when during the day. Thankfully, the discomfort is not as bad as I had first feared and, provided I ski with my legs wider apart than normal, things should be just about tolerable.

Later. The surface is far from great and my shoulder throbs with pain. For the first time on the expedition, I find myself unable to stick to the group pace and gradually start drifting behind. Incredibly demoralising. During my first lead I am very slow and find it impossible to ignore the pain in my shoulder and the problems downstairs that are getting worse. Even though the sun has returned for the first time in ages, the mercury has decided to plummet to −23°C. A stiff breeze blows straight from the south, sending the windchill the wrong side of −40°C. In these difficult conditions, exposed flesh freezes in a matter of seconds so we've got to take extra care that everything is covered up.

The cold means that each of today's pit stops is limited to about six minutes. In the afternoon I make the mistake of having my first real food fantasies of the expedition. What's the first meal I'm going to have when I get home? Roast lamb, Mum's best gravy, crunchy roast tatties, baby carrots and cabbage. Once these thoughts manifest themselves in the mind, it is very hard to relinquish them and the days become more of a mental battle. I arrive at each of the afternoon's breaks several minutes after the others, and sensing their increasing frustration I tell them that my shoulder is causing me untold agony.

'Just stick at the back and try to get through the day,' says Paul. 'We're getting slower though, so how does everyone feel about adding an extra half hour to the day?'

So Happy Hour becomes a very Unhappy Hour and a Half. Not sure whether it's the pain or the fact that we are approaching the final hurdle, but during the final session, thoughts turn to home and tears roll down my cheeks. They are not tears of sadness or happiness, just a wave of built-up emotion being set free. I'm not normally someone who shows his feelings. It's just taken a journey across hundreds of miles of icy wilderness to unlock all that pent-up emotion and make me truly appreciate what my family means to me.

The others have almost finished setting up the tents by the time I arrive at camp. A disappointing 14.4 miles gained in eight hours of travel. Call Jessy this evening to wish her happy birthday. Last night Mum and Dad took her to The Ivy for dinner – lucky devil. Salivating into the sat phone, I beg her to tell me what was on the menu, but she refuses, just saying that it was very, very good.

Text message from Patrick Ward saying that Steve Peyton was in fact 28 when he reached the Pole – a big weight off my mind. I'm furious that it took so long for ANI to provide Patrick Ward with Steve Peyton's date of birth. Paul, who can't stand all this sponsorship stuff, says the way ANI have behaved over this has created all sorts of unnecessary hassle for us over the last three days. Anyway, that should be the end of it and I hope the news will keep Hastings Direct sweet.

My lips are starting to crack.

DAY 38: FRIDAY 20 DECEMBER   139.3 MILES TO GO

Every December since university, somebody has organised a Bristol old boys' Christmas get-together where everyone dresses up in silly winter country clothing (tweed jackets, plus-twos, etc.) and has a boozy lunch in London. Today is the day of the Christmas lunch and the venue is Simpson's on the Strand. For the last few days I have been picturing exactly what they might be eating. Just before we set off, I have a surreal phone conversation with Ned.

'Hello, Ned, it's Tom calling from the Antarctic.'

'Bloody hell! I'm on the Underground on my way to the Christmas Lunch.'

'Say hello to everybody from Pat and me. We think about you all the whole time!'

'Don't worry mate, there will be lots of toasts in your honour. We've got it all planned. Stop being gay and get those kites up again! I can't believe I'm on the tube speaking to you in Antarctica and the line is this clear.' Then the phone cuts off.

Time to go to the loo. It's very cold so I have to be quick. Much more blood than yesterday. Pain is excruciating. Clear up the mess with snow wedgies before quickly coming to the conclusion that these could well be the things that triggered the haemorrhoids in the first place. Going to have to tell the others if things get any worse. I seem to remember that the French apparently blame their defeat at Waterloo on the story that Napoleon was laid up in a medical tent far away from the battlefield suffering from *'hémorroïdes diaboliques'*. I am not going to meet my Waterloo in the same way.

Thinking of food all morning. I just about keep up for the first two sessions before lagging behind again. Very disheartening. An arrival date of 28 December, which would give us the speed record, is looking next to impossible now, unless we get a few days' kiting weather. I'm just focusing on getting to the end. The South Pole is tantalisingly close but it still feels a long way off. Haven't come all this way to give up now.

It's a beautiful day – no clouds and a gentle breeze from the southeast. I've been analysing Andrew's eating habits during the day and am amazed to see he hardly eats more than a few squares of chocolate at each break. No wonder he is starving by the evening and constantly thinking about food. When I ask him why he eats so little on the march, he replies: 'I would rather binge on the extra food in the tent in the evening. It gives me something to look forward to during the day.'

Arriving at the final break 15 minutes late, I notice the others making windmills with their arms to keep warm. No sooner have I arrived than they all set off again. Whilst I have only got to know Paul and Andrew fairly recently, Pat is one of my oldest friends and I feel more let down by his lack of support than by the others'. I think back to the day in Kyrgyzstan when seven of us were making an attempt on the 16,000-foot Shining Peak. Pat was suffering from an upset stomach and quickly slipped off the pace. Whilst the rest of the team shot up the mountain, I made sure that I stayed with Pat – even though he was desperately slow. Eventually the climb proved too much for him and he was forced to make an early return to camp. Oh well.

Completely exhausted, I sit down on my sled and watch as the others file away into the distance. I allow myself a ten-minute rest before continuing. Feel dreadful. The only thing I can do is put my head down and keep plodding. It's not long before the others resemble ants on the horizon, frequently disappearing from view with all the subtle bumps and ridges in the terrain. Only once do I notice one of the others look back to check that I'm still on my feet. Maybe they are finding things just as difficult but this sudden nosedive in my performance is a real worry.

The final session is utter torture. Combination of sore shoulder and bottom – also light-headedness. Arrive into camp over 30 minutes after the others, feeling more alone than at any time on an expedition.

In the comfort of the main tent, Paul calls an urgent team meeting. I say that my biggest concern is not my own physical condition (although a major worry in itself) but that I am holding up the team. To help things out, it is decided to dish out the six-day lunch ration from my sled a day early. This will reduce the weight of my sled and should make it easier for me to stick with the others tomorrow.

27 miles ahead of the other group now. Very tired and lethargic this evening. These are dark days.

DAY 39: SATURDAY 21 DECEMBER   124.5 MILES TO GO

As we don't have enough batteries for all four of us to make hundreds of phone calls on Christmas Day, we have started telephoning our nearest and dearest. Even though I forewarned my 87-year-old grandmother I might be calling her from Antarctica, she's clearly surprised to hear me on the end of the phone this morning. In this generation of mobile phone technology, we take it for granted that we can just pick up the telephone and call anywhere in the world. I get a lump in my throat when Gran says speaking to me has made her day. Great Aunt Diana has been reading the story of Ranulph Fiennes's journey across the Antarctic continent to give her an idea of what we might be going through. She tells me she says a prayer for us every day. My final call is to Leigh Webb, a friend in London who is due to be walking down the aisle in just four hours' time. 'Webby, best of luck! So sorry I won't be there with you both on your wedding day. How are you feeling?'

'Absolutely shitting myself – but probably not as much as you guys though.'

It's a drab, overcast morning. Leave ten minutes ahead of

schedule after further binding repairs over breakfast. Feel truly awful this morning. Head all over the place and coughing like mad. The leads have been rejigged and I take over from Paul at 9.30 am. It's a real struggle and I can sense the others are getting cold and are eager to go faster. Every step I can feel the pain in my rear end and shoulder. I stop at 10 am to take some painkillers and ask Pat to take over my lead. Nobody seems overly concerned but I'm fading fast. Arrive into first break ten minutes after the others. 'You OK?' asks Paul. 'Want us to take some weight?'

'I should be alright for the next session,' I reply, trying to convince myself that an improvement is just around the corner. 'The painkillers are kicking in now and I'm going to try walking a bit as the snow looks much firmer here.'

We all set off together but I'm soon lagging way behind and watch on helplessly as the others become ever-shrinking black dots on the horizon. Feeling nauseous and really groggy. Why am I so weak? Listening to my classical compilation minidisk is not helping – every track sounds like a funeral march. The snow soon becomes softer and I am sinking in eight inches with each step. Should be on skis but don't have the energy to dig them out of my sled. A Twin Otter on its way back from the Pole passes 100 feet overhead, flashing its lights to say hello. Don't have the will to wave back.

By the time the others stop at 12.15 pm, I must be over half a mile behind. My condition is deteriorating at an alarming rate. Seemingly nothing I can do about it. Feeling increasingly nauseous and short of breath. I must tell them about the piles. Not sure if I'm going to be able to reach them. If I can just join them before they pack up to go then everything is going to be OK. Surely they won't set off without me? More exhausted than is good for me. I think back to my phone calls earlier and how positive I was about our prospects for the final leg of the expedition. If only they could see me in my sorry state now.

300 yards to go. I've decided there is no way I can continue more than a yard beyond where they are. A thick layer of ice has built up around my hood and neck – probably due to my

heavy breathing. Up ahead I can see that everyone is wearing their down jackets and throwing a ball around to keep warm. Back at Patriot Hills, I scoffed at Pat's decision to pack a tennis ball when weight was going to be so restricted but now his decision seems justified.

200 yards away and it now looks as though they are playing baseball with the tennis ball and a ski pole. All my rhythm has gone. Starting to go a bit gaga in the head. Want this all to end.

100 yards to go. I call out to them but my voice is lost on the breeze. Wave my arms frantically in the air to tell them I'm in trouble and they start walking towards me. They've been waiting nearly an hour. Staggering around like the village drunkard, I collapse to my knees. Almost there now. I pull myself up and carry on. Paul is the first to reach me and looks deeply worried. I stare back blankly, not taking in anything he says. Andrew takes my sled and after a handful more paces, I collapse on to Pat's sled. I am absolutely finished.

The day has come to an abrupt halt. The others are wonderfully supportive and set up the tent in no time. Pat bundles me inside and unpacks my gear whilst Andrew gets the stove going. Feel much better after hot chocolate and a bowl of mushroom and rice soup.

Then the discussions start. Now is as good a time as any to tell them about the piles. Genuine sympathy all round. Despite admitting to using snow wedgies for the past fortnight himself, Andrew doesn't seem too alarmed and says he will continue using them.

Paul suggests that I am probably suffering from acute altitude sickness. The low pressure system over Antarctica makes our current altitude of 9,000 feet seem more like 13,000 feet. During Paul's journey to the South Pole last year, Timo Polari apparently showed identical symptoms towards the end of the expedition, despite being the strongest member of the team. Having been the first man into camp every day, he suddenly began to struggle and was unable to keep up. Paul says: 'Your various pains are just making the whole thing worse. We'll camp here and take the rest of the day off.'

Altitude sickness, or acute mountain sickness to give it its correct medical term (AMS), is a weird one. It's caused by the thinness of the air at altitude and associated oxygen deficiency leading to fluid build-up in the lungs and brain. I normally don't suffer from AMS, despite having frequently been at altitudes of 20,000 feet or more. The only time I can recall experiencing this potentially fatal condition was on that day four years ago when I stupidly tried to climb Aconcagua on my own without allowing time to acclimatise. But here we have had 39 days to reach our current altitude, which one would think would be more than enough to adjust to it.

AMS can strike anyone at anytime. Whilst climbing in the Alps in 1999 with one of the fittest men I know, Fergus Wells (younger brother of George Wells) was struck down with AMS at the modest height of 12,000 feet. By the time Ferg was helicoptered off the mountain, he was frothing at the mouth, unconscious and at death's door. Thankfully he made a full recovery, but doctors have forbidden him from ever spending time at altitude again.

Despite the short day, the good news is that we have crossed the 88th Parallel. I am cheered further when Paul tells me that during their impromptu game of baseball, Pat's one swipe with a ski pole slashed a six-inch tear in his down jacket. And he missed the ball.

Spend much of the afternoon sleeping. Over dinner Paul says: 'Let's aim for ten miles tomorrow. We'll take some weight out of Tom's sled and take things real slow. If there's no improvement in Tom's condition within 48 hours, we'll have to think about evacuating him as there won't be enough food and fuel to get us to the Pole.'

The dreaded E word. I never thought things were as serious as this. Salvation is just a phone call away. My 'rescue' would be covered by our insurance policy and I would not have to foot any of the £50,000 evacuation costs. It would be so easy to escape. 100 years ago Scott, Shackleton and Wilson were afforded no such luxury. Despite suffering appalling hardship, their only choice was to put their heads down and keep marching. I just can't give up now. I would be letting myself and my teammates down. I must dig deep and keep pushing on, however slowly. Desperate for an improvement tomorrow. Very afraid.

We are exactly four-fifths of the way to the Pole. On my imaginary journey through Europe to Verbier, we have made it as far as the French spa town of Salins-les-Bains in the foothills of the Jura Mountains. All of a sudden the Swiss border doesn't seem so far away.

We are just 120 miles from the South Pole. I want it so badly.

Chapter Seven

POLE POSITION

Have not slept well. Racked with worry. I've got 48 hours for things to improve or the dream is over. There's nothing I can do but keep plodding on. Refuse to step onto an aeroplane until I reach the South Pole. I couldn't have wished for more supportive companions. The guys have been great, and more than willing to help take as much as 90 pounds of food supplies from my sled.

The early pace is no more than a crawl. Feelings of light-headedness return, but not as severe as of late. The rest has certainly done me good. I am embarrassed at how much lighter my sled feels and especially guilty that the others are weighed down with much of my load.

The slow going gives me a chance to reflect on the events of the last few days. Why has my condition become so fragile? How come things deteriorated so suddenly? Why me? I really don't feel there is anything I could have done to prevent what happened.

I think back to what Shackleton must have been going through during the closing stages of the Southern Journey. Not long after the three men turned for home at their furthest south on 31 December 1902, Shackleton's health took a rapid turn for the worse. As well as showing ominous signs of scurvy, he developed a hacking cough, which continued until he began coughing up blood. Wilson feared a complete breakdown in his condition and on 14 January 1903 wrote: 'Shackles has been anything but up to the mark and today he is decidedly worse, very short winded, and coughing constantly, with more serious symptoms which are of no small consequence 160 miles from

215

the ship, and full loads to pull the whole way.' Shackleton himself sounded desperately worried, commenting: 'During a halt my cough, which had been troubling me for some days, became more severe and a haemorrhage started; so I was not allowed to do any more camp work or pull ... it is most annoying. The other poor fellows have 260 pounds each to pull while I am only allowed to walk along. They are awfully good to me.'

On 18 January and with food supplies dwindling, Shackleton collapsed in his tracks after just three hours of travel. The tent was pitched and they rested until his condition improved. That night Scott wrote: 'Disappointment not to be able to go on ... It puts the old serious aspect of Shackleton's case again before us. It is no use being down about it, we must evidently be prepared to carry him.'

Although I can partially relate to how Shackleton felt about his own performance, I find it astonishing that he managed to hold himself together. I have the luxury of knowing that rescue is just a few hours away, whereas this indomitable man had no choice but to keep on marching. It is often incorrectly written that during the return journey, the men frequently had to carry Shackleton on a sled like an invalid on a stretcher. On a couple of occasions when a favourable northerly wind blew and they were able to deploy the sail, the men found that the sleds would pick up speed and slide into the back of them. To prevent this happening, Shackleton would sit on the rear sled, using a ski pole as a brake. But he was never carried.

Never one to give up, Shackleton was soon back in his harness again, although he never pulled the loads that Scott and Wilson were forced to. All three men eventually made it back to *Discovery* in one piece on 3 February – but for several weeks their safe return had been very much in the balance.

Today is the perfect day to travel, with clear skies and a light wind. After a series of short inclines in the morning, we emerge on an apparently level sastrugi-free plain, with a depthless horizon stretching in all directions. We have reached the Polar Plateau. At almost 9,000 feet above sea level now, we know that the relentless climb from Hercules Inlet is to all intents and purposes over. Compared to everything we have witnessed on our long journey so far, this is an alien world. Everything is eerily quiet and the South Pole seems tantalisingly close. God, it feels great to be here.

Since breaking camp, Pat has been a constant source of encouragement and optimism, geeing me up when I'm flagging and never once complaining about the extra weight in his sled. He and Andrew are rewarded for their unwavering patience throughout the day by being let off their leashes to set their own pace for the final session.

The day has been another struggle for me though. For much of the time I have felt lethargic and nauseous but 13.6 miles is much further than I could have hoped for when we set off and my performance has given me some encouragement. The wind is trying to shift to the east again.

I arrive into camp half an hour after the others to find Paul hopping around on one leg. It turns out that the steel pin at the front of one of his boots that clips into the ski binding has snapped off. This is the integral part of the binding system and is far more serious than our many earlier broken binding incidents. The two-inch pin is beyond repair and we have no spare boots. In the warmth of the main tent we try to work out the best way of rigging up some sort of temporary repair to the binding. Andrew is on cooking duty, whilst Pat, Paul and I fiddle around with pieces of rope and webbing in an attempt to find an effective alternative.

Two hours later and we think we have got something that will work, with various pieces of the nylon strapping screwed into the ski to hold the boot in place. Everyone has an input in the final design. The only problem is that the boot is now permanently fixed to the ski, so Paul will have to put his ski on every morning before packing up camp.

I need a haircut.

DAY 41: MONDAY 23 DECEMBER   104.1 MILES TO GO

Hoping that we might be able to get the kites up again, Andrew was up every two hours during the night to check the conditions but an easterly wind never materialised. It has been an oppressive night and despite having the tent doors wide open, I'm dripping with sweat this morning. The thermometer on my watch shows a temperature of +38°C – over 100°F. So much for this being the coldest place on Earth.

The Antarctic sun is shining in all its dazzling brilliance today and with not a breath of wind, it feels like we are in the Mediterranean. We have soon stripped down to just our thermal tops and salopettes. Although still slightly dizzy and short of breath, I'm feeling much stronger than I have done for a while.

We received a text message a few days ago, asking us to telephone Highgrove at precisely 6 pm on 23 December (1 pm Antarctica time). 'His Royal Highness would like to have a word with you,' it read. Four guys stopping in the middle of an infinite expanse of white to make a satellite phone call to royalty is about as surreal as it gets. Luckily the benign conditions mean the whole exercise of making the call in the open is as easy as speaking on a mobile phone in the middle of Hyde Park. Full of trepidation, I dial the number.

'Hello?'

I recognize the voice immediately. 'Good afternoon, Your Royal Highness, this is Tom Avery calling in from 88°23' South in the middle of the Antarctic.'

'Tom! How are you? How is everyone getting on? It must be dreadfully cold out there.'

For the next five minutes, I tell the Prince of Wales everything that has been going on since we set off. His knowledge of the polar regions is exceptional and he seems genuinely intrigued to hear how we have coped with crevasses, sastrugi and the biting polar winds. He is in the middle of thanking me for our efforts to raise money for The Prince's Trust, when I hear the telltale 'low battery' bleeps ringing in my ear. Panicking, I interrupt him mid-sentence and say: 'Sir, we better sign off now, because the batteries are running out.' I quickly thrust the phone between the others and we all shout out 'Merry Christmas, Your Royal Highness!' at the top of our voices. Just before the phone conks out altogether, I hear the Prince laughing his socks off.

For somebody as busy and important as the Prince of Wales to take the trouble to speak to us at such length means so much to us. It's the best tonic we could have had. I've never seen Paul so excited.

The rest of the day drifts by. Pat breaks a binding during the final session but at least Paul's webbing adaptation seems to have held out. Which is more than can be said for my backside. The situation downstairs is becoming more and more unbearable, and this evening I make a call to Gareth, the doctor at Patriot Hills. When I tell him what the matter is, he replies: 'You poor, poor bastard. I can't imagine what you're having to go through,' before going on to say, 'You do realise that everyone at Patriot Hills is going to hear about this.' I suppose you've got to see the funny side.

DAY 42: TUESDAY 24 DECEMBER   89.1 MILES TO GO

Another rough night – this time because an abscess the size of a football has erupted in the middle of my inflatable thermarest mattress, making sleeping particularly uncomfortable. The glue must have given way.

The change in conditions since yesterday is extraordinary. I open the tent flap to go for an early morning pee and am hit by a wave of frigid air, as if I have just opened the door to an industrial freezer.

Over the last few weeks, Andrew has given us a fascinating insight into his life in South Africa. Paul is so spellbound that he has decided to take his family to Cape Town for their next summer holiday, and over breakfast he quizzes Andrew for as much relevant tourist information as he can provide.

My condition is not as bad today, so before we break camp the fuel canisters and food bags are redistributed between the sleds so that we are all carrying the same weight. When we get going again I notice the massive increase in load and realise how much of a sacrifice the guys have made over the past 48 hours to make life easier for me. What good lads. Everyone has been upbeat and not once have they complained of the extra work.

The battery in my minidisk dies only half an hour into my 'Rock Mix' compilation, just as 'Money for Nothing' is kicking in. So with only the noise of the wind to accompany me this morning, thoughts turn to home and what will be going on in the Avery household on Christmas Eve. Dad will no doubt be cursing the Christmas tree lights which have fused – again – whilst Leo's mood will be determined solely by Arsenal's performances over the busy holiday football schedule. Mathematics has never been Mum's strong point and she'll be getting her knickers in a right old twist working out the time she will have to put the turkey in the oven. Jessy will be trying to avoid the temptation of sneakily opening a few presents on Christmas Eve. I miss being with everyone dreadfully.

Later. I am plodding along, minding my own business, when I hear a high-pitched drone buzzing around my ears like a swarm of angry mosquitoes. This is quickly followed by the dramatic sight of a Twin Otter en route to the South Pole flying less than 100 feet over our heads. We stop in our tracks as the little ski plane banks to make another pass. The smell of aviation fuel is overpowering. It is the first smell away from the tent I have been aware of since we arrived in this pristine land nearly seven weeks ago. As the Twin Otter makes its second approach, I can clearly make out the faces of grey-haired tourists peering through the windows. They are all taking photographs of us. Just as the plane passes overhead for a second time, the back door opens. We watch as an anonymous hand throws out a black package onto the snow no more than a few yards from us. I wonder what it is. Christmas cards? Whisky? More food perhaps? Clean underpants? Pat hurries over to retrieve the mystery package and we all gather round in eager anticipation.

As the plane disappears over the horizon, we find there's nothing inside but a small white box. On closer inspection in big scary writing are the words: 'PREPARATION H. SUPPOSITORIES FOR THE TREATMENT OF HAEMORRHOIDS'.

Well I've heard of manna from heaven but this is ridiculous. The other three are gutted that all we have been given is a box of suppositories.

The day comes to an end and we have covered 14.4 miles in eight hours. All hope of this speed record has long gone (unless of course there is an unexpected change in the wind). For the first time in ages I feel relatively normal today and am just about managing to stick to the group pace. I have been very short of breath but, touch wood, it looks like I am over the worst of the altitude problems. There are now more pressing medical matters to attend to. After supper, I open the Preparation H box to reveal a magazine of a dozen bullets, encased in shiny metallic packaging. My eyes water as I read the instructions:

1. Tear down the perforation to remove one suppository from the strip.
2. Gently peel down wrapping to reveal suppository.
3. Remove suppository from wrapping and insert as far as possible into the rectum, rounded end first. This is best done in a stooping position. [Just in case there is any confusion, there is a graphic illustration to show how things should be done.]

The instructions also provide very helpful information on how to prevent the onset of piles:

1. Try not to overstrain your bowels.
2. Get into a habit of opening your bowels naturally and easily every day.
3. Eat food that is rich in fibre on a regular basis.
4. Drink plenty of fluid.
5. Careful cleansing and removal of irritating matter.

Interestingly, there are no warnings about the use of snow wedgies.

A tent full of people is no place to pull one's pants down and assume a stooping position so I step out into the cold to give myself a bit of privacy. As the whole nasty business is carried out, the guys can't contain themselves and burst into raucous laughter.

The whole episode offers a bit of light relief from what has been another tough day. We broke two more bindings this afternoon and are completely out of spares. The frostbite has returned to my face and my heels are flaking off. My feet have turned an alarming shade of purple and I've had no feeling in my big toes for over a week. Our equipment and bodies are falling to bits – the end can't come soon enough.

DAY 43: WEDNESDAY 25 DECEMBER   74.7 MILES TO GO

We have ourselves a White Christmas. Other than that, it feels decidedly unfestive and everyone is deflated. The ordeal of my morning suppository insertion has done nothing to cheer me up. A large snowdrift has built up against the windward side of the tent, making things much darker and colder than usual over breakfast.

I'm still not up to full strength and Paul suggests I begin the day at my own pace whilst the others take down the tents, the theory being that over the course of the morning they will gradually catch me up. I am all harnessed up and about to clip into my skis when Pat shouts out: 'Tom, come here and give Andrew and I a hand with the tent. We may as well all leave together.'

I tell him that's not the plan we had agreed earlier but he's already turned his back to the wind and can't hear my protestations. Absolutely fuming, I take off my harness and walk over to lend a hand. After packing up his own tent, Paul comes over and asks why I am still here. I point a mittened hand directly at Pat and carry on folding up the flysheet.

Today is without doubt the coldest day of the expedition,

with the windchill approaching −50°C. Paul's early pace is much quicker than normal to stop us from getting cold. It's too quick for me, and after half an hour I have dropped back about 50 yards. I am in a filthy mood. This would never have happened if Pat hadn't stopped me going off ahead as had been agreed.

Earlier on in the expedition, a minor incident like this would not have bothered me in the slightest. Because I'm finding it difficult to drift off to my private world of daydreams, my mental state is deteriorating every day. And even though I am extremely fond of them, I'm starting to vent the frustrations of my health and variable performance on the other guys. I know that barring a disaster I can still make it to the South Pole, but every stride is going to be a miserable one.

We all manage to stick together for most of the second session until ten minutes before the end of my lead Pat storms ahead saying that the pace is too cold for him. Paul and Andrew stick with me and the three of us arrive at the 12.15 pm break together.

Everyone is starting to get on each other's nerves. I tell Pat there's no wonder he is so much faster because he is carrying less weight than everyone else. He offers to settle the dispute by swapping sleds for the next session. To my utter delight, Pat's sled feels as light as a feather and I have no problems at all keeping up with everyone. I'm sure it's more psychological than anything else and I do my best not to gloat. It's these little mind games that are helping me through these difficult times.

Some days ago we decided that provided we had enough food reserves, we would give ourselves some time off to enjoy Christmas Day. To everyone's relief, the day's sledging comes to a halt at 2.30 pm. A lazy afternoon is spent in the tents trying to celebrate Christmas Day as best we can. We've got a veritable feast to get through so we all share the cooking duties. Christmas Lunch begins with nougat and peanuts, washed down with a few gulps of whisky. This is followed by a main course of spaghetti bolognaise, complete with grated cheese. Paul pulls out a packet of cured 'Turkey Jerky' from his sled, so even here we can have a proper Christmas dinner. Spirits are lifted further after he rustles up a surprisingly good cranberry-filled rice pudding from some of the extra dinner and dried fruit rations. After the hardship of the past week all this indulgence feels, well, just like Christmas.

Our sense of wellbeing must be similar to how Scott, Shackleton and Wilson felt on this day exactly a century ago. During their ten-mile march that day, a spectacular pyramidal peak came into view off to the southwest, which they named Christmas Mountain. After pulling the sleds for seven hours, they treated themselves to triple rations, biscuits and jam and a small hot plum pudding. Shackleton had squirrelled a sprig of holly all the way from England and this was ceremoniously planted on top of the pudding. For the first time in weeks, they went to bed with their bellies full.

We all make telephone calls home, play cards and read our books. The tent is filled with its customary banter until bedtime. With batteries recharged, we are all set for the final 65 miles. Our aim is to do this in four long days of pulling. The good news is that we have crossed the Swiss border and are fast approaching Lake Geneva. Verbier seems just around the corner.

Looking forward to Marmite and a hot bath – not necessarily in that order.

DAY 44: THURSDAY 26 DECEMBER   65.2 MILES TO GO

Hardly slept a wink. I was hot and bothered overnight fretting over our ambitious plan to cover over 16 miles a day in four ten-hour days. Not sure that I'm up to the mark yet. Matters made worse by three ferocious attacks of diarrhoea before breakfast, inflaming the haemorrhoids further.

Later. I set off five minutes before the others today and manage to maintain a sizeable gap for my full hour. Not only does it feel great to be out in front in my own space for a change but it does wonders for my morale, as this is the first sign that I am at last returning to full strength.

Throughout Pat's session, I keep glancing over my left shoulder at a dark bank of cloud in the northeast that has been inching towards us all morning. I am particularly excited as I can start to feel the faintest of breezes on my left cheek. There are signs that this weather front will bring about a change in wind direction and we'll be able to go kiting again.

Pat's sled comes to a halt at 10.30 am precisely. I pull up alongside him and ask: 'Are you thinking what I'm thinking?' He's already grinning from ear to ear as he begins to nod enthusiastically. The others are soon with us and after some initial hesitancy from Paul, we are soon unpacking the kites and putting our harnesses on. The wind is blowing at no more than five knots but it should be enough to get going. I just hope Paul's makeshift boot binding is up to the rigours of kiting.

By the time we're under way, the cloudbank has caught up with the sun and the light is deteriorating fast. It's also snowing a little. I tug on the handles and watch anxiously as my kite grudgingly lifts itself off the ground. We're moving, but only just. For the next two hours, we drift through the murk, working the kites like mad to generate enough power to keep us moving. It's not clear if the hassle of setting everything up and all this hard work is actually paying dividends. However, the smooth surface of the Polar Plateau is a joy to kite across and makes a welcome change from the last time we tried the kites in these conditions, when I spent much of the time on my backside. Furthermore, we have crossed the 89th Parallel – the last line of latitude before the Pole.

The wind picks up in the afternoon. This coincides with the sun dissolving away into the most dramatic sky I have ever seen. The sun is surrounded by not one, but two perfectly circular rainbows, or parhelia to give them their technical name. Around the edge of the inner sphere we can see four smaller suns at three, six, nine and twelve o'clock. The six o'clock sun tries desperately to burn through some wispy clouds in the far distance, giving the illusion that the southwestern horizon is ablaze. As if that wasn't enough, a horizontal white ring which looks not unlike an aircraft's vapour trail circles the sky above us, bisecting our ring of suns precisely at three and nine o'clock.

Impossibly fine ice crystals rain down from a deep azure sky, as if a magician has zapped this special place with his wand. One of Mother Nature's great celestial displays of light and colour is unfolding around us.

Our incomparably beautiful sky provides the perfect backdrop for our afternoon's kiting. We're going along at a fair old lick now and really eating up the miles to the Pole. Andrew seems to be finding the kiting a little harder today and on several occasions we have to wait for him to catch up. He's also having difficulty following the same course as the rest of us, drifting further west than we would like. But any delays are very short, and now with a moderate wind we are averaging well over twice the speed we would be doing if we were pulling our sledges. We have all found a wonderful rhythm with kites, bodies and skis moving along in perfect unison. God, this is so much fun!

Just as I start to harbour thoughts of the wind blowing us all the way to the Pole, the wind dies down. It's 6 pm and we've covered a staggering 28 miles (not all of it in the right direction) and now find ourselves just 41 miles from the Pole itself. It feels so close. Surely nothing can go wrong now.

DAY 45: FRIDAY 27 DECEMBER   40.8 MILES TO GO

We set off under a rich royal blue sky, with a gentle headwind blowing in our faces. The terrain has completely changed since we arrived on the lofty Polar Plateau. Thanks to the calmer conditions up here, the sastrugi have almost entirely disappeared and the snow is as fresh and powdery as if it fell overnight. But whilst the flatter surface means we can steer a much straighter course, the sled runners sink into the soft snow, making the sled itself feel much heavier than it actually is. Getting the things to move at all requires more of an effort than we're used to – a job made all the more exhausting in the thin air. Luckily the suppositories seem to have done the trick and with much less discomfort in the downstairs department, my leg movement is unrestricted.

After the first break, Andrew sets off uncharacteristically slowly. We've only been going for five minutes and he turns round to ask if the speed is OK. Sensing everyone's frustration at our current crawl, I ask him to speed things up a bit. For reasons known only to him, he promptly goes from second gear into fifth. I've never seen him go this fast. In a desperate bid to keep up, I'm soon panting and sweating uncontrollably. Part of me feels like yelling at him to slow down but on the other hand I don't want to give him the gratification of seeing us unable to keep up. For half an hour we all manage to maintain his ridiculous pace before Paul comes up alongside me and says: 'This is way too fast. I want to slow down myself and I think you should too. I don't want you breaking down again. Let's leave him to it.'

Moments later Pat too drops back, leaving Andrew to tear off into the distance. I'm spitting mad. Maybe he feels he has something to prove after lagging behind several times during yesterday's kiting. We've drummed it into his head countless times how unproductive these aggressive spurts of his are, but he seems determined to ignore us. By the time his stint has come to an end and we have eventually caught up with him, I completely blow my top. 'What the bloody hell do you think you're trying to do? You were practically running back then. We're supposed to be working as a team and you had us all strung out like ants.'

Andrew mutters sheepishly, 'But you told me to speed up.'

Paul joins in, saying, 'But not that much! That was way too fast, Andrew. Now is not the time to start sprinting ahead.'

I feel much better to have let off a bit of steam. The going is still tough but the South Pole is just around the corner and I can't wait to get there. I'm munching away on a particularly chewy piece of flapjack at the second break when Pat turns to me and says, 'Tommy, if we have a big day today and another one tomorrow, we'd be pretty much at the Pole.'

'Say that again.'

'I've been thinking about this all morning. If we put in an eighteen-mile day today, we could have a good night's sleep and polish off the remaining twenty-three tomorrow. And we've always said how cool it would be to cover the same distance as a marathon in a single day.'[1]

I pause for a moment before saying, 'You know what, Pat, that's the best idea you've ever had. I think we could do it but we would be absolutely knackered.'

The idea of putting in an extra spurt to get to the Pole a day early fills me with excitement and I lead off the next session full of beans. Rather than knocking off the remaining mileage in three relatively straightforward legs of just under 14 miles each, we would be finishing the expedition with two long, tiring days. Although we probably won't feel it at the time, by arriving at our final destination with nothing left to give, we would have the satisfaction of knowing we had given our all to reach the Pole. We would be going out on a real high.

The afternoon flies by and it's soon 3.45 pm – the last break of the day. Paul pulls out his GPS and announces we've covered 13.2 miles in $6\frac{1}{2}$ hours. I'm tired but keen to press on.

I lean across to Andrew. 'I've been thinking about Pat's ambitious little scheme and I'm well up for it. What are your thoughts?'

'I don't see the point,' he replies, looking decidedly miserable. 'We've got our plan and I think we should stick to it.'

I'm gobsmacked. Ever since the start of the expedition, Andrew has been a powerhouse – the strongest member of the team. He's not a particularly big guy but I have never come across someone with such a high level of natural fitness and endurance. When he was growing up in South Africa, his mother was so worried about his abnormally high energy levels she made him take a daily dose of the tranquilliser drug Ritalin to calm him down. There have been times when I wish I could have slipped a couple of tablets into his water bottle myself. I have lost count of the number of times one of us has had to tell him to slow down but now he wants us to take things easy. I just don't understand.

[1] 23 nautical miles equates to 26.5 statute miles.

'If we wanted to, we could just keep going until we get there.' It's the first time Paul has spoken in hours and everyone turns to him in disbelief. 'You've always said how you wanted to end the expedition with a bang.'

It's not clear if he's pulling our leg or not so Pat pulls back Paul's goggles and face mask so we can see his face. He's grinning from ear to ear.

'You're not being serious are you?' asks Pat.

'Absolutely. We've got twenty-seven miles still to go, which will mean seven or eight two-hour sessions. It will be the longest day of my polar career but I think we can do it. Conditions for travel are superb and I think our bodies are up to it. Have a think about it over the next two hours.'

With not another word spoken, we clip into our bindings and pole away. What Paul is proposing seems like utter madness – a final leg of 41 sleepless miles would represent nearly *two* marathons, not one. It all makes Pat's earlier idea seem like a stroll in the park. Nobody has ever attempted to reach the Pole from this far out in a single push. It would represent one of the longest continuous marches in polar history. And if we make it before tomorrow evening, we would be the fastest team to make the journey to the South Pole. Talk about finishing with a bang.

My mind is made up when far ahead of me I spot a flash of light just above the horizon. The long grey smudge behind it tells me that I'm looking at a Hercules aeroplane coming in to land at the American science base at the South Pole. Moments later, another plane comes in to land. Although the buildings at the base remain out of view, for the first time on the expedition it feels as though the end is in sight. An ugly streak of aviation pollution is a long way from the image I had built up of our first view of the Pole but I now know that I will make it. But I'm also fully aware that the next 20 or so hours are going to be the most demanding of my life.

6 pm. Decision time. Everyone gathers round for a team get-together. Paul is first to speak. 'The way I see things, we've got three options. One, we stick to the original plan, camp here and have two gentle days of about twelve miles each. Two, we go

for Pat's idea, push on for another two hours tonight, camp and have another long day tomorrow. Or three, we camp for a couple of hours now, have a bite to eat, fill up water bottles and set off for the Pole later this evening. Tom?'

'I think we should go for the Pole tonight. I'm tired but I feel good enough to carry on. As long as you think we're capable of doing this.'

'I think we can do this.'

Andrew now seems to have come round to the idea of pushing on. 'I'm pretty keen. Let's get some food down us and go for it.'

Pat's turn comes next. 'Yeah, I feel the same as the other guys,' he says unconvincingly, before some doubts start to creep in. 'But do you really think we can make it, Paul? I'm already pretty bushed and not so sure I'm up to this. We could always pitch the tents in the middle of the night if we started to get really tired.'

This does not go down well with Paul. He believes that once we set out to do something as ambitious as this, we have to abide by that decision until that aim is achieved. If one of us decides to throw in the towel early on, it would completely defeat the object of what we are trying to do. It was just the same on the first day of the expedition when he asked for our full commitment in taking full sleds to Hercules Inlet and avoiding the Patriot Hills camp on our way south.

Speaking to us in an almost Churchillian manner, Paul goes on: 'This is a key moment in the expedition. If we're going to go for this, we cannot go about things half-heartedly. We all need to be committed one hundred per cent. Once we make the decision to go, we go. We only stop if there's a rapid deterioration in the weather or if somebody injures themselves. Is everybody in?'

Just as a collective decision has been made to go for our all-night assault, I start feeling faint and stumble back onto my sled.

After a couple of light-headed minutes wondering whether we have made the right decision, I am back on my feet helping the others set up the tent for dinner.

Both Jason and Jamie are on the line when Paul makes the evening sat-phone call to Patriot Hills. After giving them our present position of 89°36'S, Paul says: 'We're just going to carry on for a little bit and pitch camp a few miles further south.'

Once he's hung up, I ask, 'Why didn't you tell them what we're really up to?'

'They wouldn't like it. Nobody's tried to do what we're attempting and Jamie would try to dissuade us, particularly as they know you have been ill. And besides, I can't stand other people trying to run my expeditions from hundreds of miles away.'

Over the course of a hurried dinner, we get the real explanation why Andrew decided to burn off in front this morning. 'You told me that my pace was too slow. I was feeling pretty sweet, so I decided to crank it up a bit. And shortly after Tommy and Paul had dropped behind, Pat, who was clearly struggling to keep up goes, "Mate, slow down. You're losing the others." I just thought to myself, "Yeah, well any moment now, I'm going to lose you as well."' That guy is officially the most competitive I have ever met.

9.30 pm and we're out of the tent again packing up the sleds – possibly for the final time. Thanks to a hearty meal of chicken soup and spaghetti bolognaise, our batteries are fully recharged and we're ready to go. I'm more nervous than I have been in weeks, but raring to go. Goodness knows how things are going to pan out. We all shake hands, wish each other the best of luck and then, with no further ado, we set off into the bright sunshine of the polar night.

DAY 46: SATURDAY 28 DECEMBER   ABOUT 20 MILES TO GO

Antarctica is unrecognisable at this early hour. The skies are clear, the winds are calm, but the sun is no longer behind us. It's midnight and the sun has swung round to the south. Even with dark ski goggles on, the light is blinding and we are forced to look down at our ski tips. I never expected that I would feel the warmth of the sun's rays this close to the South Pole. The

Polar Plateau appears to be much more uneven than before, with even the smallest hummocks and troughs accentuated by the effect of the shadow.

2 am. We're having navigational problems. Because all the lines of longitude converge towards the Pole, it's becoming increasingly difficult to follow a particular gridline and maintain a straight course. Have to make constant checks with the compass and GPS. Right idiots we're going to look if we get the direction-finding so wrong that we end up skiing right past the Pole and missing it altogether.

I'm looking at my watch far too regularly – it feels as though time is standing still. For every minute that ticks by, we are about 100 strides or 60 yards closer to the Pole. We have made nearly 1,500,000 strides to get this far but these final few thousand are by far the hardest. Must stop counting down the clock but finding something else to distract me is impossible. Feel totally brainwashed and light-headed. It's as if I'm being slowly tortured. The end will come but it's a long way off.

3 am. Been going for some time now and I'm starting to feel very tired. The legs are still working fine but my head is all over the place. It feels detached from the rest of my body. My INXS and Dire Straits minidisk has done a great job in keeping me going for the last few hours, but the battery has run out and the only sounds are the metronomic glide of the skis and the whine of the wind.

All my powers of determination are needed to keep my ski tips glued to the back of Andrew's sled. It's like I'm driving along an empty motorway in the middle of the night with no car stereo. There's nothing to look at or listen to and it's a constant battle to keep my eyelids open. It would be so easy to shut them for just a few seconds. Sporadic whiffs of spaghetti bolognaise drift over from Andrew's salopettes and are impossible to avoid. The aroma is utterly foul but surprisingly it helps me stay awake.

4.30 am. Clunk. Too comatose to realise Andrew has decided to stop, I ski straight into the back of his sled and almost fall over. It's time for a break. We've done three two-hour sessions since dinner, during which time we've covered 11 miles. Just over 13 more to go. On my map of Europe, that puts us near the town of Martigny at the foot of the Swiss Alps – the long climb up the hair-pinned road to Verbier promises to be an arduous one. Pat and I are finding these stints too much to bear and ask for them to be reduced to $1\frac{1}{2}$ hours each.

5.15 am. We're halfway through my lead. Even harder to stay awake with no sled in front to distract me. With the sun way off to the left now and its glare greatly diminished, I am able to look ahead. We should be catching our first glimpse of the Pole soon, and throughout my shift I keep my eyes peeled in the hope of being the one who spots it. And then suddenly there it is – three dark rectangular specks appear in the distance. I stop in my tracks and start waving my ski poles jubilantly. 'Guys, there it is – it's the bloody South Pole!'

Andrew pulls up alongside me. 'I don't see anything.'

'Can you not see those three buildings on the horizon?'

'Erm, maybe. Not quite sure.'

We're still some way out but my speed increases noticeably, buoyed up by my discovery. For the next ten minutes I keep my eyes locked on the buildings ahead, desperate not to lose sight of them. They are getting closer all the time.

Just as I'm starting to think how refreshing it feels to have a visible goal to set our sights on, I hear shouting behind me. I turn round to see Andrew and Pat pointing their ski poles at three black objects on a bearing a good 30° west of where I have been leading them. The shapes are clearly manmade with the sun reflecting off their metallic sides. What an absolute plonker. Moments later it turns out that my buildings were no more than innocuous lumps of sastrugi. We nearly skied right past the South Pole after all.

7 am. Don't think I can take much more of this. No longer able to keep with the pace and now a good 200 yards behind Paul and Andrew. Pat also struggling and some distance behind me. The water bottles have been empty for some time so we're going to have to stop soon to melt more snow. Dry mouth and parched throat are only making feelings of giddiness more

acute. Morale plummets further when we drop into a giant depression and the buildings disappear from view altogether. Feet in agony and leg muscles tightening with every stride.

7.45 am. Impromptu breakfast stop nine miles short of our goal. Sudden diarrhoea attack forces me to drop my trousers before I've even had the chance to unclip from my chest harness.

Once the tent is set up, we all collapse inside, wearing everything bar our outer boots. Pat and I are in absolute pieces and unable to say a word. Paul is amazing and prepares hot chocolate for everyone, whilst at the same time melting snow for the water bottles. I am utterly incapable of doing anything and within minutes I'm drifting off into a deep sleep.

Paul quickly wakes me. 'Tom, you must stay awake at all costs,' he says, before thrusting an unappetising bowl of muesli in my lap. It's no use. Soon I'm asleep again, spoon still in hand. Paul refuses to give up and slaps me across the leg. Pat is also trying to nod off.

10.15 am. We're under way again. I feel much better with some food and fluid inside me. For the first time in ages the weather closes in, and I've soon lost all sense of direction. We'll have to make regular compass and GPS checks until the buildings re-emerge. I hope we don't make any more wrong turnings. The canyon seems to go on for ever and it's a good two hours before we emerge on the far side and the buildings come into view again.

The true scale of this sprawling scientific complex soon becomes frighteningly clear. Even though I've read much about the American base at the Pole, nothing could have prepared me for the sight ahead of us. Countless blue, green and yellow structures are dotted haphazardly over a wide area, like portacabins on a construction site. At the far right-hand end of the sprawling monstrosity is a long line of radio masts, which run alongside the snow runway. At over two miles in length, it's one of the longest runways on Earth. To the left there's a large geodesic dome, not dissimilar to the Eden Project in Cornwall, alongside a large yellow building on stilts. The place looks like something from a Doctor Who movie. This is the first sign of human civilisation we have seen in nearly seven weeks and even though we knew that we would find it here, it paints a sad picture. When Captain Scott finally reached the South Pole on the 1910–12 *Terra Nova* Expedition he wrote: 'Great God, this is an awful place.' If only he could see the place now.

1.45 pm. Three miles out from the Pole we ski past an old meteorological balloon, embedded in a snowdrift. It's a sorry sight. Ten minutes later, we all have to help Andrew untangle a long elastic cord from some sort of discarded radio box that has wrapped itself round one of his skis. All my childhood fantasies of a romantic arrival at the Pole are quickly evaporating.

I'm going to put the feelings of disappointment to the back of my mind and try to savour the final moments of the journey. We are no more than three miles away from the South Pole now, the place I have wanted to be so badly for so long. I think of the obstacles we have overcome to get here and what we have achieved, and as I think of Mum and Dad and how proud this will make them, my eyes well up with tears. I remember with great fondness the laughs we have had and the camaraderie we have shared. I think how lucky we have been to have such a special person as Paul at the helm.

I cannot imagine a better bunch of guys to have shared this adventure with. Out here every character flaw is exposed for all to see. We've had our fair share of discomfort and hardship, but in over 600 miles of sledging my friends have never once complained, stopped smiling or lost sight of our goal. They have been great companions. Being able to laugh at our own inevitable misfortunes, and not taking ourselves too seriously has probably helped us to keep our sanity. We have had the time of our lives, but soon the expedition will be over, we will go our separate ways and I know things will never be the same.

2 pm. I'm not a picture of health and have to make a couple of emergency roadside diarrhoea stops, which leave me trailing behind the others. I arrive at our second break since breakfast to find Andrew bent over double and complaining about stomach

cramps. It turns out he ate three bowls of muesli this morning and he looks far from comfortable.

3 pm. Not long to go now. I cannot begin to imagine how much Scott and his men had already suffered by the time they arrived at this place on 17 January 1912. The sight of Amundsen's discarded tent at the Pole must have come as a hammer-blow, as it told Scott that somebody had beaten him to the ultimate prize. As if that wasn't bad enough, his despondent party then had to turn around and retrace their tracks all the way back to McMurdo Sound. To put Scott's final journey into perspective, he was on the move for 146 days – today is only our 46th. It's kind of spooky to think that his body lies entombed somewhere in this vast volume of ice and snow beneath our feet. I wonder what he would have made of our amateur little escapade.

3.20 pm. 800 yards from the Pole, we approach the long line of radio masts and a sign which reads 'WARNING. DO NOT CROSS RUNWAY WHEN RED LIGHTS ARE FLASHING.' Fortunately, no lights are flashing and we carry on our way. With no more than 400 yards left, Paul breaks another binding. It just had to happen. We're out of spares so swap the broken ski with one of Pat's kiting skis.

3.30 pm. Depending on which way up you're looking, we're approaching the bottom of the planet. With the weight of the world on top of me, I can't help but feel a little bit like Atlas. Not far from the base's main building, a four-foot-high steel rod protrudes through the ice. It precisely marks 90 degrees south, the place where the Earth's lines of longitude and all its different time zones meet. From this timeless spot, the only direction is north. The globe spins around this exact point. Any minute now we will be able to walk right round the world in just three seconds. With just one sunrise and one sunset each year, and an average temperature of −49°C, it is a unique place. The Antarctic Treaty stipulates that nobody owns the South Pole, but one could easily be fooled by the conspicuous Stars and Stripes fluttering in the breeze beside the polar marker.

3.34 pm. We cover the final few yards four abreast, my heart beating like crazy. Right on cue the cloud starts to melt away and we are bathed in watery sunshine. Two scientists, kitted out in red overalls and goggles, wait for us a few yards from the Pole, clapping us in. It's all very surreal. We stop a couple of paces short of the Pole itself and place our hands round a single ski pole. After a few words from Paul, it is planted in the snow. We hug, laugh and slap each other on the back. We've made it.

Chapter Eight

GREAT SCOTT

Sunday 28 December 2003

Twelve months have passed since we unclipped from our skis
and removed our sled harnesses for the final time, and I have
found the process of returning to the normality of everyday life
a real struggle. For the best part of two years I had been totally
focused on reaching one precise spot on the map. Nothing else
seemed to matter. But the moment we arrived at the South Pole
and my dream had been fulfilled, my life had no obvious path
to follow. I was overwhelmed by a feeling of lassitude, often
finding it too much effort to talk or even think.

Within five minutes of arriving at the Pole, most of the
Amundsen-Scott base's 200 residents spilled out onto the ice,
and gathered around us. Much to our initial confusion, a man
clutching a tape-measure announced: 'We've got to move the
Pole.' They hadn't come to greet us after all. We were told that
the ice at the Pole drifts towards the coast at a rate of precisely
32 feet and $3\frac{1}{2}$ inches a year, so every year the polar marker has
to be returned to the exact spot that represents 90 degrees south.
If it were left alone, the South Pole would drop into the sea in
120,000 years' time. By a complete coincidence, the Pole-moving
ceremony takes place on the final Saturday of the year and we
were on hand to help the scientists move the South Pole to its
rightful position.

We camped a snowball's throw away from the new Pole,
happy in the knowledge that we had become the fastest team
in history to get here. Thanks to a phenomenal kiting day and
our refusal to fall asleep on the last day, we had covered the
final degree of latitude in just 53 hours – a full day faster than
anyone had managed before. The 'fastest team' record was

more than a little tenuous however. In 1996–7, the Norwegian Borge Ousland reached the Pole a full *ten* days before us. What made his feat all the more astonishing was the fact that he was travelling solo and unsupported from the Weddell Sea coast – 125 miles further away from the Pole than Hercules Inlet. And as if that wasn't enough to qualify him for the 'hardest man that ever lived' award, he then continued all the way to the other side of Antarctica. But because Ousland was travelling on his own, we could just about get away with calling ourselves the fastest team.

Paul had entered the record-books himself by becoming the first man to reach three Poles (the South twice, the North once) in a single calendar year – a phenomenal achievement that will probably never be repeated. However, he seemed more excited about arriving in such good time because it meant that he could get back to Montreal to make his Rolling Stones concert.

Paul's achievement notwithstanding, our records count for next to nothing in the grand scheme of polar exploration, so I was completely taken aback with the huge volume of media calls I had to field that night. The first person I spoke to was an enthusiastic Terry Lloyd from ITN. 'Tom, I knew all along that you would do it! Many congratulations to you and your team. I'm chuffed to bits for you.'

It was great to hear from Terry again. I was up until the early hours giving interviews (most of which were live) to radio stations, television news channels and newspaper reporters, when all I wanted to do was go to bed. Unbeknown to me at the time, our story had hit the headlines, and for the best part of two days television crews and an assortment of journalists were camped out on the driveway at my parents' home in Sussex, desperate for more news from the 'intrepid adventurers'.

The day after arriving at the Pole we were given a tour of the base, culminating in a 40-minute presentation by Jerry Marty, the base's chief scientist, about the environmental and astrological research the Americans do. Maybe it had something to do with the stale artificial light and balmy temperature of the room into which we were herded, but I felt decidedly queasy throughout his lecture. Everything we were told went in one ear and out the other and I was soon half asleep. As we walked round the base that afternoon, we kept our eyes peeled for Angela, the legendary red-haired snow-plough driver who Devon had told us to look out for. Sadly she was nowhere to be found.

After 24 hours at the South Pole a Twin Otter was dispatched to take us home. There was very little talking during the six-hour flight back to Patriot Hills. As we skimmed over the exact route across which we had spent the last 45 and a bit days slogging our guts out, all four of us sat glued to our windows, lost in our own private thoughts. 20 minutes after takeoff, we passed Matty's team, waving ski poles like mad, and I couldn't help but think I was happy not to be down there with them. They would eventually become the first team to reach the Pole in 2003, arriving five days after us, and a fortnight before our American friends Will Cross and Jerry Petersen.

Our flight north was utterly spellbinding, particularly as we knew the route so intimately. The instantly recognisable figures of the Lewis Nunatak and the Ice Escarpment first came into view, quickly followed by the frozen splendour of the Thiel Mountains. The treacherous blue ice around Windy Corner seemed to have lost its menace, shimmering in the midnight sun like a tropical lagoon. Even though our cruising altitude was no more than 300 feet above the polar snows, the terrain beneath us appeared completely flat. There was no sign of the sastrugi or steep climbs that had been the bane of our lives for so long. Antarctica now appeared very tame. Soon we would be touching down at Patriot Hills, where we would wait for the Ilyushin to bring us back to civilisation.

The flight from the Pole was the first of seven that we needed to make before we would be back on home soil. It gave me the chance to reflect on our great journey and what it meant to me. There were many times before and during the expedition when it seemed highly unlikely that we would ever make it to the South Pole. Altitude, errant boots, untamed kites, forgotten skis, depthless crevasses, sponsorship dramas, broken bindings, a malicious mug, and a plethora of snow wedgies had all threatened to terminate the expedition for one or all of us. Then just when it looked as though the dream was over, things took a marked turn for the better. Maybe somebody had been looking down on us, or maybe we just got lucky.

Deep down I knew that it had been worth it, and as I looked across at my three friends I knew they were going through similar emotions. I had experienced the spectacular white crucible of the frozen continent that had drawn Captain Scott south a century before us. I knew now what it was like to be alone on the largest ice cap on Earth with a team of close companions, to live in a tent for weeks on end and to pull a sled for hundreds of gruelling miles. I had felt the raw polar winds on my face and the numbing cold in my fingers. As I looked down at the snowfields for a final time, a place that, despite some difficult moments, had given us so many happy days, I knew that I would miss it. For the first time in my life I felt that I understood Antarctica and could judge for myself the place, and the men who first ventured there. I felt privileged to have been given this unique opportunity but at the same time I was relieved that it was all over. I felt content.

Less than an hour before we were due to leave Chile, Santiago was rocked by an earthquake. At the time I was sitting on the loo by the departure gate at Santiago Airport, and felt more terrified and vulnerable than I ever had been in Antarctica. As dust started to fall around me and with people in the corridors outside openly screaming, I joined in the general sense of panic and dashed out of the cubicle, desperately trying to pull up my trousers at the same time. Expecting the Gents to have emptied immediately, I was surprised to see an old man still there, mopping the floor and smoking a cigarette. He calmly told me that 'the terminal won't fall down' and I should go back to finish what I was doing.

We touched down at Heathrow during the worst snowstorm to hit the capital in a decade. Despite being surrounded by snow for nearly two months, it was a sight that still filled me with childish wonder. Four inches of fresh powder lay on the ground – more snow than had fallen during our entire time in the whitest continent on Earth. The whole world had gone topsy-turvy. I learned that the country was on the verge of invading Iraq and the nuclear stand-off in North Korea had reached crisis-point. Most terrifying of all, six of my friends had decided to get engaged whilst we had been in Antarctica, and another two had become pregnant. It was as if I had been gone for years. It all just added to my feelings of disillusionment and general confusion about the hectic world that I had returned to. I was suffering from culture shock in my own back yard.

For some time I didn't know what to do with myself. I seemed to spend most of January making visits to the physiotherapist, who successfully managed to put my damaged shoulder back together again. Readjusting to everyday life took longer than I anticipated. It took some time to rediscover my knife and fork skills, whilst sleeping in the dark just didn't feel normal. The frostbite marks on my cheeks refused to go away, although they proved to be useful conversation-starters at dinner parties.

Whilst it was great to catch up with family and friends again, being transported from a seemingly empty continent to the most overcrowded city in Europe left me shellshocked. Civilisation now seemed restricted, superficial and boring. People routinely commented on how 'spaced out' I had become and how my attention span had reduced to that of a toddler. I had to escape. Within three weeks of coming home, I abandoned all the grown-up ideas I had harboured on the Ice about finding a proper job, withdrew the meagre funds from my savings account and headed out to my beloved Verbier for the rest of the winter to ski, climb and start work on this book.

One year since we arrived at the South Pole and I feel as though I am just about back to my usual self again. Having vowed that the Commonwealth South Pole Centenary Expedition would be my last big adventure, I have found myself putting together the next trip – to the North Pole in early 2005 with much the same team. It will be an adventure very different from our southern journey and I can hardly wait.

*

Trawling through diaries, expedition reports and archive photographs from the *Discovery* Expedition has given me a fascinating insight into how those men survived on the Ice for over two years and what drew them into the unknown. Whilst writing this book, I have often asked myself what would have happened if Scott, Shackleton and Wilson had pushed even further south than they did. Had Michael Barne's team not been sent back to the ship so early, the Southern Party would have been much more appropriately supported for the journey across the Ross Ice Shelf. The dogs would not have become so tired and disheartened, negating the need to shuttle the supplies in exhausting relays. The men would surely have reached the mouth of the Beardmore Glacier, a little over 100 miles beyond the point of their furthest south. Not only would their discovery have proven conclusively that Antarctica was a continent, but it would also have shown the men the gateway to the South Pole. With another season's sledging ahead of them, Scott could well have changed the expedition's plans altogether and launched an all-out assault on the Pole the following spring.

But their unveiling of Antarctica would have also led to complications. If we assume that the Southern Party would still have turned for home around the same date, 31 December 1902, and that Shackleton would have succumbed to scurvy at the same time, then an already fraught return journey would have been made even more perilous. The chances of Shackleton covering the extra mileage and making it back to the ship alive would have been very slim indeed. One even has to question whether the increased distance would have proved too much for Scott and Wilson. Should something like that have occurred, as it so nearly could have done, the whole course of polar history would have been drastically altered.

Ten days before the Southern Party returned to the ship, *Morning*, a relief ship sent by Sir Clements Markham in case *Discovery* had run into difficulties, dropped anchor in McMurdo Sound. Large amounts of fresh food, fuel and other provisions were delivered, along with a year's worth of mail to the ship's crew. With twelve months to go before *Discovery* itself was due to leave Antarctica, the extra provisions, particularly the fruit and vegetables, proved very welcome.

The arrival of *Morning* also gave Scott the chance to send back any individual whose health might be put at risk by a second season's sledging. After the three men had had a chance to recover from the ordeal of the Southern Journey, they were given a thorough medical examination by the expedition doctor, Reginald Koettlitz. Whilst he deemed that Shackleton had practically recovered from his earlier breakdown, he added, 'I cannot say that he would be fit to undergo hardships and exposure in this climate.' Wilson appeared to agree with the doctor, writing, 'It is certainly wiser for him to go home.'

On 2 March a reluctant and dejected Ernest Shackleton was helped aboard *Morning* before the ship embarked on her long voyage back to England. Scott and the entire shore party waved from the ice edge as the wooden whaler steamed out of the bay. For Shackleton, the humiliation of being invalided home was too much to bear, and shortly after the assembled gathering had disappeared from view he broke down in tears.

It has often been written that Scott forced Shackleton off the ice because he felt threatened by the presence of another strong and determined character amongst his team. Scott's hostile biographer Roland Huntford went so far as to say, 'No leader can tolerate a rival ... There was no place for Shackleton and Scott on *Discovery* and Shackleton had to go.'

In my view, the reality is very different. There is no evidence of there being any bad blood between the two characters. If Scott disliked his companion so much, then sending him home to face the British press would have posed a far greater threat to the public image of his expedition and the credibility of his leadership than keeping him on the Ice. Indeed, in his account of their great southern effort, Scott wrote, 'As much as I regret parting with him, I do not think the health of an executive officer should be in any doubt,' before going on to say, 'Shackleton, who returns much to my regret, should be of the greatest use in explaining the details of our position and our requirements for the future.' In all of Shackleton's public and private writings about his experiences in Antarctica, there is no evidence of bitterness, or of unfair treatment by Scott, only heartfelt praise.

Discovery's work continued for another year. For the last two months of 1903, Scott led a small party due west from *Discovery* along a route pioneered the previous summer by his second-in-command, Albert Armitage, that led through the Transantarctic Mountains to the high plateau of Victoria Land. It had still to be proven whether Victoria Land was just a large sub-Antarctic island, or if it was part of a much larger continent. Scott, along with two of his fittest men, Bill Lashly and Taff Evans, pushed on at a punishing speed, pulling their sledges beyond Armitage's 'farthest west'. They hoped to find the western shore of Victoria Land, if indeed one existed. Despite making a formidable return journey of nearly 600 miles, most of it at altitudes of 8,000 feet, no coastline was ever sighted. Scott reasoned (correctly) that the ice cap continued for hundreds of miles and that it was probably part of a larger continent – his Terra Incognita.

At the same time as Scott was making his westward push, other sledging journeys were launched from *Discovery* that would also yield significant results to help solve the mystery of the frozen continent. Michael Barne led a party south towards the inlet at 80°S that now bears his name. He discovered that an immense glacier (now called the Byrd Glacier) filled the channel, not the flat ice shelf that he was expecting. This suggested that the coastline, discovered by Scott, Shackleton and Wilson the previous summer, was continuous and not the polar archipelago that was initially believed. Barne also collected pink and grey chunks of granite, proving the coastline's continental nature.

A sledging journey led by Hartley Ferrar to Finger Mountain would add yet more weight to the possible existence of a southern continent when he discovered fossilised plant remains. Fossils had never been found so far south. Unbeknown to the young geologist at the time, his find would prove that Antarctica once had a temperate climate and was part of the supercontinent of Gondwanaland. Ferrar was working some years before the science of plate tectonics was fully understood, which would eventually show that continents could drift across the face of the globe over the course of millions of years.

Other noteworthy scientific discoveries showed that the Great Ice Barrier was a floating ice shelf hundreds of thousands of square miles in area, which flowed inexorably northwards. New species of wildlife were discovered and others were studied in much greater detail than they had ever been before. On a bitterly cold September visit to the emperor penguin colony at Cape Royds, Wilson made the astonishing revelation that these incredible birds lay their eggs in the depths of the Antarctic winter. Magnetic observations made throughout the two years that *Discovery* was moored in McMurdo Sound helped pinpoint the exact location of the Magnetic South Pole – a vital aid to navigation in the southern seas. And to cap it all off, during his descent from the high plateau of Victoria Land, Scott stumbled upon the magnificent Dry Valleys – otherworldly ice-free canyons which have seen no rainfall in over two million years. It was one of the expedition's great geographical finds.

Scott knew that the mountain of evidence collected during the previous two years strongly hinted that Antarctica was indeed the vast southern continent that he had hoped. His belief would later be confirmed by the scientific establishment in London, which heaped lavish praise on the young officer. The Norwegian explorer Fridtjof Nansen described the expedition's findings as 'magnificent'. As *Discovery* weighed anchor on 17 February 1904 and turned for home, Scott must have felt delighted and proud of what his expedition had uncovered. And rightly so. As well as answering some of the most pressing scientific questions of the day, he had penetrated deep into the heart of the unknown continent and opened the possibility for a future assault on the Pole.

Back in England, Scott became an overnight hero. At a time when national pride had suffered a dent after the setbacks of the recent Boer War, the gruelling sledging journeys of Scott's men caught the public's imagination. The British National Antarctic Expedition of 1901–4 gave birth to the period known as the Heroic Age of Antarctic Exploration, which culminated in the race for the Pole and Shackleton's dramas aboard *Endurance*. The exploits of *Discovery* and her crew have since been largely obscured by the tragic events of Scott's final expedition, which have propelled him to immortality. Today, the story of the death of Scott and his men has almost become part of the national curriculum and I bet that most schoolchildren in the country would be able to finish the famous line, 'I'm just going outside . . .'

However, in the last 25 years, critics have set out to denigrate Captain Scott's qualities as a leader, a scientist and an explorer. It has become a popular British pastime to knock our nation's heroes and Scott has not been spared. Cynical biographers with no experience of polar travel have deliberately misrepresented diaries and expedition reports to produce an image of Scott as a bumbling fool. This misconception has blossomed with the recent idolising of Shackleton as the greatest leader of men that ever lived. In boardrooms throughout Britain and America, it has become a craze to use Shackleton's leadership as a model of successful corporate management. Films have been made, documentaries produced, books reprinted and his journeys recreated, all of which must have contributed to Shackleton coming eleventh in a nationwide BBC poll in 2002 to decide who was the 'Greatest Briton' of all time. For the record, Captain Scott came 54th behind the likes of Boy George and Michael Crawford and only two places above Cliff Richard.

Yes, Shackleton was an inspirational leader who was able to get the very best out of his men, particularly when the chips were down. But as an explorer, I would have to rank Scott as the greater of the two – if only by a hair's breadth. Both had their faults and during their careers made decisions that would ultimately lead to the deaths of men under their command. Nevertheless, they were men of enormous courage and extraordinary willpower whose achievements far outweigh their failings. Their place in shaping the history of both Antarctica and Britain is well grounded.

*

Skiing to the bottom of the world was a pilgrimage for me. Robert Falcon Scott was never far from my mind and the admiration I hold for my childhood hero has grown markedly since we touched down on the frozen continent at the end of last year. Although the Antarctica which we skied across is just as colossal, empty, crevassed, cold and windy as it was a century ago, it would be folly to even mention our expedition in the same breath as the journeys made by the early Antarctic pioneers. Whilst the time we spent trudging across the polar snows was the most gruelling of our lives, modern developments in clothing and equipment, nutrition, transport, communication and navigation have not only made polar travel a more comfortable and much less hazardous experience than it once was, but have made the Pole more attainable for amateur adventurers such as ourselves. Reaching the farthest corners of the planet is no longer a mission reserved for the likes of Superman.

Our time in the South has given me a much more balanced picture of Antarctica than the sinister place I had imagined it to be from years of reading polar books. Ever since I was a young boy, I have found it impossible to think about Antarctica without conjuring up images of ferocious cold and hardship, as experienced by Captain Scott and his fearless companions. Their terrible deaths, recorded so poetically in Scott's diary, have gone down amongst the bravest and most noble in the history of the human race. It is that picture of the hardiest of men freezing to death in their tents, etched indelibly into the consciousness of our nation, which has given Antarctica its image as one of the most dangerous places on Earth.

But it could all have been so different. Had Scott survived the return journey in 1912 (as he probably would have done had his party not encountered such an unseasonably cold March), he would not have been accorded his mythical status, and the public perception of Antarctica would be nothing like as subjective as it is.

Antarctica is the same hostile and desolate place that it always has been, but dealing with the harsh polar environment is less of an ordeal than it once was. Following his epic crossing of the Antarctic continent in 1992–3, Sir Ranulph Fiennes wrote that, 'The changes in relevant foods and clothing made in the eighty years that had passed between Scott and ourselves treading the Beardmore had unfortunately been minimal.' Our experience ten years later was that we wouldn't have swapped our Gore-Tex jackets, super-light fleeces or delicious freeze-dried meals for anything.

Of course Antarctica is not without its hazards. One needs only to look back to our crevasse encounters a few hours into the expedition to see that danger is never far away. But crevasses are only found in certain parts of the continent and most can be easily avoided. If you were left on the ice for a long period of time and out of contact from the rest of the world, the major threats to your life would come from frostbite and starvation. However, the introduction of one single piece of machinery has drastically reduced the great risks of polar travel – the aeroplane. Given reasonable weather conditions and a moderately flat surface at the take off and landing sites, a rescue operation can be mounted in a matter of hours to any point on the continent. If only Captain Scott had had the luxury of being able to ring up his base camp team on the satellite phone … 'Lads, we've pretty much run out of food and fuel and the first signs of frostbite are starting to appear. We're not going to be able to make it back to Cape Evans. Please send the Twin Otter out to pick us up immediately. I'll turn on the GPS to give you our exact position.' Whilst people are killed on the slopes of Mount Everest every year, the last person to perish on a South Pole expedition was Captain Scott himself.

Since returning home I have been astonished by the number of friends who have asked me 'How was your trip to the North Pole?' or 'Did you run into any polar bears?' or even 'Was Santa waiting for you at the Pole?' To many people, the two places seem impossible to differentiate. But aside from the cold, the Poles have very little in common. Antarctica is a continent buried by millions of years of snow, the Arctic a vast sea cloaked by an eight-foot-thick blanket of ice, which cracks and crumples with the ocean currents. The Arctic also has a native human population, and bears, seals and whales are sometimes sighted as far north as the Pole itself.

Another popular misconception, and a legacy of the Scott myth, is that Antarctica is far more treacherous than the Arctic. What makes Arctic expeditions particularly grisly is that explorers travel during the bitterly cold winter months before the pack ice starts to break up. Furthermore, there is precious little daylight at this time of year, making open water and pressure ridges all the more treacherous to negotiate. Oh yes, and there are the polar bears to contend with too. The Arctic is an evil place and most days in the frozen North are a battle for survival. On those special occasions during our southern journey when the winds abated and the clouds dissolved away, Antarctica seemed more like a friend to us than the serial killer we had been anticipating.

Whilst a large proportion of Arctic expeditions have failed to generate much in the way of media coverage, every British team that has reached the South Pole in the last 20 years has become headline news. Maybe this is because we Brits were right in the thick of things during the race to the South Pole and we still feel as though the place is ours. Dozens of British expeditions were sent north during the nineteenth century, but they were searching (in vain) for a northern sea route to the Pacific – the North-West Passage. The prize of the North Pole was left for the Americans to squabble over. Antarctica was our domain. Today, characters like Scott and Shackleton are almost as identifiable amongst the British public as Posh and Becks, and this could be why the press continue to write freely about them and the icy continent they made so famous.

Adventurers from North America and Europe look at our media with a touch of envy when it comes to Antarctic travel. During one of our many evening tent discussions, Paul remarked, 'It's so much easier for you guys to get the funding for your expeditions because you are guaranteed the media coverage. A sponsor would be mad not to get on board.' This partially explains why 27 of the 115 people who have ever reached the South Pole on foot from the edge of the Antarctic continent have been British. I am sure there are thousands of would-be explorers around the world who would leap at the chance to ski to the South Pole, if only they could raise the money. We have been immensely fortunate.

But our helpful press only partly explains the large number of Brits who venture into the South. For centuries, we have been a nation of seafarers and explorers who have gradually filled in the empty spaces on the map in a quest for knowledge, wealth and fame. The 'conquest' of Antarctica, pioneered by Cook and Ross, and completed by the crew of *Discovery*, was the crowning glory of British imperialism, and the frozen continent has held a special place in our hearts ever since. Shortly before Scott embarked on his final Antarctic expedition, the President of the Royal Geographical Society said at his team's farewell dinner: 'Scott is going to prove once again that the manhood of our nation is not dead and that the characteristics of our ancestors who won the Empire still flourish among us.' The British Empire is no more, but that thirst for knowledge and adventure remains part of our cultural identity and continues to draw us to these faraway lands.

But to find the real reason, we have to look much further back in time. Barely 600 generations ago, the British Isles would have looked very similar to Antarctica. The great ice sheets of the last Ice Age covered over 80 per cent of the land, forcing people to travel vast distances in search of food and shelter. The adaptability and resourcefulness of our resilient forefathers was enough to survive the worst of the polar climate before the ice eventually receded from our shores 10,000 years ago. We modern-day Brits are children of the Ice, and I would like to think that a deep-rooted calling to the cold remains, compelling so many of us to head to the great Antarctic ice cap.

*

Over the past year, I have been asked two questions more than any others: 'How did you go to the loo in Antarctica?' and 'Why did you go to the South Pole?' Whilst my responses to the first line of questioning are growing more elaborate by the week, the second still defeats me. Sometimes I wish I had a succinct answer up my sleeve like George Mallory who, when asked what was the point in climbing Mount Everest, famously proclaimed: 'Because it's there.' But my reasons for skiing across a flat, featureless ice cap are far more complex than that. So much so that I feel no matter how much explaining I try to do, there are some who will never truly understand. Sir Edmund Hillary's customary reply to the 'Why?' question was: 'If you need to ask the question, you will never understand the answer.' I know exactly what he means.

To me, there seems to be a five-stage plan in life. From an early age, we are encouraged to make the most of our education, find ourselves a good job, buy a house, get married and start a family. Some of my close contemporaries have already progressed to stage five and I hope that one day I will be able to follow in their wake. Our aspirations in life seem to revolve around that plan, but this can sometimes give us a narrow-minded view about the world in which we live. Twenty-first-century Britain is a very cosy and secure place, and to many people crossing the road is the biggest hazard they will face. When people choose to satisfy their own desires and step outside the norm by deliberately pursuing dangerous challenges, they are often considered totally insane. But in discarding the safety net of modern life, expeditions give me a unique sense of freedom that I don't get from working behind a desk. The only time I feel in complete control of my life is when I am up a mountain or on the Ice. Pursuing my dreams through expeditions is at times a pretty selfish existence but it allows me to escape from life's many constraints. Expeditions help to give me direction and a well-balanced view of the world. They define the person I am.

Expeditions are no more than glorified adventures, and ever since I was a young boy I have loved adventure. My adventures progressed from climbing bookshelves and trees, to mountaineering and then to perhaps the ultimate adventure there is –

a journey to the bottom of the world. Nothing makes me feel more alive than organising my own adventure to some far-flung corner of the planet. The complete adventure should be demanding, full of uncertainty, set amongst breathtaking scenery, and contain an element of risk. In Antarctica we found all these exciting ingredients in abundance. But what made our polar adventure so special was being able to enjoy it with close friends. The bond that is forged when a close-knit team shares the intense experiences of a long expedition is the real essence of adventure and is why we will keep coming back for more.

Whilst our time in Antarctica was an enormously happy one, our polar odyssey was also the toughest challenge we have ever experienced. Many months ago, we began the seemingly impossible task of trying to reach the South Pole, one of the coldest, most remote, least hospitable spots on the planet – the last place on Earth. We had next to no relevant experience, we didn't know what we were letting ourselves in for, but against all the odds, we did it.

Our journey to the South Pole has given us all a new inner confidence we never had before. No matter what challenges we set ourselves in our future lives, I feel that nothing is impossible. But it is as clear to me as the air beyond the southern seas that our own achievements don't hold a candle to the exploits of Scott, Shackleton, Amundsen and all those glorious characters before them who unlocked the frozen door of Antarctica for the rest of us to enter. They are the true heroes of the South. We just feel incredibly fortunate to have followed in the footsteps of these courageous and brilliant men.

COMMONWEALTH SOUTH POLE CENTENARY EXPEDITION PROGRESS CHART

Camp	Date (2002)	Latitude	Longitude	Compass deviation (°)	Hours travelled	Daily mileage	Accumulated mileage	Elevation (feet)	Elevation gain (feet)
	Nov 13	80 01.655	79 29.426	39				398	
1	Nov 13	80 10.579	79 43.191	39	6.5	9.25	9.25	1,830	1,432
2	Nov 14	80 19.485	79 56.704	40	7	9.21	18.46	2,594	764
3	Nov 15	80 28.992	80 04.661	40	6.75	9.55	28.01	2,541	−53
4	Nov 16	80 38.725	80 11.026	40	7	9.88	37.89	2,539	−2
5	Nov 17	80 49.356	80 11.405	40	7	10.7	48.59	2,667	128
6	Nov 18	81 00.573	80 14.360	41	6.75	11.3	59.89	2,629	−38
7	Nov 19	81 12.142	80 13.518	41	7.5	11.6	71.49	2,568	−61
8	Nov 20	81 24.150	80 05.047	41	7.5	12.1	83.59	2,458	−110
9	Nov 21	81 36.445	80 09.365	41	7.5	12.4	95.99	2,513	55
10	Nov 22	81 48.149	80 10.562	42	7.5	11.8	107.79	2,736	223
11	Nov 23	82 00.106	80 24.312	42	7.5	12.2	119.99	2,832	96
12	Nov 24	82 00.106	80 24.312	42	0	0	119.99	2,832	0
13	Nov 25	82 13.381	80 38.328	42	7.5	13.4	133.39	3,036	204
14	Nov 26	82 25.937	80 43.798	43	7.5	12.6	145.99	3,497	461
15	Nov 27	82 39.832	80 57.936	43	7.5	14.1	160.09	3,619	122
16	Nov 28	82 53.019	81 05.917	44	7.5	13.3	173.39	3,777	158
17	Nov 29	83 07.142	81 31.402	44	7.5	14.5	187.89	3,905	128
18	Nov 30	83 21.006	81 54.236	45	7.5	14.2	202.09	4,139	234
19	Dec 1	83 35.724	82 16.535	45	7.5	15	217.09	4,252	113
20	Dec 2	83 50.684	82 41.665	46	7.5	15.3	232.39	4,600	348
21	Dec 3	84 05.613	83 13.945	47	7.5	15.4	247.79	4,740	140
22	Dec 4	84 20.955	83 56.922	48	7.5	16	263.79	4,817	77
23	Dec 5	84 36.497	84 31.486	48	7.5	16	279.79	5,044	227

Wind (am) Direction	Wind (am) (knots)	Wind (pm) (knots)	Temp °C	Weather	Surface conditions
SSW	10	15	−7	Sun	Blue-ice, sastrugi & crevasses. Big climbs.
SSW	20	10	−19	Sun	As before. Fewer crevasses pm.
SSW	18	14	−12	Sun	Continuing improvement. Moderate sastrugi.
SSW	12	5	−14	Sun	As before.
SSW	10	3	−6	Sun	1 short, steep climb. Good surface.
SSW	3	1	−9	Sun	Several large banks of sastrugi. Long descent.
SSW	15	8	−10	Sun	Good surface.
SSW	4	5	−12	Cloud	A few sastrugi. Otherwise good surface.
SSW	4	5	−12	Sun	Moderate sastrugi.
SSW	15	12	−15	Sun	Long, gentle climb am. Some sastrugi.
SSW	17	11	−14	Sun	Good surface.
SSW	40	10	−9	Cloud/sun	N/A.
SSW	8	12	−16	Sun	Good surface. Short climb pm.
SSW	5	4	−12	Sun	Series of long climbs. Moderate sastrugi.
SSW	5	5	−8	Sun/cloud	Short, steep climbs am. Frequent sastrugi.
SSW	10	8	−11	Cloud/sun	Regular banks of big sastrugi.
S	9	8	−18	Sun	Moderate sastrugi. 2 short climbs pm.
S	10	10	−12	Sun	Long, gentle climb am. Frequent sastrugi.
S	10	10	−12	Sun	Hard surface. Patches of powder. Big sastrugi.
S	5	5	−12	Cloud/sun	Mega sastrugi. 3 short climbs. Hard surface.
S	3	2	−12	Sun	More large sastrugi.
S	8	8	−15	Sun	Surface improving.
S	10	5	−15	Cloud	Several banks of big sastrugi. One long climb.

Camp	Date (2002)	Latitude	Longitude	Compass deviation (°)	Hours travelled	Daily mileage	Accumulated mileage	Elevation (feet)	Elevation gain (feet)
24	Dec 6	84 52.003	85 23.602	49	7.5	16.3	296.09	5,000	−44
25	Dec 7	85 06.259	86 53.359	51	7.5	16.4	312.49	5,109	109
26	Dec 8	85 12.007	87 54.455	51	3.75	7.78	320.27	5,250	141
27	Dec 9	85 12.007	87 54.455	51	0	0	320.27	5,250	0
28	Dec 10	85 23.683	86 40.188	51	7.5	13.2	333.47	4,973	−277
29	Dec 11	85 37.253	86 18.894	51	7.5	13.7	347.17	5,077	104
30	Dec 12	85 50.874	86 04.872	51	7.5	13.7	360.87	5,491	414
31	Dec 13	86 04.664	85 43.591	51	7.5	13.9	374.77	5,837	346
32	Dec 14	86 17.040	85 36.387	52	6.5	12.4	387.17	6,112	275
33	Dec 15	86 41.011	87 54.414	54	12.5	25.5	412.67	6,548	436
34	Dec 16	86 51.530	87 42.984	54	5.75	10.6	423.27	6,827	279
35	Dec 17	87 14.663	89 15.803	57	9.0	23.7	446.97	7,586	759
36	Dec 18	87 27.164	88 21.906	56	7.5	12.8	459.77	7,859	273
37	Dec 19	87 41.533	88 22.751	56	8.0	14.4	474.17	8,325	466
38	Dec 20	87 56.186	87 58.294	56	8.0	14.8	488.97	8,555	230
39	Dec 21	88 03.017	88 05.244	57	3.5	6.8	495.77	8,650	95
40	Dec 22	88 16.577	88 16.033	57	7.5	13.6	509.37	8,878	228
41	Dec 23	88 31.526	87 46.270	57	8.0	15	524.37	9,055	177
42	Dec 24	88 45.862	87 37.053	57	8.0	14.4	538.77	9,050	−5
43	Dec 25	88 55.299	87 18.927	57	5.5	9.5	548.27	9,101	51
44	Dec 26	89 19.343	90 49.285	59	8.5	24.4	572.67	9,155	54
45	Dec 27	89 35.808	87 56.927	61	8.5	16.6	589.27	9,380	225
46	Dec 28	90 00.000	00 00.000	66	13.25	24.2	613.47	9,301	−79

Wind (am) Direction	Wind (am) (knots)	Wind (pm) (knots)	Temp °C	Weather	Surface conditions
S	12	8	−15	Sun	Good, hard surface. Fewer sastrugi.
S	16	4	−16	Sun	As before.
S	0	1	−18	Sun	As before.
S	1	1	−10	Cloud	N/A.
SE	4	20	−10	Sun	Mega sastrugi, blue-ice. Short, steep descent.
SE	18	3	−12	Sun/cloud	More large sastrugi.
S	13	7	−15	Sun	Several climbs in waves. Sastrugi everywhere.
SE	5	5	−12	Sun/cloud	3 short, steep climbs pm. Some blue-ice pm.
E	5	2	−12	Sun	New snow. Soft surface. Fewer sastrugi.
E	16	9	−15	Cloud/sun	Uphill all day. Several large banks of sastrugi.
E	5	3	−15	Sun	Improving surface.
E	10	5	−11	Cloud	Mega sastrugi in middle of day. Big climbs.
E	2	3	−12	Cloud	Worst sastrugi so far. More climbs.
SSE	8	10	−23	Sun	Several climbs in waves. Moderate sastrugi.
SSE	10	5	−19	Sun	Improving surface. 1 long, gentle climb pm.
SE	5	5	−16	Sun/cloud	Soft surface. Fewer sastrugi.
SE	8	3	−14	Sun	3 short, steep climbs am. Soft, flat surface pm.
SE	1	0	−14	Sun	Improving conditions.
SW	8	8	−24	Sun	Good, flat surface. Sastrugi almost all gone.
SW	16	8	−24	Sun	As before.
NE	5	3	−14	Sun/cloud/sun	As before.
S	4	4	−21	Sun	Several gentle climbs in waves. Good surface.
S	2	3	−23	Sun/cloud/sun	Long descent, followed by climb. Soft surface.

INDEX